The American Poet
at the Movies

By the same author

The Flying Machine and Modern Literature
*Ruins and Empire: The Evolution of a Theme in Augustan and
    Romantic Literature*
The Three Gardens (poetry)
Altamira (poetry)

Edited volumes

Seasonal Performances: A Michigan Quarterly Review *Reader*
The Female Body
The Automobile and American Culture
    (coedited with David L. Lewis)
Writers and Their Craft: Short Stories and Essays on the Narrative
    (coedited with Nicholas Delbanco)

The American Poet at the Movies

A Critical History

LAURENCE GOLDSTEIN

ANN ARBOR

THE UNIVERSITY OF MICHIGAN PRESS

Copyright © by the University of Michigan 1994
All rights reserved
Published in the United States of America by
The University of Michigan Press
Manufactured in the United States of America
⊚ Printed on acid-free paper

1997 1996 1995 1994   4 3 2 1

Library of Congress Cataloging-in-Publication Data

Goldstein, Laurence, 1943–
     The American poet at the movies : a critical history / Laurence
Goldstein.
          p.   cm.
     Includes bibliographical references and index.
     ISBN 0-472-10508-6 (alk. paper)
     1. American poetry—20th century—History and criticism.
     2. Motion picture actors and actresses in literature. 3. Motion
pictures and literature—United States.   I. Title.
PS310.M65G64   1994
811'.5409—dc20   93-48036
                                                                  CIP

A CIP catalogue record for this book is available from the British Library.

For permission to reprint complete poems, the author is grateful to the following
publishers: Black Sparrow Press for Wanda Coleman, "Invitation to a Gunfighter,"
copyright © 1979 by Wanda Coleman; reprinted from *African Sleeping Sickness, Stories
& Poems,* reprinted with the permission of Black Sparrow Press; Grove Weidenfeld for
"To the Film Industry in Crisis" from *Meditations in an Emergency,* copyright © 1957
by Frank O'Hara; Harcourt Brace & Company for Carl Sandburg, "In a Breath," from
Chicago Poems (1916) by Carl Sandburg, reprinted by permission of Harcourt Brace &
Company; Houghton Mifflin Company for Archibald MacLeish, "Cinema of a Man,"
from *Collected Poems 1917–1982,* copyright © 1985 by The Estate of Archibald
MacLeish, reprinted by permission of Houghton Mifflin Company, all rights reserved;
Liveright Publishing Corporation for Robert Hayden, "Double Feature," reprinted
from *Collected Poems* by Robert Hayden, edited by Frederick Glaysher, by permission
of Liveright Publishing Corporation, copyright © 1985 by Erma Hayden; Macmillan
Publishing Company for Winfield Townley Scott, "Dream Penny in the Slot at 6 A.M.,"
from *Collected Poems 1937–1962,* copyright © 1962 by Macmillan Company; New Di-
rections Publishing Corporation for Delmore Schwartz, "Metro-Goldwyn-Mayer,"
from *Last & Lost Poems of Delmore Schwartz,* copyright © 1989 by Kenneth Schwartz,
reprinted by permission of New Directions Publishing Corporation; W. W. Norton &
Company for Adrienne Rich, "Images for Godard," reprinted from *Collected Early
Poems 1950–1970,* by Adrienne Rich, by permission of W. W.. Norton, Inc., copyright
© 1993 by Adrienne Rich, copyright © 1984, 1975, 1971, 1969 by W. W. Norton, Inc.;
Wieser & Wieser for Karl Shapiro, "Hollywood," copyright © 1941, 1987 by Karl
Shapiro by arrangement with Wieser & Wieser, Inc., New York.

Preface

Readers of modern poetry will have noticed that a certain type of poem has become steadily more popular during the twentieth century. It is a poem that speaks about some favorite movie, or movie star, or the movies in general. It may refer glancingly to a cinematic figure, as when it says of some boys that they are "falling down a lot like Laurel and Hardy" (Maxine Kumin) or describes a woman "tossing her hair in imitation of Bacall" (Rita Dove). It may flaunt the terminology of cinema in a knowing way, confident that the reader shares its semantic comfort with this specialized field of knowledge. Like poems about popular music, with which they share an obvious kinship, such poems at first walked the line between a condescension to "low" culture derived from the old days when such topics were indecorous, and a defiant blazoning of the new subject matter as a badge of membership in the modern generations. More recently, poems about the movies appear in books and journals with neither defensiveness nor fanfare. There are now too many of them to provoke any special surprise. Like poems about love or landscape, they appeal to readers, or not, by the way they use their ever-expanding repertory of conventions.

The content of this new genre is becoming more visible to us as the categories of highbrow and lowbrow continue to be redefined by a postmodern generation of authors and editors eager to contest the ideology of modernism. That ideology has never been a monolithic one because the authors who comprise the canon did not agree on the desirability of popular culture as a literary subject. Ezra Pound's contempt in *Hugh Selwyn Mauberley* for what "the age demanded"—something less monumental than alabaster and the sculpture of rhyme—sounds reactionary to postmodern ears, as Pound meant it to be in an era when the revolt of the masses seemed to find its mirror image in the "accelerated grimace" of mass culture. A more tolerant stance toward the popular arts is associated with the work of William Carlos Williams and Robert Frost, and a multitude of writers since midcentury who have ceased to resist what is in any case irresistible. For better or worse, the supposedly more ephemeral productions of the modern period have achieved a central status in our culture, and every poet of my generation knows that more nuances of meaning can be conveyed by an allusion to *Casablanca* or *Rebel Without a Cause* than to "King's Treasuries" and the *Milesian Tales*.

The variety of movie poems in this century can be sampled in a recent anthology, *The Faber Book of Movie Verse*, which collects some 340 specimens. It would not be accurate to say that this assemblage is only the tip of the iceberg, but neither is it entirely comprehensive, for it excludes many poems, especially longer poems, of the genre. Nevertheless, this anthology, and a forthcoming one titled *Screen Gems*, signal the presence of a vast unstudied tradition that should cause us to rethink our usual generalizations about the viability of poetry in a visual culture. I have undertaken this book to provide not only a chronicle but an analysis of that tradition in modern American literature. Though I glance occasionally at non-American works, I have largely confined myself to native examples because they constitute the single most extensive national group of poems written on the topic, and because significant intertextual relations are so much easier to document. My purpose in devoting a book-length study to these fascinating poems is not to invert literary history, not to claim that low should be high. Rather, I believe that a familiarity with this previously unstudied category of literary discourse will expand our understanding of how American poets have created a working partnership with a new technology, and a new art, that seemed to threaten their niche in the cultural environment. The diversity of ways in which poets have been attracted to and repelled from the movies not only clarifies the course of American literary history in this century but foretells the contours of that history in a twenty-first century dominated by mass communications. As I write, the air is full of commentaries on "the end of history," "the end of nature," and even "the end of culture." What will surely not end is the movies, and the continuum of poems about the movies. Why such poems have become so vital and enduring a part of our literary heritage is the question this book seeks to answer.

Like my study of the flying machine and modern literature, this interpretive account began as an essay, and then grew. I am grateful to the following people who helped me with parts of the manuscript, or read the whole of it with scrupulous care: Michael Anderegg, Rudolf Arnheim, Charles Baxter, Leo Braudy, Philip French, Roger Gilbert, William Paul, Alan Wald, and Susan White. Doris Knight aided me in understanding how computer technology can simplify the preparation of the manuscript. Ned Creeth read the final proofs with his meticulous eye and once again saved me from embarrassment. Portions of the book appeared in a different form in the *Centennial Review*, the *Iowa Review*, the *North Dakota Review*, and *Parnassus*. I am grateful to the editors of those publications for permission to reprint. My wife Nancy remained a cheerful partner on my scholarly quest and a patient auditor of my evolving ideas. My teenage sons Andrew and Jonathan deserve credit for some shrewd, if offhand, insights about the impact of movies on the generation following mine. Finally, I have profited enormously from my seminars on film and literature at the University of Michigan. I hope, for more reasons than one, that my former students find their way to this book that benefited so much from our spirited discussions.

I owe a special debt of gratitude to the Horace Rackham School of Graduate Studies at the University of Michigan, for awarding me a fellowship and a travel grant at a crucial stage of my research.

In writing poems about the movies I have always recognized that my private motive for metaphor is the memory of my early life in Culver City, California, known as "The Heart of Screenland" because it was the home of M-G-M Studios. This book, too, draws upon powerful emotional wellsprings located in that sacred place. I dedicate the book to Michael Anderegg, my classmate from age five in the Culver City schools, my fellow scholar of film history, and my lifelong friend.

Ann Arbor, Michigan
September 1993

Contents

Real life is only a reflection of the dreams of poets. The strings of the lyre of modern poets are endless strips of celluloid.

Franz Kafka

the poet is at the movies
dreaming the film-maker's dream but differently
free in the dark as if asleep

Adrienne Rich

Andy Warhol, *Marilyn,* 1962. Of all movie stars, Marilyn Monroe has been the most popular subject for artistic representation since the 1950s. "It might be the birth of a new Venus among us," Delmore Schwartz wrote in a celebratory poem of 1955. "A nation haunted by Puritanism owes her homage and gratitude." (From *Warhol,* a catalog of the Tate Gallery exhibition, 1971.)

Introduction

In talking with friends about how this book on poems and movies came to be, I sometimes found myself recounting a memory that has nothing to do with either poems or movies. As an act of trust in the intuitive powers of the mind during conversation, I'll set down the memory here and then trace it out to the furthest reaches of this unusual project. The site is Los Angeles in 1962, when, a sophomore at UCLA, I was exploring Southern California in every direction, and especially the territory north of Culver City, my hometown. I would drive up La Cienega Boulevard to Sunset, turn left toward Beverly Hills or right toward Hollywood, and cruise for hours waiting for something exciting to happen. Mainly I got tangled in traffic jams with hundreds of other cars piloted like mine by teenagers looking for action.

One summer evening I noticed a crowd in front of the Ferus Gallery on La Cienega between Melrose and Santa Monica boulevards. I stopped, and saw in the window some paintings of Campbell's soup cans in the pop art style currently making a splash in New York. Another gallery down the street featured a window display of real Campbell's soup cans and a sign, Two for 39 cents. Don't Overpay. (The paintings were $300 each.) I found myself instantly of two minds about this exhibit, pulled in one direction by the latter gallery's insinuation that the paintings were a hoax, a stunt, and in the other direction by my hunch that something important for the history of American culture was being proclaimed in the gallery with the thirty-two red-and-white canvases. Like the other sightseers I could not take my eyes off Andy Warhol's pastiches, any more than visitors to a media event can keep from watching the action on the TV monitor rather than at center stage. The banal deflation of the artistic subject, and the implied mockery of the spectator's taste, took my breath away. I went home both exhilarated and troubled.

A year later, when I saw Warhol's famous image of Marilyn

3

Monroe, I had the same mixed feelings, at a higher level of complexity. As the culture's chief figure for the movies, Marilyn shared some attributes with Campbell's soup; she was another pop icon promising sensual pleasure to the hungry consumer. This much Warhol had discerned. And yet she was also a real person whose emotional turmoil offscreen had involved nearly everyone on the planet in her career choices and finally in the pathos of her recent suicide. Now I felt that Warhol's art of surfaces was insufficient, undeserving of the fanfare that had welcomed this derivative work. He had been right to deny imaginative depth to the commodified American value system signified by soup cans, and by the dollar bills, Coke bottles, Cadillacs, Brillo boxes, airmail stamps, S & H Green Stamps, and dance diagrams he also produced as serials. But his provocative extension of these ready-made commercial designs into the world of celebrities—he would go on to silkscreen photo-reproduced images of Elizabeth Taylor, Elvis Presley, Jackie Kennedy, Mao Tze Tung, Marlon Brando, and others—was nothing more than a Johnny One-Note routine that flattened the cultural horizon. The joke was not on the famous subjects of these portraits, and not even on the communications media that knowingly exploited them. The joke *was* on those who overpaid for these garish canvases and exhibited them in living rooms or museums to people who knew in their hearts that Marilyn and Elvis were more, much more, than these representations evoked.

Who these stars were seemed to matter a great deal in the early 1960s, and nothing in our national history since then, needless to say, has diminished the desire of serious artists and their audience to see through the tinsel of Warhol-like surfaces and down to the depths of popular idolatry. It is the argument of this book that the movies were the catalyst for an engagement between artists and popular culture that is unprecedented in its magnitude and intensity, an engagement best studied in poems that have sought to dramatize with maximum sophistication the moments of contact between poetic and cinematic realms of being. Until recently such poems were written very much against the grain of literary decorum. In the first sixty years of this century poets were warned away from the popular arts and scorned when they went slumming in nickelodeons and movie palaces alike. Many intellectuals, especially of the Frankfurt School and the conservative wing of the *Partisan Review* and other quarterlies, persistently denounced what they called mass culture, perhaps because it kept turning up people like Andy Warhol. Such culture produced only kitsch, they claimed, a degraded form of authentic art that degraded its admirers in turn. Dwight Macdonald's remark is representative: "Since Mass Culture is not an art form but a manufactured commodity, it tends always downward, toward cheapness—and so standardization—of production."[1] But a populist strain of commentary, rising after the 1960s to dominance in the literary world and the academy, has argued that works of popular culture, even in genres like the romance and western, have originality, variety, and even profundity. To put it in a double-edged way, they have the same structure as the emotional life of their consumers. Movie criticism may be said to have pioneered this belief, starting with Hugo Munsterberg's *The Photoplay: A Psychological Study,* published in 1916. After his seminal work, writers in all fields began to delve into the deep imagery of the movies and claim with differing tones of authority that there was more to visual narrative and film iconography than met the eye.

Dwight Macdonald's remark about the commodification of culture in a mass society reminds us that the response of poets to the cinema is part of a larger story involving the love-hate relations of intellectuals with machine technology in the twentieth century. In its most demonic form, technology has been seen as a Futurist juggernaut overrunning humane values and reconstituting art itself according to the collaborative, assembly-line conditions of modern production. Walter Benjamin's indispensable essay of 1936, "The Work of Art in the Age of Mechanical Reproduction," dolefully predicted "the liquidation of the traditional value of the cultural heritage" as a result of film technology.[2] Film renders the spectator passive before its shocking, motor-driven rush of imagery, he argued, thereby wiping out the habit of sustained aesthetic contemplation a viewer has developed by communing with, say, paintings by Leonardo or Picasso. When a critic of our own time remarks that "Warhol correctly foresaw the end of painting, and became its executioner,"[3] he is likewise expressing the sense that art has lost its humanistic aura because of techniques of reproduction and marketing beginning before the Industrial Revolution and culminating in Warhol's "Factory," as he called his film studio and workshop. The alternative way of looking at this matter is to defend the modern arts, whatever their nature, as agents of renewal in a soulless (because exhausted) culture. Art is a techne, a craft, a fabrication of the imagination no less than a flying machine or an automobile. Authors who comment on the pleasure-enhancing technology of a new art like cinema often endorse it as a kindred part of the evolution of the democratic spirit, a modern form of the sacred.

One aspect of this story has been told many times: the impact of film techniques on modernist narrative, especially on Joyce and Dos Passos, and the reciprocal efforts of moviemakers to adapt fiction into film. Harry Geduld's anthology, *Authors on Film,* demonstrates how avidly writers like Howells, Tolstoy, Woolf, Gide, Mann, Sartre, and others reported their experience of cinema. Their sporadic enthusiasm for the new medium has been overshadowed, however, by the amply described experiences of Nathanael West, F. Scott Fitzgerald, Aldous Huxley, and William Faulkner in Hollywood. Following the success of cruder efforts in the genre of the Hollywood novel, Carl Van Vechten set his playwright Ambrose Deacon loose in the movie factories of Culver City in *Spider Boy* (1928), and Carroll and Garrett Graham followed suit in *Queer People* (1930), their novel about "the most peculiar, and often the shadiest industry of all time." Ever since, the novelist has anatomized the film colony with much-studied disdain.[4] But aside from some suggestive commentary by Robert Richardson in his pioneering *Literature and Film* (1969), no scholar has chronicled the total experience of the American poet as spectator and critic of film history. That is the story I have undertaken to tell in this book.

"Every American is a film critic," writes Louis Simpson in one poem. "We come by it naturally. / They don't have to teach it in school."[5] American poets, nourished on Whitman's omnivorous embrace of the social arts, have showed themselves more apt at movie criticism, in Simpson's sense, than poets of other countries. But there are odd exceptions. If, as Stanley Cavell argues, "film is *the* modern art, the art to which modern man naturally responds,"[6] we would expect even more response from American poets than we get. It may not surprise us that aristocratic men of letters like Saint-John Perse, Yeats, and Rilke, spending their formative years in an almost preindustrial culture, eschewed reference to an art as vulgar as early cinema. It is more surprising that Wallace Stevens, given his fascination with the philosophical questions raised by artifacts, did not bend his magisterial attention to the movies. Nor Ezra Pound, who wrote

often about new painting and sculpture. And that even William Car-
los Williams, that *bricoleur* of all things ordinary, who began his career
by asking, "How shall I be a mirror to this modernity,"[7] kept the
movies out of his specular verse. One of the pleasures of writing this
book has been to rediscover some fine poets neglected by the canoniz-
ers of modern poetry, and to make thematic and formal connections
between poets rarely associated in the standard histories but who
shared an interest in the phenomenology of film. As with other stud-
ies I have undertaken, this book engages the problematics of literary
history by proposing a revised reading list, if not a canon, for readers
who appreciate the importance of technology in the formation of
post-Enlightenment culture.

Such a study inevitably begins with Vachel Lindsay, whose im-
portance in this tradition cannot be overestimated. Lindsay saw at
once what other writers did not see for many years, that movies
would take on the same aura of spirituality that formerly belonged
to poetry and song. Movies would do so by sponsoring a mythology
of iconic figures that would eventually rival the ancient legendry
favored by poets before Edison and Griffith. This mythology would
become a source of tactical allusions for poets who required at key
moments in their verse both deep and superficial images shared by
the literate community. In 1915 Lindsay offered Mae Marsh and
Mary Pickford as examples; Hart Crane would soon employ Chaplin.
By 1926 Eugene Jolas, in a volume of poems titled *Cinema,* would
exclaim, "O Dreamer of God, show us the Cinema of the Angels."[8]
How quickly popular entertainment challenged classical culture in
American texts! Henry Taylor notes how "the old allusions to Zeus
and Apollo give way to allusions to Bogey and . . . Valentino, say."
David Lehman, after cataloging some of his favorite movie roles,
remarks that "they, the actors and the characters they play, are part
of our collective consciousness, the closest thing we have to a public
mythology."[9] In his poems and in his treatise *The Art of the Moving
Picture* (1915), originally titled "The Religion of the Movies," Lind-
say anticipated and endorsed the practice of poets throughout the
century who take it for granted that movies can serve as the principal
subject matter and the occasional tropes of even their most ambitious
and visionary work.

Once the movies were acknowledged as the chief art medium of
this century, the Matter of Hollywood became more suspect, for

subsequent poets recognized that Lindsay had perhaps too uncritically welcomed the most formidable rival imaginable into their fraternity. The ascendance of film in the hierarchy of the arts prompted not only misgivings and jealousies but guarded meditations by poets on the deep nature and profound consequences of the popular newcomer in their midst. For one thing, the desirability of "cinematic form" in poetry became a subject for debate, as modernist authors boldly experimented with discontinuous jump-cutting in lyric and narrative modes. The sudden dominance of cinema guaranteed that when poets made use of montage or collage as a structural principle, they could depend on its intentions being recognized by a reading public accustomed to the fluent mobility, surprising juxtapositions, and abstraction of screen imagery. As we shall see, poets like Archibald MacLeish and Carl Sandburg wrestled with the political implications of cinematic form. Was montage compatible with a liberal-reform ideology, they asked, or did it mock the efforts at rational order upon which social reform depended? Poets who went to school at the cinema were sensitive to the critique of movies by the Left in the 1930s, when fast-paced musicals and romances especially were denounced as a conspiracy to pacify needy audiences and dampen social protest. The addiction of multitudes to movies during the Depression seemed a disturbing phenomenon, and poets like Winfield Townley Scott and Delmore Schwartz undertook to examine the pathology, as they saw it, of movie audiences that included themselves.

Poems about movies, then, quickly changed from being a starry-eyed mode of praise to a form of cultural criticism. Poets have always been not only makers of aesthetic objects but monitors of the aesthetic habits of their society. Where bad taste prevails, poets have insisted on connections between aesthetic and social degradation. (One thinks of Pope's *Dunciad,* or Wordsworth's "Preface" to *Lyrical Ballads,* or the strictures of Emerson and Arnold, Eliot and Pound.) In an era of mass communications, a critique of the mediated vision serves the public welfare by testifying to the rightful place, as each poet sees it, of moviegoing, or TV watching, in the economy of everyday life. How much of the affection for visual media is a healthy expression of the audience's democratic right to experience the mysterious other world projected by actors, and how much is an illicit gaze of envy, hopeless yearning, and self-delusion? Poets had written plentifully around this question in previous centuries, especially when dramatizing their responses to painting, sculpture, and the kind of artifact typified by Dryden's "Medal" and Keats's Grecian urn. It should not surprise us, then, that modern poets have recourse to the prestigious examples of their neoclassical and Romantic ancestors when they engage in cultural criticism, or that they write didactic essays and fiction on occasion to explore the impact of the movies. Or that they are influenced by the commentaries on film of nonpoets when they compose their poems. I have felt free to contextualize my readings by making use of all these materials as powerful texts pressing upon the poems central to the tradition.

Karl Shapiro, for example, has written extensively in prose about the set of social and literary concerns, one might almost say obsessions, that informs his encomiastic lyric of 1942, "Hollywood." And a poem like Wanda Coleman's "Invitation to a Gunfighter" owes much to the protest literature of the Black Arts movement from which it emerges and which it critiques. In each chapter, proceeding chronologically from Lindsay's time to the present, I have placed a poem as a central text and explored the issues raised by the poem, issues that involve the whole of American society as well as the poet as representative author in a culture of film. Case studies are the best way of exhibiting the variety of poetic responses to an aesthetic of motion artists have treated as both beneficial and threatening to social order. That some poets sought to ingratiate themselves to a moviegoing readership, enhancing their own appeal by reflected glory, and others raged against the subjection of the spectator to the seductions of the screen, and that the whole of modern literature eventually became implicated in the contact between these two art forms, proved to me the need for extended presentation of this history.

Of course, one of the major objects of study must be the movies themselves. The poems I study are examples of film criticism, film history, or film theory, among their other virtues. Twentieth-century poems do not influence movies, as fiction has often helped to shape innovative structures and provide plots. But they do model for readers of poems the complex dynamics by which movies change the consciousness of spectators. Readers discover things they never knew about the movies, and their movie-made culture, when a talented poet chronicles his or her complex engagement with them. That movie poems have played a unique role in articulating black, gay, Jewish, and feminist sensibilities is another reason in the 1990s for constructing a taxonomy of poetic interventions into this realm of popular culture. In a society of spectatorship like ours, what the minority poet observes in his or her nation's favorite pastime can percolate to the furthest reaches of everyday discourse. This is especially true at a time when there is an explosion of film and video materials in contemporary literature, and in academic theory, causing all authors to consult every form of media critique as a guide to their own. With their fine ear for the multiplicity of verbal responses to the whole of human experience, poets can be trusted to enunciate in memorable and partisan speech what their readers need to hear in order to counteract the aesthetics of immediacy sponsored by popular culture. The unique take of poets on the movies will often rescue stories and stars from the simplistic, unthinking approach typified by entertainment journalism and pop art, which share an antihistorical mentality.

If, for example, a poet wants to write about Marilyn Monroe, what resources would prove useful in framing a fresh and meaningful perspective? What rights to the subject could a poet convincingly claim comparable to Andy Warhol's appropriation of a studio publicity still for his "Gold Marilyn" and "Turquoise Marilyn"? Warhol compels us to see the star presence as a glitzy, one-dimensional object mass-distributed by the commercial media; her full potentiality even as a star is circumscribed into a stereotyped image. A poet can challenge the monolithic power of such iconography by rescuing Marilyn into a different mode of portraiture, a different convention of interpretation. Here is Edith Sitwell's prose description of the actress, whom she met once in Hollywood: "In repose her face was at moments strangely, prophetically tragic, like the face of a beautiful ghost—a little spring-ghost, an innocent fertility daemon, the vegetation spirit that was Ophelia."[10] One might complain that such a passage types Marilyn just as much as Warhol's glamour pic; but how well it fits the Monroe of *Bus Stop, The Misfits,* and so many of the moody photographs from the beginning to the end of her career. Ophelia is an after-the-fact-of-suicide characterization, but the more one thinks about the connection between these two ill-fated women, a connection amplified by the mythic references of Sitwell's passage, the more it has the effect of remaking Marilyn, and our everyday relation to her memory, according to the most profound understanding of human nature provided by the literary tradition. Sitwell's version is no less essential than Warhol's, especially if we seek to understand why Marilyn has survived so much more hauntingly in the public imagination than Jean Harlow and Rita Hayworth, to whom she was so often compared in her lifetime. Similarly, Delmore Schwartz, in his poem "Love and Marilyn Monroe," has recourse to an immensely suggestive model for his portrait, Christopher Smart's eighteenth-century poem, "For I will consider my Cat Jeoffry." Feeling himself drawn into the vortex of insanity that enveloped Smart when he wrote the poem in a madhouse, Schwartz mimics the boisterous litany of his ancestor:

> Therefore let us praise Marilyn Monroe.
> She has a noble attitude marked by pride and candor
> She takes a noble pride in the female nature and torso
> She articulates her pride with directness and exuberance
> She is honest in her delight in womanhood and manhood.[11]

And so forth. Like Smart's wholesome and joyful cat that "counteracts the powers of darkness," Marilyn comes to represent all that is natural and unselfconscious in an age of anxiety increasingly tormenting to the nerve-racked poet. And to the extent that Marilyn was an international figure, a sign of America's cultural imperialism, Schwartz's praise aligns him with the prevailing middle-class and gentile multitude of his nation. As so often, a movie poem is a means of making common cause with the mainstream folkways of a self-confident culture.

As one who has written poems about movies, I have a long-standing interest in this topic. I have taken care to narrate this history from a reasonable distance without poking my head persistently in front of my own camera. Nonetheless, in the fashion of recent critical texts, I have felt it necessary and desirable to introduce myself, especially in the Intermission and the Conclusion, as a participant in the story I am unfolding. It is my story in more ways than one. Culver City and Hollywood were not merely metaphors for me, but localities I knew intimately, so that the use of them as sites of conflict in American poems (and fiction) always resonated in my personal experience. I was immune to oversimplified rhetoric about my native ground, and at the same time unusually susceptible to homages and satires directed at the movies. Finding a voice for my own poems, and subject matter rooted in the popular culture about which I continue to feel much ambivalence, has enhanced my sensitivity to the struggles of modern poets to position themselves in the zeitgeist as working partners of moving pictures. Has this affected my choice of texts to interpret? Undoubtedly it has, but I am confident that no masterpiece has eluded me, and no eccentric example is inflated beyond common sense. I do feel somewhat guilty for not attending to so-called underground film, but here I follow the lead of American poets, who have shown almost no interest in this worthy tradition of the avant-garde. Knowing some good poems on the subject by Michael Collier, James Merrill, Richard Tillinghast, and others, I was tempted to address the question of home movies as a unique form of filmed reality. But it seemed essential to focus instead on the American poet's engagement with artworks addressed to the entire society if this book was to have coherence as a description of the mediated reality we all share.

Reality. This word bedevils the subject of film criticism and poetry criticism alike. One thinks back speculatively to the period before the movies (and then television) took on their awesome power to declare what reality is. The earliest appearance of moving pictures in an important American literary work is a scene in Frank Norris's *McTeague* (1899) where "the crowning scientific achievement of the nineteenth century, the kinetoscope," as the playbill calls it, provides some brief footage of street traffic in San Francisco as part of a stage show featuring jugglers, comedians, and singers. Some years later Edith Wharton casts an even more fleeting glance at a "cinemato-graph...apparatus" in *The House of Mirth* (1905).[12] A minuscule amount of reality is granted to that device on the periphery of the Van Osburgh marriage where Lily Bart receives some lessons about the limits of her social acceptability. The home movie to be made from the wedding is simply a private memorial of the event. When in the second and third decades of this century the movies take on a public, independent life and offer sustained scenarios of their own to rival the reality of social beings, writers still try to keep the boundary as secure as possible in an effort to fence off cinema from actuality. Here, for example, is the earliest poem about the movies to appear in an anthology, in 1917. Titled simply "The Movies," these two trimeter quatrains by Florence Kiper Frank schematize the moviegoing experience sharply:

She knows a cheap release
   From worry and from pain—
The cowboys spur their horses
   Over the unending plain.

The tenement rooms are small;
   Their walls press on the brain.
Oh, the dip of the galloping horses
   On the limitless, wind-swept plain![13]

Those walls that press on the brain, like the constricting verse form, represent the oppressive confines of the working-class spectator's felt life. They signify the worry and pain that compel "release" or escape to some romantic elsewhere, a fantasy wilderness. Even to indulge for a moment in the visual pleasure of this pastoral alternative is to undergo the ecstasy summoned in the ejaculation, "Oh." When the poem was reprinted in an anthology of 1923, *The Soul of the City,* the binary division became almost eerie. In the midst of so much naturalistic detail in the many poems of the anthology, the cowboys and horses strike the reader as a hallucinatory presence set in opposition to an all-too-solid urban reality.

And yet, somebody photographed those cowboys, just as somebody photographed the Van Osburgh wedding; the implied faith of the speaker is that her visionary moment in the movie theater is an awakening from the sordid dream of her life into a more authentic and satisfying reality. "To deny that it is ever reality which film projects and screens is a farce of skepticism," writes Stanley Cavell.[14] When poets much more sophisticated than Frank consider the movies, they find themselves driven to formulations recognizably related to this early effort. Whatever is screened *will* have the authority of perceived fact, for poets as well as other moviegoers. My epigraph from Kafka suggests how indelibly cinematic imagery and editing technique are impressed on everyday consciousness, so that the poetic eye, as it ages in a culture of film, routinely selects, frames, and recreates a reality (over)determined by the primal texts of the visual imagination. That is why the crisis of the film industry in the 1950s, when audiences turned to other forms of recreation, initiated a boom in movie poems. Experts in nostalgia, poets set out in large numbers to reclaim and revive the delectable "reality" they had shared as children and adolescents with movie personalities during a golden age. "The poet is at the movies," as Adrienne Rich will say, because the poet is not only a monitor of reality but a rigorous moralist in determining whether the *lived* world is sufficiently informed by the utopian pleasures of the *seen* world. A reality as bifurcated as the Frank poem offers, duplicated in Rich's poem by the gaps she discerns in *Alphaville,* cannot satisfy twentieth-century poets whose longing for a more perfect union of the real and ideal has been partly nourished by movies themselves.

The book concludes with Jorie Graham's poem "Fission" and the rise of television, two topics that take me into the dramaturgy of semiotics that is postmodernism. One of the intentions of this study is that the reader clearly recognize the origins of postmodernism in the anxieties about image multiplication, self-definition, and cultural power that begin in the second decade of this century. Movies are alert to their power to contaminate the culture, and they have transmitted that alertness to audiences by means of cautionary tales all the way from Chaplin's shorts set in movie studios and Keaton's *Sherlock Jr.* to *Sullivan's Travels* and *Sunset Boulevard,* and beyond them to *The Purple Rose of Cairo, Barton Fink, The Player,* and *The Last Action Hero.* The Hollywood novel and its long-distance cousins (dating from Luigi Pirandello's novel of 1916, *Shoot: The Notebooks of Serafino Gubbio, Cinematograph Operator,* to Manuel Puig's fantasia of 1979, *Kiss of the Spider Woman*) likewise chronicle how a society of spectators too avidly introjects the products of the dream factory. A similar tradition exists in the movie poem; indeed, it is the ultimate function of a movie poem to encourage our wariness of visual media by modeling their nearly irresistible attractions. Frank O'Hara exults, "Roll on, reels of celluloid, as the great earth rolls on." At the same time he compares himself as moviegoer to Leda being raped by a god of light. It's gratifying to think that poets will always be there to keep an "eye of power," to use Foucault's phrase, on the pleasure-giving medium that leaves its phantom traces in each and every one of us. When Jorie Graham analyzes the traumatic awakening of sexuality and selfhood occasioned by *Lolita,* or Sharon Olds writes a poem on the deep meaning of Marilyn Monroe's death, they implicitly contrast the profound effects of cinema to the superficial images made for poster display and glib journalism in the marketplace. Movie poems are *not* a form of pop culture, but batteries of formal resistance to the fantasy bribes offered by the well-financed manipulators of desire. Poems that frame complex responses to film are some of the few securely rooted sites of order and meaning in the postmodernist carnival. One would like to think of filmmakers consulting them, as D. W. Griffith and his actresses read Lindsay, and as Chaplin pondered Hart Crane's "Chaplinesque."

This book, then, is not another story about the triumph of the movies but about the triumph of the poet. Often the narrative arc of the chapters that follow carries a poet from enthusiasm about the movies to devaluation of them in favor of . . . (what else?) poetry. Because language is its substance, movie poetry cannot be content to simply replicate its object of desire, as Warhol did in offering pictures supposedly worth a thousand words. But it must also be said that movies helped to teach (at least some) modern poets how to retool the mirror of art into a projector of visionary authority. The earliest filmmakers were the forerunners of the pop artist who made movies like *Sleep* and *Haircut*. They simply cranked a camera in front of a banal event: a sneeze, a train's arrival, a factory at quitting time. When they outgrew these straightforward *actualités* the movies began to frame more complex narratives that would be incomplete until their admirers sought both to mimic and to understand their personalities, their coded plots, their revelatory montage. Poems about the movies are acts of reflection, acts of completion, asking in turn for readers willing to engage *their* unique and complex reality. What follows, then, is the first effort to undertake the journey down to the mouth of Plato's cave and speak with several generations of emerging poets about the mysterious shadows inscribed in the living body of their imagination.

Mae Marsh as Vachel Lindsay liked to think of her, in *Paddy the Next Best Thing*. In what Lindsay called "the glorifying eye of the camera," Marsh and other actresses took on the mystique of deities, and the civilizing social function formerly performed by poets.

Chapter 1

An American Millennium: Vachel Lindsay and the Poetics of Stargazing

Mae Marsh, Motion Picture Actress
(In "Man's Genesis," "The Wild Girl of the Sierras,"
"The Wharf Rat," "A Girl of the Paris Streets," etc.)

I

The arts are old, old as the stones
From which man carved the sphinx austere.
Deep are the days the old arts bring:
Ten thousand years of yesteryear.

II

She is madonna in an art
As wild and young as her sweet eyes:
A frail dew flower from this hot lamp
That is today's divine surprise.
Despite raw lights and gloating mobs
She is not seared: a picture still:
Rare silk the fine director's hand
May weave for magic if he will.

When ancient films have crumbled like
Papyrus rolls of Egypt's day,
Let the dust speak: "Her pride was high,
All but the artist hid away:

"Kin to the myriad artist clan
Since time began, whose work is dear."

The deep new ages come with her,
Tomorrow's years of yesteryear.[1]

—c. 1917

Vachel Lindsay was reaching the height of his powers when
he began to consider the movies as something more than mere recrea-
tion. In 1912, at age thirty-two, he tramped the western states trading
poems for bread and absorbing with his meals the spiritual hunger
of fieldhands, small-town shopkeepers, factory workers—all the sim-
ple folk Whitman had claimed as his constituency. While in Los An-
geles Lindsay wrote the poem that established his reputation, "Gen-
eral William Booth Enters into Heaven." This tribute to the founder
of the Salvation Army was published in the fourth number of Harriet
Monroe's magazine *Poetry* in January of 1913 and became the title
work of Lindsay's first important volume later that year. After the
fall of 1914, when *The Congo and Other Poems* appeared from Macmil-
lan, and *Adventures While Preaching the Gospel of Beauty* from Mitchell
Kennerley, Lindsay was a star of the first magnitude. Shortly before
his suicide in 1931 he would look back nostalgically at "that famous
1912 New Poetry Fire kindled by the good and great Harriet
Monroe"[2]: at Edgar Lee Masters, who would be his first biographer,
at Edna St. Vincent Millay's premier volume *Renascence,* at Ezra
Pound's and Amy Lowell's sponsorship of Imagism, at Robert
Frost's first appearance in England and Carl Sandburg's muscular
poems about Chicago. But better known than any of these was Lind-
say himself, who would be featured by the ever-vigilant Sinclair
Lewis in his novel *Free Air* (1919) as the epitome of American poetic
genius and invited throughout the Jazz Age to declaim his poems in
manic performances across the country.

Of all his contemporaries in the poetry world, Lindsay was sin-
gular in one respect: "I am the one poet who has a right to claim for
his muses Blanche Sweet, Mary Pickford, and Mae Marsh."[3] Lindsay
was infatuated with the movies, like the rest of America, and without
a thought for the indecorousness of doing so he incorporated them
into his work and into his public image. He wrote poems about the
actresses named above, and about John Bunny, and about the "rest-
less Kinetoscope vigils" he kept with acquaintances on the road

(2:740). In 1915 he published the first book of film theory in the English language, *The Art of the Moving Picture,* which was reprinted in 1916 before a second edition appeared in 1922. D. W. Griffith appreciated Lindsay's praise and invited the poet to be his guest at a screening of *Intolerance.* In letters of that period Lindsay discerns his influence on that work of "Epic Poetry," as he called it, though film critics, beginning with Eisenstein, pointed to more obvious sources like Victorian melodrama, the novels of Dickens, and, if poetry must be mentioned, Shakespeare. As college courses gradually adopted Lindsay's pioneering commentary, he continued to discourse on the subject, briefly as the first film reviewer for the *New Republic.* He authored a second book of film criticism, never published, in which he applied his theories to films like *The Thief of Bagdad, Scaramouche, Peter Pan, The Covered Wagon, Monsieur Beaucaire,* and *Merton of the Movies.* Lindsay claimed with justice that he was the one poet of the silent period who could speak with authority about the two mediums. When in 1925 the University of California asked him to teach a course in Los Angeles, he proposed "Movies and Poems."[4] Who else of his contemporaries could have taught such a course?

If we ask why it is that Nicholas Vachel Lindsay, the physician's son from Springfield, Illinois, should be the most noteworthy poet in the first two decades of this century to treat the cinema in verse, we confront a knot of explanatory data not easily untangled. First, there is the problem of conflicting opinion about film as art in Lindsay's generation. Film was routinely condemned by artists and intellectuals for its inane story lines and its vulgar appeal to the lower classes. A typical case against film that attracted Lindsay's attention and influenced his arguments in *The Art of the Moving Picture* was an essay by Walter Prichard Eaton, a newspaperman and afterward a professor of theater at Yale. Titled "Class-Consciousness and the Movies," the essay argued that films were limited in quality because of the low educational level and unrefined taste of their proletarian audiences. Eaton compared the crude sensationalism of films with current theatrical works, which could and did assume a more literate and sophisticated public. He pronounced the film play "infinitely inferior" and "spiritually stultifying."[5] In the same spirit Ezra Pound noticed the new medium long enough to castigate mass vulgarity in *Hugh Selwyn Mauberley* (1920) as a "prose kinema" that militated against the sculpted beauty of great literature. "The age demanded

an image / Of its accelerated grimace," sneered the inventor of vorti-
cism. Sympathetic to photography, Pound drew the line at moving
pictures, except as he could use their undeniable narrative possibilities
as a stick to beat narrative poets with. In the heyday of "flickers," the
movies seemed to the heirs of Matthew Arnold, the self-appointed
custodians of a rich humanistic tradition, closer to anarchy than cul-
ture.

Even to mention Pound and Arnold, however, is to half explain
why Lindsay gravitated to a defense of the new medium. By upbring-
ing and temperament Lindsay disdained the eastern seaboard and elite
Old World standards of taste. His populist sensibility led him to
embrace not only the astonishing innovations of modern technol-
ogy—the flying machine, the automobile, the skyscraper—but vul-
gate forms like the billboard and the comic strip as eruptions of the
common language into a moribund world of refined discourse. He
was attracted on the visceral level to movies, and on an intellectual
level to the claims of filmmakers that film constituted a revolutionary
art. Griffith proclaimed in 1915 that because of film "the human race
will think more rapidly, more intelligently, than it ever did. It will
see everything—positively everything."[6] With the knowledge pro-
vided by the universality of gesture and story, audiences of silent film
would gather to themselves a power they could wield against the
cultural and socioeconomic hegemony of Old World hierarchies. A
scenario-writing guidebook of the late teens and 1920s put it this way:

> Film has all of the fascinating charm of youth. It belongs to the
> new order. It thrills with the latest creative impulses. It is *democ-
> racy*. It speaks the universal language and belongs to all classes,
> all races and all nations. Someone has said that the last century
> discovered electricity, and that this century would discover life.[7]

An article from a 1913 issue of *Moving Picture World* expresses the
same sentiment:

> The motion picture has emancipated the gallery. I might say the
> gallery is having its revenge on the boxes and loges, but there is
> no question of revenge. The facts merely show that no single
> factor in our modern civilization has done more to emphasize the
> brotherhood of man than the motion picture. No single factor

has done more to create that sympathetic understanding between individuals and nations which is really an asset of the whole race and which does more for the preservation of peace among the nations than The Hague Tribunal or the Peace Society.[8]

In such manifestos, which could be quoted indefinitely, we find what has been called "the solar myth" of the Enlightenment, culminating in the early phase of the French Revolution. Just as the Enlightenment seemed to its early advocates a glorious conquest of the darkness of tyranny and superstition, so "Edison's goodliest toy," as Lindsay called it (2:740), promised a new dawn in which nations and peoples would link hearts and minds in millennial solidarity.

Lindsay's poem on Mae Marsh, then, is prophetic in the strict sense, a poem written by one who offers revelation to a class of people in need of enlightenment. The choice of Mae Marsh—and of Blanche Sweet and Mary Pickford—represents the first of what would become a tradition of actresses cast by poets for this redemptive role. Lindsay is entirely conscious of the cultic significance he is investing in the maidenly Mae Marsh. Much of his poetry before and after 1917 is devoted to the revered figure of a semidivine woman who exercises supreme power over a worshipful community. His favorite subject is the Virgin Mary, both as Christian literature imagines her and as she was more recently represented in the writings of Henry Adams. Though Lindsay resented the snob medievalism (as he saw it) of Adams's fondness for Old World cathedrals, he would have understood the lament in Adams's autobiography about the sense of emptiness he experienced in the Hall of the Dynamos at the 1900 Paris Exposition. Before technological progress harnessed human will to worship of the dynamo, Adams noted, the goddess had captivated whole societies by her imperial presence. The Virgin embodied the ultimate force imaginable, the force of sexuality and reproduction, and as mother of Christ the force fundamental to the creation and dissolution of all things. But according to Adams, "in America neither Venus nor Virgin ever had value as force. . . . The woman had once been supreme; in France she still seemed potent, not merely as a sentiment but as a force. Why was she unknown in America?"[9] Lindsay answers this question by locating the enthralling power of the "madonna" in her New World incarnation. Moreover, as a product of technological progress the cinema reconciles Virgin and dynamo, the "dew flower" and "hot lamp." The motion picture industry, by extension, becomes a secular church devoted to the perpetual re-creation and adoration of the love goddess—a responsibility gladly embraced by the studios once they realized that their own power would be enhanced by a star system and star vehicles.

Indeed, the *naming* of Mae Marsh in the poem's title is an act of prime significance. Only a few years before the poem's composition movie actresses, unlike stage personalities, either worked without credit or with titles like the Biograph Girl (Florence Lawrence) and the Vitagraph Girl (Florence Turner) that subordinated their identities to the institution that employed them. After 1909, for a variety of reasons, film actors began to be named by the studios and glorified in publicity articles that stimulated moviegoers to compulsive stargazing. The subtitle of Lindsay's poem is important because it identifies Mae Marsh as a recognizable personality in many films, an intertextual agent with a special relationship to the loyal fan. "The more films the spectator saw," Richard deCordova remarks, "and the more she or he focused on the actors, the richer the associations would be. The fame of the picture personality was something the audience could feel it was actively participating in."[10] The connection of actress to authorship, then, goes beyond being "kin to the myriad artist clan," as Lindsay asserts in his poem. Lindsay calls attention to his own unique vision by a glowing close-up of Mae Marsh in imitation of Griffith's practice, and he does so to make the same bid for recognition and reward in the marketplace. Lindsay gladly granted Griffith importance as an auteur, but in his verse he asserted his claim that the relation of the spectator to the actress is the primary and essential experience of cinema, obligating the poet to mix his welcome of the new medium with a fan's devotion to the self-defining figures so recently nominated by Hollywood for adoration.

The naming of Mary Pickford in Lindsay's other poem cinches the connection with the Virgin even tighter. In his prose book of 1915 Lindsay had argued that "the people are hungry for this fine and spiritual thing that Botticelli painted in the faces of his muses and heavenly creatures. Because the mob catch the very glimpse of it in Mary's face, they follow her night after night in the films."[11] This Mary is more than America's sweetheart; she is a fantasy intermediary between moviegoers and the higher creative powers located in the Golden State. When Mary Pickford married Douglas Fairbanks,

Lindsay's favorite actor, Lindsay declared Pickfair, their joint estate, the heavenly Olympus of the American nation, worthier of fealty than cities like New York and Boston hallowed by literary traditions.

If Lindsay was inspired by the virgin-heroines of Griffith and early filmmakers, it must be said also that he had disciplined himself to receive the glory of such a vision when it occurred. What he called his "Hothouse Period" of adolescence was devoted to the romantic proposition that, as one early poem puts it, women are stars of the heart. "I am on my knees to woman, because she is mysterious," says another poem, and continues: "O woman, to you I build myriad altars. . . . Let me never forget that woman is holy" (1:3). Lindsay did not need Freud to explain this obsession: "All of you smile the mother smile" (1:6–7). A celibate poet who filled his work with imagery of fairyland, magic, sorcery, and the miracles of children's literature, Lindsay embodied his hunger for beauty in the Eternal Feminine as manifested both in women of his own time—film actresses, Anna Pavlova, Isadora Duncan, Sara Teasdale (whom he wooed and lost)— and in women of history like Joan of Arc, Cleopatra, and Queen Elizabeth as Gloriana. Often his poems become erotic fantasies in which he costars, in propria persona or in transparent disguise, with one of these glamorous creatures. "A Doll's 'Arabian Nights'" (1919), for example, is subtitled "A Rhymed Scenario for Mae Marsh, when she acts in the new many-colored films." In this poem Lindsay escapes his spectatorial status and mingles with the actress of his dreams. "I walked into the screen," he writes well before Buster Keaton does so in *Sherlock Jr.* (1924). "Like Alice through the looking glass, / I found a curious scene"—and by the time this inter-active story is finished he has become a sultan and won the lady (1:369–72).

Wooing the actress is a form of gratitude for favors received from her films. In his poems on Mary Pickford ("doll divine") and Blanche Sweet, Lindsay chronicles the "reverent passion" passing between star and audience, and how the rudeness of the latter is softened and purified by the grace of the former: "Mobs of us made noble / By her strong desire . . . / by her . . . / Royal romance-fire" (1:223). It is a fairy transformation of the kind poets habitually practiced before they lost their audience to fiction, and then to film. If Blanche Sweet is a "Great Queen" it is partly because she has dominion over the emotions of the populace and will not cede them to poets no matter how long and eloquently they court her. The triumph of film, then, represents a crisis in the poetic vocation that Lindsay responds to in different ways throughout his career. In the 1912-1920 period he is content to imp his wing upon the object of his reverence, in the manner of devotional literature. The "romance-fire" cannot burn him, only inflame him to match the glory of his muse by poems worthy of her notice and welcome to her admirers. Everywhere in his work he cites the models of Shakespeare and Cleopatra, Dante and Beatrice (and Mary), Swinburne and Dolores, and, moving across the Atlantic, Poe and the mysterious Ulalume (Lindsay's favorite poem). As Hart Crane will later attempt in his poem of Pocahontas and the Bridge, Lindsay aspires to write the first great American poem centered on Woman, the figure Henry Adams called "the animated dynamo."

This ambition, fundamental to an understanding of the Mae Marsh poem, is spelled out explicitly in a letter of 1923 to a student admirer Lindsay idealized and almost married, Elizabeth Mann Wills. As part of his courtship, Lindsay praises Wills as an incarnation of the feminine in history. He proclaims himself her troubador, her bard, her priest, and in a surprising turn asserts that he is the superior poet to Whitman because Whitman lacked such a perfect woman. "America hungers for a Virgin Queen to glory in," he writes, "as she did in the days of Virginia when Virginia was named for Queen Elizabeth. . . . America is like me waiting for something exquisitely beautiful and virginal to which to bow down. . . . The poorest, sickest, lowest family in the slums may produce one pretty child capable of moving [making?] a Movie-Queen more delicate than all the heroines of Whitman." The movies, then, endow an aristocracy of presence; they offer genuine democratic vistas by presenting to poets, as to everyone, figures proleptic of a golden age. In a culture of film the poet still has a chance of securing an audience made submissive and receptive to eternal beauty by the screen image of some Cinderella raised to splendor. "Even a Mary Pickford . . . would have made Whitman the poet his followers claim he is—the poet of *total* democracy," Lindsay says in the same letter.[12]

In Lindsay's poem the "madonna" becomes an idol of the community spirit, though she calls her followers to a destiny beyond the confines of conventional society. A modern sphinx, this remote, untouchable image offers itself as a reminder of man's immemorial desire. She is both more fundamental than civilization and a *symboliste* dream of the pleasure that civilization might bestow in some transfigured, utopian form. Lindsay's opposition of the "gloating mobs" to the proud female image reflects Griffith's use of Mae Marsh as the virginal symbol of the frail virtues that barbarism seeks to violate. In *Man's Genesis* she is the prehistoric cave girl Lilywhite beloved by Weakhands, a protointellectual who saves her from the bestial clutches of a caveman named Bruteforce. In *Birth of a Nation* she is the innocent Little Sister who leaps to her death rather than be ravished by a black renegade. In *Intolerance* she is Dear One, the patient and virtuous wife and mother enduring her husband's unjust imprisonment. She is too good for the mob, which is why it desires her. Lindsay discovered on the road that Americans hungered for an undefiled beauty, the kind that only presences like Mae Marsh could satisfy. He wrote in his film book: "If it is the conviction of serious minds that the mass of men shall never again see pictures out of Heaven except through such mediums as the kinetoscope lens, let all the higher forces of our land courageously lay hold upon this thing that saves us from perpetual spiritual blindness."[13] If executives of the movie companies read Lindsay's prose, and his poems, they must have rejoiced to hear these words. They did what he told them; they built more theaters and produced more films to carry compelling faces like Mae Marsh's across the country.

If Lindsay is a minor poet it is in part because he did not analyze the psychological and sociological effects of such enthusiastic utterances. When the heat is turned up on the "romance-fire" of cinema sexuality, who gets burned? The question does not occur to Lindsay because he is focused so entirely upon the innocent doll figures of Mary Pickford and Mae Marsh. Griffith's treatment of Mae Marsh was certainly less innocent than Lindsay understood. Molly Haskell calls his use of girl actresses "nympholeptic," part of the tradition of leering perversity encouraged by the camera eye's intrusive peeking into the private spaces of adolescent female sexuality. Marjorie Rosen likewise comments on Griffith's "nymphophilia," as expressed, for example, in his insistence that Mae Marsh appear with limbs exposed in *The Sands of Dee,* and that another actress forego panties to enhance her sex appeal.[14] Lindsay's one recognition of this tendency occurs during a review of Mary Pickford's film, *A Romance of the Redwoods* (1917), in which he remarks on the way Mary is "sometimes . . . innocent eight, sometimes dangerous sixteen."[15] Mae Marsh's no less dangerous sexuality, which Griffith exploited boldly, is kept entirely out of Lindsay's commentaries upon her, in prose and verse.

Likewise, Lindsay keeps clear of Lillian Gish, whose "energy of sublimated sexuality," in Haskell's phrase, is so often foregrounded by directors like Griffith.[16] It is interesting to look at an essay on Gish by the novelist Joseph Hergesheimer, in the April 1924 issue of the *American Mercury,* to appreciate what Lindsay excludes from his idealizing of Botticelli-like actresses. Hergesheimer enthuses about Gish in Lindsay's manner, and confesses that he has modeled some of his fictional characters after her. Now he wants to write a screenplay that will elevate her above "the tyranny of mob sentimentality" into a story worthy of her awe-inspiring presence. The essay depicts the humorous effect when he makes his proposition to her directly. As he builds castles in the air for her to glide through, she queries about financing and choice of director, and the most effective way of presenting her charms. Despite the arch tone, his tribute to her is heartfelt:

> you have the quality which, in a Golden Age, would hold an army about the walls of a city for seven years. Helen might be different from you in every apparent particular, from the ground gold in her hair to her dyed feet, but you are one at heart. Listen, in this picture none will ever possess you, dragging you down to the realities of satisfaction. You will be, like the April moon, a thing for all young men to dream about forever; you will be the immeasurable difference between what men have and what they want.

Hergesheimer playfully inflates his diction as he makes his mock offer to write a story that will render all young men "forever dissatisfied with reality" and cast Gish as the femme fatale who enacts this terror upon them. And yet he has confessed to having been burned by just such a flame in his lovelorn worship of Gish. Had he not punctured his own hyperbolic tone by allowing Gish her unromantic responses, he would have confined her to some transcendent identity, belle dame sans merci or maiden goddess. Instead, Hergesheimer depicts a professional businesswoman who obligingly wears whatever pagan or puritan mask male authors fix upon her for the entertainment of

archromantics like himself. Placing Hergesheimer's double-voiced ar-
ticle next to Lindsay's poem, we can measure the acute limitations of
Lindsay's unself-conscious cultivation of the feminine mystique.

One anecdote on this topic is irresistible. Anita Loos, a scenario
writer for Griffith in the late teens and a good friend of Mae Marsh,
tells of the actress's anxiety about fan letters she received from Lind-
say. She felt that out of common politeness she needed to respond to
his ardent tributes. "'But,' said Mae, 'I wouldn't know what to say
to such an intellectual gink.'" In Cyrano de Bergerac fashion, Loos
wrote return letters to Lindsay over Mae Marsh's signature, until
finally the lovesick poet arranged a meeting with the actress (and
Loos as chaperone) in Loos's New York apartment, formerly a
brothel and still floridly decorated. When Lindsay appeared, Loos
reports, "He resembled neither Byron nor Shelley. From head to toe
he failed to conform. . . . The most accurate image I can conjure of
poor darling Vachel is that of the red-headed ventriloquist dummy
called Mortimer Snerd." Though Lindsay overwhelmed them in a
rush of eloquence, he could not persuade Mae Marsh to retire with
him to Springfield. This Chaplinesque incident might have served a
more sophisticated writer, like Hergesheimer or the Eliot of "Portrait
of a Lady," as the source of a self-mocking modernist piece. But
Lindsay could not step back from the comic scene and listen with an
unromantic ear to his flourishes of rhetoric.[17]

Indeed, a significant constraint on Lindsay's encomiastic poem
is the conventionality of its style. His philosophy of beauty inherited
from Poe and Pre-Raphaelite models inclined him toward the melodi-
ous quatrains, the refrain, the monotonous iambics, and the mild
rhymes of "Mae Marsh," rather than the dynamic kinesis of his more
famous lyrics. When Lindsay celebrated masculine personalities in the
public sphere, he wrote with a wild freedom. In "Bryan, Bryan,
Bryan, Bryan," for example, the American idiom refreshes his enthu-
siastic praise; he places the fiery orator among "The plop-eyed bunga-
roo and giant giassicus / . . . The rakaboor, the hellangone, / The
whangdoodle, batfowl and pig." Animal nature of every kind seems
to rise up in the poem with the energy of a new language in order to
aid Bryan's attempts to smash the eastern establishment. The buoyant
spirits and revolutionary fervor of Bryan's 1896 appearance in
Springfield are enacted in the oral flourishes of the varied lines. This
is the syncopated verse that roused audiences who spent their eve-

nings watching Chaplin shorts and the Keystone Kops. But Lindsay's pietistic devotion to film actresses mandated a more conventional structure; likewise, his memorial poem on the slapstick comic John Bunny has the heightened diction appropriate for the elegiac mode. Only in private correspondence could Lindsay see Mae Marsh and Mary Pickford plain, as ordinary and not very interesting people with pretty faces rather than as icons of the infinite.

Lindsay's high style reflected his belief that the ages had chosen him (not Whitman) to be the American bard who would reveal what he called "the secret of democratic beauty."[18] The adjective is crucial, for it separates his quest from that of contemporaries like Pound and Eliot, who considered democracy and beauty incompatible. Lindsay searched through history for models of the new order he wished to imagine into being by poems like the one on Mae Marsh. He claimed that the old beauty had been democratic too. Cro-Magnon cave painting—a discovery of Lindsay's generation—had conveyed to the tribe charismatic models of beauty and power. The men who "carved the sphinx austere" had presented to a wondering public the most compelling visual images of the preclassical age. Democratic art, in Lindsay's view, must be nonliterate, the art of pictures, or, in verbal expression, the "Higher Vaudeville" (as he termed it) of oral recitation. As Pound discovered in the Chinese written character a model of precise description, so Lindsay turned to Egyptian hieroglyphics for a universal alphabet based on pictures which could restore to man the powers of precise expression of which abstraction had deprived him. Egyptian art preserves the secret of beauty in visual form available to all. And one could say that the massive effort required to erect the pyramids and sphinx represented a universal participation in the mysteries, as Henry Adams claimed for the erection of the great European cathedrals.

Lindsay began his career as an artist, and never ceased to insist that his poems *were* pictures, or hieroglyphs, comparable to the stained glass of Chartres or the pictorial language of the pyramids. Like Blake, he designed books in which graphics and text were combined for occult visual effects. In an introduction to his *Collected Poems* he wrote mystically of the hieroglyph as "the minute single cell of our thought," a new visual alphabet for a symbolic language inspired by the movies. "The reason I am so mad over hieroglyphics," he remarked in a letter, "is simply that I am movie satu-

rated. . . . Such movie training is a surprising initiation into the whole
Egyptian psychology of hieroglyphics."[19] Because this connection
did not take in the history of modern poetry, and has been treated as
little more than debased Imagism, we may miss its principal function
as a means of justifying the movie scenarios Lindsay versified in his
later years. By the late 1920s, however, there is evidence that Lindsay
was trying to free himself from his obsession with visual media. This
is a period when he wrote no poems about movie figures. "We are
sweeping into new times," he remarked in his unpublished movie
book, "in which the eye is invading the province of the ear, and in
which pictures are crowding all literature to the wall, and if some of
the dressed-up steerage passengers had their way, they would crowd
all history to the wall" (22). Similar sentiments in his letters from the
early teens indicate that Lindsay felt intermittently that films were a
threat as well as a blessing, and that poets must not be so drawn into
the maelstrom of their appeal that they lose the ability to sustain an
independent voice, a vision creative of, but not entirely created by,
popular culture.

    (Who, parenthetically, are the "steerage passengers" that threaten
to extinguish history from modern consciousness? In such a phrase
we glimpse the xenophobia that is the dark side of Lindsay's mid-
western patriotism. The context suggests that Lindsay is thinking of
immigrants like Adolph Zukor, Carl Laemmle, and Samuel
Goldwyn, that is, movie producers who were the agents of revolu-
tionary change Lindsay elsewhere celebrated. A late essay complains
about the "smutty" films of the 1920s and lays the blame for their
sinfulness on the producers: "The movie men, poisoned by easy
money, have lock jaw of the mind. I, for one, will be delighted if
they are tied up one and all, and fed through a tube called Censorship.
It will do them good. No, there are no exceptions."[20])

    Lindsay, like many other writers of the teens and 1920s, held
contradictory opinions about the dynamism of a mass society ser-
viced by popular media. On the one hand, he was appalled by the
Brownian motion of citizens caught up in a frenzy of getting, spend-
ing, and recreating. He saw this hectic activity reflected in the
"speeded-up, unreasoning hieroglyphics" of silent film, with its
montage of often loosely organized images. As an expression of a
materialistic civilization, the movies threatened to degenerate into a
"lavish department-store basement gone wrong" and the spectator's

mind into "a Ringling circus, a gigantic spectacle but not set in order, not harmonized by a stage manager" (24–25). Whitman had exerted his poetic powers to contain and order the prolific spectacle of commodified objects and behaviors by means of his catalogs and the inspired sequencing of his discrete impressions. But Lindsay saw himself and contemporary poets in danger of being overwhelmed by the anarchic conditions of modernity signified by the moving pictures of the Roaring Twenties.

Where Whitman called the United States the greatest poem, offering himself as equal to the task of apprehending and articulating its structure, Lindsay states as "my general proposition that the United States is a great movie. . . . All American history past, present and to come, is a gigantic movie with a Pilgrim's Progress or hurdle race plot" (130, 205). The significance of such statements can hardly be overestimated. If history is imagined as a purely *visual* structure, then the bardic ambition of Whitman and Lindsay must yield to the "fine director's hand" capable of rendering that history in its appropriate form. However concerned he is about history and poetry being pushed to the wall by the triumph of movies, Lindsay defers to artists like Griffith who aspired to become the sole interpreters of American experience, and by doing so make verbal literature superfluous. Here are sample comments by Griffith from an interview of 1915.

> [Audiences] have the good old American faculty of wanting to be "shown" things. We don't "talk" about things happening, or describe how a thing looks; we actually show it—vividly, completely, convincingly. It is the ever-present, realistic, actual now that "gets" the great American public, and nothing ever devised by the mind of man can show it like moving pictures.
>
> The time will come, and in less than ten years . . . where the children in the public schools will be taught practically everything by moving pictures. Certainly they will never be obliged to read history again.[21]

There is nothing surprising in Griffith's ambition to marginalize historiography and literature in favor of his own technics. But Lindsay's acceptance of a diminished role for poetry in the volatile, often disordered movie scenario of American history testifies to his decreasing confidence in the legitimacy of his enterprise, indeed of his professional life.

In Lindsay's oscillating feelings about the art of the cinema we see the paradigm for many poets to come. Sensing in himself the evacuation of that old-time religion, and of the Romantic worldview as well, Lindsay played the role of some new John the Baptist heralding the coming of a liberating spiritual force that would weld together the American Zion into a joyful and entirely modern civilization. As a spectator Lindsay could participate in the new mysteries, and he documented his affinity for the art of surfaces all the way into the sound era, hailing *Broadway Melody* as a satisfying entertainment in one of his last commentaries on film. As a poet, however, he felt himself increasingly estranged from the culture as it followed his lead in situating movies at the center of national life. The more keenly he felt himself an outsider, the more he sought out movies to assuage his lonely separation from the common folk who no longer cared for his poetry. On his last unsuccessful reading tours on the East Coast he went to the movies compulsively, in every town and village, rejoicing in the thought that somewhere in the West a new imagination of history was being created. "Hollywood is the real American capitol, not Washington D.C." (13), he wrote. Hollywood was the promised land he never revisited before he took his life in Springfield, the city of Lincoln.

The Whitmanian dream of American literature is that space might replace time, that the linkages between place and place—railroads, canals, telegraph lines, bridges—might usurp the time cycles of events as principal facts of everyday consciousness. In claiming that Mae Marsh and her descendants would penetrate every local community and bring them joy and wisdom, Lindsay made their presences one with the "orchard god" Johnny Appleseed, whom he apotheosized in poem and tract as a democratic Christ. The growth of Southern California as a moviemaking center served Lindsay's mythology, for it perpetuated the westering impulse of pioneers who decentered the nineteenth-century sites of American power in favor of the frontier. Lindsay affirmed that "Edison is the new Gutenberg. He has invented the new printing. The state that realizes this may lead the soul of America, day after tomorrow."[22] Los Angeles would achieve in artistic terms what according to Lindsay the Panama Canal had accomplished in 1915; his commemorative poem is titled "The Wedding of the Rose and the Lotus." The last westward drive, in Lindsay's own time, had found the most convenient passage to India, and Los Angeles deserved to succeed the European and eastern American cities as the fulcrum of a new world empire.

In effect, then, Lindsay announced "An American Millennium," to use a phrase from his poem on Alexander Campbell, founder of the Disciples of Christ in the nineteenth century (1:406). Lindsay's family belonged to this church and raised Nicholas Vachel to be on the lookout for signs and wonders that would fulfill the hopes invested in the New World by the centuries. Lindsay was not the only poet to recognize in cinema the agency of a continuing Enlightenment. One of John Berryman's earliest published poems, "Homage to Film" (1940), begins:

> The sun of another medium
> Comes up the East, mechanical
> As any art, slow, but it will come
> Faster and at last find
> Its noon an Argus brain that shall
> Center all complexities in mind.

Berryman praises the Dionysian qualities of film, its ability to release "ecstasy in the bone / Of all men always, in city, / Hills or in a wilderness of stone."[23] Film refreshes the exhausted spirit in the waste land by organizing, or centering, the capacity for love and joy. Berryman, too, backed away from the implications of such an apocalyptic claim, one that would obligate him to greater homage than he was prepared, then or ever, to offer the new medium. His next great "Homage" was to another originary figure, whom he featured in a book-length poem sixteen years later. Anne Bradstreet, the first American poet, becomes his inspirational object of devotion. Lindsay found no muse of poetry to sustain his later career, though he tried in the 1920s to find a successor to Mae Marsh and Mary Pickford, too womanly by then to serve as his Beatrice and (Virgin) Mary. "There is emerging a motion picture Muse," he wrote hopefully in the late 1920s, "a somewhat abstract lady, no doubt, but she is in many ways a sister of Mary Pickford" (222). He was attracted to Bebe Daniels but decided she didn't qualify, and finally he left the position vacant.

He would not have felt comfortable predicating a new age on the likes
of Clara Bow, Gloria Swanson, or Joan Crawford.

"Mae Marsh" follows the analogy of Egypt to its melancholy
conclusion, a significant difference from the optimistic final chapters
of *The Art of the Moving Picture*. And yet "The deep new ages" that
come with Mae Marsh, though she herself be buried by them, will
owe their luster to her contribution. Because of the corrosive chemis-
try of nitrate stock, Mae Marsh seemed in 1917 unlikely to survive
"ten thousand years" except as a name, a Romantic image on stills
or pottery, an object of regard in poems like this one. Ironically, she
has been preserved and lovingly retouched and restored by film histo-
rians, and by a growing audience enamored of silent film, while most
of Lindsay's mythmaking has been buried by the custodians of the
modern tradition in literature. His poems and prose urging the gospel
of beauty as a response to the spiritual crisis of his era have mingled
with the dust of other new-century modes of edifying literature. But
this modest poem survives as a memorial of the country's first heady
engagement with "today's divine surprise."

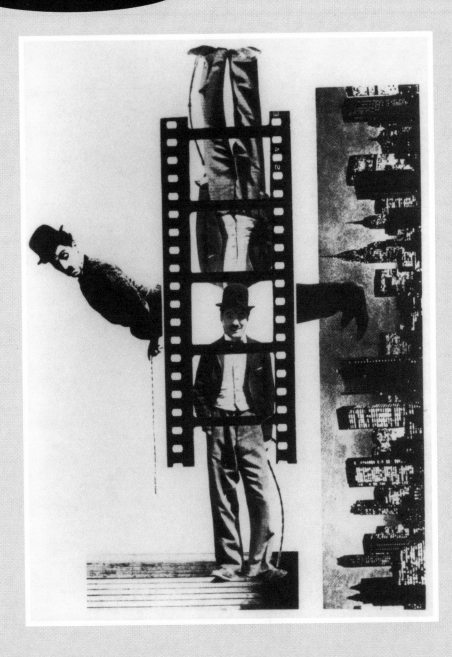

Mieczyslaw Berman, *Chaplin II,* 1928. Charlie Chaplin in a photo-collage construction. His feet dangling above the city of skyscrapers, Chaplin defies the laws even of gravity thanks to his cinematic essence. The worldwide symbol of silent film, Chaplin cast a spell on many modern poets. (From *Dada: Photographie und Photocollage,* ed. Carl-Albrecht Haenlin [Hanover: Kestern, 1979].)

Chapter 2

Hart Crane: Speaking the Mot Juste in the Age of Silents

CHAPLINESQUE

We make our meek adjustments,
Contented with such random consolations
As the wind deposits
In slithered and too ample pockets.

For we can still love the world, who find
A famished kitten on the step, and know
Recesses for it from the fury of the street,
Or warm torn elbow coverts.

We will sidestep, and to the final smirk
Dally the doom of that inevitable thumb
That slowly chafes its puckered index toward us,
Facing the dull squint with what innocence
And what surprise!

And yet these fine collapses are not lies
More than the pirouettes of any pliant cane;
Our obsequies are, in a way, no enterprise.
We can evade you, and all else but the heart:
What blame to us if the heart live on.

The game enforces smirks; but we have seen
The moon in lonely alleys make
A grail of laughter of an empty ash can,
And through all sound of gaiety and quest
Have heard a kitten in the wilderness.[1]

—1921

39

In the 27 February 1915 issue of the *New Republic,* George Santayana joined the spirited debate about poetic diction aroused by the New Poetry movement. Should the language of verse be more like common American speech? Santayana speculated on how Shakespeare's Sonnet 29 would sound if it were written in the vernacular. Instead of the memorable opening, "When in disgrace with fortune and men's eyes / I all alone beweep my outcast state," we would have "When times are hard and old friends fall away / And all alone I lose my hope and pluck," and so on down to the resonant closure, "For if you care for me, what need I care / To own the world or be a millionaire?" The antic revision is aimed at the newspaper verse of Eugene Field and Eddie Guest, but his satirical point applied to all writers who called for a rejection of the so-called grand manner. Ever since Walt Whitman declared his contempt for "art-writers" and lifted his barbaric yawp over the rooftops of America, writers had felt pressured to take their lead from the lower reaches of the social world. Santayana's satirical prescription would be taken up affirmatively by Alva Johnston in a biography of Samuel Goldwyn; he asserted that if Shakespeare were alive in modern America he would be writing scripts for the movie producer and be subjected justly to criticism for his high-toned dialogue. Reviewing Johnston's claim, Edmund Wilson was moved to take up the conservative's cudgel: "Mr. Johnston must know as well as anybody that Mr. Goldwyn would not be able to do anything for the least of Shakespeare's plays except turn it into something different and worse."[2]

Santayana's polemic was a counterrevolutionary one, for literary history had always privileged the higher idiom and the more complex artifice as the voice of civilized society and cast the defenders of plainer and more "natural" writing as discontents. The high style—an elevated vocabulary often arranged in unconventional syntactical combinations—presumed to articulate truths that transcended common understanding. It had thematic complexity and intensity. It shared itself with a select audience educated to the habit of textuality. But like the hierarchical society it represented, it dared not separate itself from the practical energies and good sense of the demos; indeed, it required the infusion of common blood to keep it from unhealthy inbreeding, lest poetry "talk like books" in an ever more rarefied poetic discourse. Alexander Pope had undertaken the revolutionary's role in the early eighteenth century when he set his wit against the baroque locutions derived from Milton and Shakespeare or the more extreme word choices of Metaphysical verse. In his prose essay *Peri Bathous,* subtitled *The Art of Sinking in Poetry* Pope had lampooned poets like Theobald and Blackmore who translated the most common utterances into pompous speech. Pope complains that for a simple phrase like "Light the fire" the oracular bard will write:

> Bring forth some remnant of Promethean theft,
> Quick to expand th' inclement air congealed
> By Boreas' rude breath . . .

And for "Snuff the candle":

> Yon Luminary amputation needs,
> Thus shall you save its half-extinguished life.[3]

As the champion of a plainer style, however, Pope would feel himself suspended uncomfortably between a hallowed tradition of lofty idioms and the fresher but more ordinary diction of his London contemporaries. He would register his mixed feelings in *The Rape of the Lock,* which deploys the grand manner to underscore the triviality of its narrative events but at the same time draws a line against Homeric and Miltonic epithets ("glittering Forfex" for scissors, and the like) on behalf of his sophisticated urban audience. Wordsworth would do the same in his 1800 "Preface" to *Lyrical Ballads,* where Thomas Gray's midcentury attempt to revive the golden style is subjected to withering scorn, and a chastened "language of real men" held up as the preferred speech of modern poetry. It is the triumph of Wordsworthian principles that Santayana is deploring, albeit with good humor, in his redaction of Shakespeare's sonnet.

In the decade before Santayana's essay, the movies were struggling with the same kind of bifurcated sensibility. Moviegoers were tempted one way by filmed stage plays acted in the histrionic style appropriate to huge theaters, and another way by the unpretentious kinesis of realistic drama and slapstick. The history of motion pictures shows a toning down by directors and actors of the grandiloquent body language inherited from the stage toward more natural mannerisms, and more lifelike tempo, from scene to scene. Though silent movie acting of the 1920s elicits laughter in theaters of the present day, the stylistic codes of the acknowledged masterpieces actually represent simplifications of the more exaggerated styles that mandated, say, raising the back of the hand to the brow to express anguish, and the hand clutching the throat to express fear. As the more streamlined films quickly found favor with audiences, filmmakers gladly chased the high style off the screen by travesties. Charlie Chaplin, especially, punctuated his films with burlesques of the grand manner, as he had learned them in the British music hall tradition stretching back to the early eighteenth century.

No doubt one reason Vachel Lindsay disliked Chaplin was that he resented the irreverent satire on stylistic models he emulated in his own verse. What is the diction of "Mae Marsh" ("Ten thousand years of yesteryear") but the literary equivalent of Sarah Bernhardt trying to perpetuate the grand manner of the Victorian stage in the Film D'Art vehicle *Queen Elizabeth* (1912)? Lindsay advised mankind to go down on its knees before the sacred image of woman; the early Chaplin was more likely to give a pretty girl a kick in the backside. Lindsay never felt at home with the parodic and irreverent, the modernist style as it would take form in the writing of Eliot, Stevens, Cummings, and in the films of Chaplin and Keaton. Watching Chaplin cavort, he must have felt that here was no great-souled artist but merely some talented street yokel of the lower vaudeville.

Hart Crane, however, saw something very different in Chaplin's sportive comedies. What he saw was an animated performer whose "fine collapses" and "pirouettes" distinguished his activity from the quotidian body language of his contemporaries. What is remarkable in Chaplin's early films is the excess of gesticulation, the bravura gestural performance that bewilders his coactors and surprises his audience into a pleased alertness. The continuous stream of invention in the films cannot help but impress the poet as similar to the linguistic play he practices in excess of what is minimally required by the declarative character of his address. The occasion for Chaplin's kinetic frenzy is a lyric one, and the momentary mayhem he causes or the fleeting pathos he evokes, have all the rich conventions of the pierrot act in the commedia dell'arte tradition, as it is honored in the poems of Jules Laforgue, some of which Crane translated. If Lindsay yearns for Mae Marsh because she embodied the romantic ideal of beauty, Crane, drawing on the same fin-de-siècle sources for different effects, admires Chaplin for his modernist subversion of that same ideal.

Though Lindsay and Crane both introduce a movie star into the
pantheon of illustrious Americans as a model of vitality for the new
century, Crane makes use of a different register of idiom in order to
distance his verse equally from what he considered the decadent prac-
tice of the grand manner and from the homespun diction derided by
Santayana.

A glance at the phrasing of "Chaplinesque" shows us the ostenta-
tious peculiarity of Crane's word choices. Crane is not writing a
straight golden style of the Keatsian kind, or the baroque of Milton,
but rather a form of burlesque, as the suffix of the title reminds us.
(And there is a helping of "grotesque" as well, whose meanings in-
clude "a clown, buffoon, or merry-andrew" and "fantastically ex-
travagant, bizarre, and quaint.") "Burlesque" has these associations:
"That species of composition which excites laughter by caricature of
serious works, or by ludicrous treatment of their subjects." The
poem's phrasing is certainly a comedy of language, but does it depre-
ciate at the same time it pays homage to Chaplin? Does it accept
Chaplin's naive simplification of social reality into the kitten, the
cop, and the wilderness? The diction does not give the reader an easy
purchase upon these questions, for it is both *like* Chaplin's fantastical
comedies and *unlike* them because of its elliptical structure and com-
pressed locutions. One can imagine Pope or Wordsworth creeping
up on the third and fourth stanzas, pin in hand, ready to puncture the
inflated rhetoric of "and to the final smirk / Dally the doom of that
inevitable thumb / That slowly chafes its puckered index toward us"
or "Our obsequies are, in a way, no enterprise," where the phrase "in
a way" is a propitiatory gesture to keep the line within hailing dis-
tance of common speech. Most English-speaking people will lead
their whole lives without uttering the word *obsequies*. The question
is not what such phrases mean, in the sense of what they translate
into, but why it was important for Crane to position them within a
poem honoring an artist who never constructed a scene or sequence
of comparable difficulty.

Malcolm Cowley remarked to Crane about his early poems,
"You write with a bombast which is not Elizabethan but contempo-
rary, and you are one of two or three people who can write a 20th
century blank verse about other subjects than love, death, and night-
ingales."[4] "Bombast" is perhaps the more precise term than "bur-
lesque," for the iambics of "Chaplinesque" offer an expansive diction

deliberately in excess of its sentimental subject. If Vachel Lindsay had written the poem, or Edna St. Vincent Millay, the effect would have been very different. Crane had written in his adolescence the kind of Poe- and Swinburne-haunted verse of these high-emotion poets, and no doubt the figure of, say, America's sweetheart Mary Pickford was a temptation to the author of "My Grandmother's Love Letters." But Chaplin helped Crane escape from the decadent romanticism to which so many of his contemporaries succumbed. *The Kid,* especially, was a revelation to Crane of how to express legitimate emotion without bullying the audience into an automatic or stock response to formulaic situations. First of all, there was the humor that leavened the sentiment by making Charlie a more complex figure than simply a walking trope of lovelorn yearning. Such a view would have made the sentiment one of bathos, susceptible to all of Pope's strictures against rhetorical inflation. And then there was the astonishing ingenuity of the film, with all its unrealistic turns of plot and its signature Chaplinesque tricks and transformations. Sergei Eisenstein, in his essay on *The Kid,* praised the "unusual eyes" that permitted Chaplin a childlike vision of the world as "monstrous and distorted." "In thinking about Chaplin," he wrote, "one wants above all to delve into that *strange* structure of thought which sees Phenomena in such a *strange* fashion and replies to it with images of equal *strangeness*" (emphasis added).[5] Images of strangeness translate effectively into a poetic language of strangeness, making Chaplin an appropriate model for the idiosyncratic phrasing, supple and preening, of Crane's poem.

Indeed, Crane insisted that the poem is centrally about the poet and poetry in a world that treats its ancient claims as risible. Crane wrote to a friend, "poetry, the human feelings, 'the kitten,' is so crowded out of the humdrum, rushing, mechanical scramble of today that the man who would preserve them must duck and camouflage for dear life to keep them or keep himself from annihilation."[6] Every word tells in this remark. As a practitioner of a primordial and honored art form, Crane has the poet's anxiety about modernity, for every cultural change necessarily threatens an entrenched medium or style. As noted, Pope and Wordsworth advocated significant adaptations to a vernacular mode empowered by dynamic social and economic changes in their times; and yet both expressed the same anxiety Crane projects in poem and letter. Pope turned his mixed feelings about the new society into comedy, often low comedy as in *The*

Dunciad, where the epic conventions crush the witlings of Grub Street who threaten poetry and human feeling alike. (Daniel Defoe is one of the writers disparaged in *The Dunciad,* and by the time of the poem's composition, 1728, Defoe's fiction had helped to establish the new art form of the novel as firmly as Chaplin had established film by 1921.) Wordsworth would dramatize his anxiety about modernity in the dream scene of book 5 of *The Prelude,* when an Arab horseman in the wilderness undertakes to guard a stone and a shell, the latter a symbol of "Shakespeare and Milton, laborers divine," from being overwhelmed by a tidal wave gathering at the horizon. The Arab is described as also being Don Quixote, for the task is a madman's desperate, perhaps absurd, attempt to preserve a tradition of eloquence from the apocalyptic new wave of democratic culture engendered by the French Revolution and its barbaric demiurge, Napoleon.[7]

Crane's adjectives "humdrum, rushing, mechanical" tell us what social forces worried him in the new century. They are recognizable likenesses of the dynamic forces that disturbed those polemicists for the plain(er) style, Pope and Wordsworth: the accumulation of humanity in cities, the transformation of work and leisure by international trade and the Industrial Revolution, as well as the degraded taste for mass entertainments, addictive sensual pleasures, and violence. This is the signified context of "the fury of the street" in "Chaplinesque." Chaplin had opened his early films to all of those anarchic forces, and before settling on the genial figure of the Tramp or "The Little Fellow," he had often joined the most belligerent of the bullies in beating down bystanders innocent or otherwise. But in *The Kid* Chaplin offers "random consolations" to the victimized, whose condition he knew from personal experience. Chaplin's immense popularity suggested to Crane that such "gaiety and quest" was not futile, not the absurd daydreaming of a Quixote, but viable in an increasingly harsh and uncaring world. Chaplin appeals to him as a resourceful maker who can use technique to transform the objective world into a subjective style. Crane wrote that he was moved by *The Kid* "to put Chaplin with the poets (of today); hence the 'we'."[8] Crane will adopt Chaplin's repertoire of idiosyncratic props— "the ample pockets . . . pliant cane"—as signs of artistic privilege and social concern. By doing so Crane effects a community of purpose that permits him to share vicariously in the mythology Chaplin created, a mythology in which he reigned as the working-class hero, the first citizen in a commonwealth of new democratic beings joined in solidarity. Crane's "we" in the poem looks back toward the aspirations of "We the People" in forming a new constitution for the nation.

It may be useful to pause and further examine this "we" that Crane calls attention to as the linguistic sign of his fellow feeling with Chaplin. On one level it is a simple declaration of his identification with the comedian as artist, specifically the Chaplin who renders the feelings of the human heart by means of inventive performative technique. "You know I worship Chaplin's work," he wrote to a friend. "Think he is the greatest living actor I've seen, and the prime interpreter of the soul imposed upon by modern civilization."[9] But Thomas E. Yingling argues that "Chaplinesque" is "an allegory of homosexual desire" precisely because "the 'we' . . . is constructed in sight of the practice of homosexuality, its alienations and consequent nostalgias."[10] That is, the same erotic passions recognizable in Lindsay's reverence for Mae Marsh can be located in Crane's "worship" and re-creation of Chaplin's presence. Chaplin's fondness for scenes of gender confusion in which he plays, literally or by implication, the part of a coquettish woman, would make Crane's male gaze at the comic more empathetic. This reading is worth noting because we will find so many gay poets writing about film, such as Parker Tyler, Frank O'Hara, Edward Field, Allen Ginsberg, John Ashbery, James Baldwin, and Paul Monette, to name only a few. Is there something about the experience of filmgoing and the experience of writing poetry that is symbiotic with the homosexual imagination? The connection might be identified, at this point, as the sense of poet as outsider, alienated from mainstream society by his crystallization of a countercultural sensibility. Delmore Schwartz supplies the logical connection when he writes, "The more the poet has cultivated his own sensibility, the more unique and special has his subject, and thus his method, become. The common language of daily life, its syntax, habitual sequences, and processes of association, are precisely the opposite of what he needs, if he is to make poetry from what absorbs him as a poet, his own sensibility."[11] By this perspective, the narcissistic "we" of the poem binds together not only Crane and Chaplin, but also Crane and the reader, who is incorporated as part of the body of Crane's vision, watching Charlie invent an evasive (rhetorical) strategy to defy the upraised thumb of a powerful authority. The campy ostentation of the diction and syntax, then, constitutes part of the evasion of "the common language [and codes] of daily life" that has alienated poet and homosexual alike.

Crane writes this poem just at the time when Chaplin is deliberately changing his style to rid himself of the vulgar mannerisms of the Keystone, Essanay, and Mutual comedies, and achieve the more genteel, sophisticated pantomime of the features he will direct in the 1920s and 1930s. As Charles Maland has demonstrated, Chaplin made himself available to the intelligentsia as a kindred spirit, and by 1921 had effectively separated himself from the mass of moviemakers and film stars as a special case, a hybrid of clown and poet. *Poet* is the word used constantly in the panegyrics of the period, even in the mass media. The poet Benjamin de Casseres, for example, conducted an influential interview in the *New York Times* in 1920 in which he calls Chaplin "a poet, an esthete . . . a man infinitely sad and melancholy . . . a Puck, a Hamlet, an Ariel." Chaplin fills the interview with sentiments designed to endear him to that elite audience dwelling in the Axel's castle of the American experience: "the dream-world is . . . the great reality; the real world is an illusion," he remarks, and later, "I am oppressed . . . by world-weariness."[12] He wants only to retire to an Italian lake with volumes of Keats and Shelley.

This episode of public relations, in which an entertainer tells an intellectual just what he wants to hear, cannot be given too much weight. And yet it helps fix for us the image of Chaplin most appealing to poets, then and now. Chaplin's films, with the low figure of the Tramp as a putative everyman, would *seem* to be straightforward examples of egalitarian style and storytelling. But literary commentators chose to emphasize the extra-ordinary quality of his movies. Parker Tyler remarks, "the image of grace in clumsiness; of articulacy in inarticulacy. . . . This was Charlie's art of caricature . . . *aristocratic style at any price.*"[13] Edmund Wilson compares Chaplin to E. E. Cummings, whose balletic and comic poems seem to affirm solidarity with all good-hearted people but whose technique keeps a mass reading audience at a distance. R. W. B. Lewis argues that Chaplin is the model for Wallace Stevens's quixotic poet-protagonist in the (mock) grand-manner masterpiece "The Comedian as the Letter C."[14] With or without Chaplin's remarks in periodicals, it was possible to think that his films lent support to the modernist enterprise that set unusual

language against the tradition of natural speech bequeathed by
Whitman and watered down to Crane's—and Stevens's—disgust by
poets like Masters, Sandburg, and other midwestern discoveries of
Harriet Monroe.

Indeed, Chaplin's image was appropriated for the international
language(s) of modernism; his name and picture appeared in a multi-
tude of artworks, especially in photocollage and commercial graph-
ics, as an irrepressible sign of the zeitgeist. As an unthreatening,
indeed ingratiating symbol of American mass culture, Chaplin se-
cured an audience for the nervous agility and inventiveness of mod-
ernist style in all the arts. "Chaplinesque" owes at least some of its
popularity as an anthology piece to the celebrity of its subject, as
Alfred Kreymborg noted in his influential *A History of American Poetry*
(1929). "In going to school with Chaplin, Crane has attended a better
school than Harvard or Yale," Kreymborg asserted. "The diminutive
tragi-comedian has more knowledge in his flopping feet and 'pliant
cane' than a lamplit eye can find in encyclopedias."[15] It was not just
American poets who sought, and were encouraged by the likes of
Kreymborg, to ground their knowledge of human experience in the
screen rather than the literary tradition. Spanish poet Rafael Alberti's
poem "Buster Keaton Searches through the Forest for His Sweet-
heart, a Full-Blooded Cow" (1929) achieved an enhanced currency
in surrealist circles by its deference to another widely admired Ameri-
can comedian. Likewise, in Bertolt Brecht's "A Film of the Come-
dian Chaplin" (1944), the sentimental film *A Face on the Barroom Floor*
helps to crystallize Brecht's self-pity about his unhappy years in Hol-
lywood and the fate of the artist in a society indifferent to his suffer-
ing and his genius. Such poems advert attention to the antic models
of their verbal play. As advertisements for the modern, they restage
the rupture of past and present that cinema, the supreme art of imme-
diacy, enforced in the new century.

It is part of our story that Crane imagined he could make a living
writing titles and evaluating scripts for the movies. American poets
had been wary about personal involvement in cinema, but as the new
art form gained respectability, especially in Europe, poets began to
lend their talents to it. H. D., for example, not only helped in the
editing of the film journal *Close-Up* but acted in two experimental
films by Kenneth Macpherson, *Foothills* (1927) and *Borderline* (1930,

costarring Paul Robeson). Crane was no actor, but he may have fantasized a screenwriting career on the model of well-known fiction writers, like F. Scott Fitzgerald and Ben Hecht, who were profiting from piecework in the dream factory. He journeyed to Hollywood in 1927 to make his fortune, while at the same time aiding his mother who was living there in straitened circumstances. If Lindsay idealized Los Angeles as a site where the prophet wizards were building the New Jerusalem, Crane found only the phantasmagoria of a Babylon—as in this letter to his friend Slater Brown:

> Besides which I have met the Circe of them all—a movie actor who has them dancing naked, twenty at a time, around the banquet table. O André Gide! no Paris ever yielded such as this— away with all your counterfeiters! Just walk down Hollywood Boulevard some day—if you must have something *out* of uniform. Here are little fairies who can quote Rimbaud before they are 18—and here are women who must have the tiniest fay to tickle them in the one and only way! You ought to see Betty C—shake her tits and cry *apples* for a bite![16]

This paragraph has all the density of Crane's poetry, and all the wit. Here is a different congeries of poetry, film, and homosexuality than can be found in "Chaplinesque." The gay movie actor called Circe and the abandoned Betty C frame the paragraph as degenerate forms of film personality. In the previous paragraph Crane had passed along a rumor that burlesque comedian Bert Savoy was sporting a black eye after a midnight spat with "a mariner." Crane himself would pursue sailors for sex, and here he contrasts them to fairies "out of uniform," professionals for whom Rimbaud, the type of the young homosexual poet, is an exotic turn-on, a pander for their ostentatious—and to Crane repellent—sexuality. As the reference to Gide's novel *The Counterfeiters* suggests, Hollywood not Paris is the modern locus of a debased copying of the genuine artifice. Hollywood proved to be part of that "fury of the street" Crane had opposed to the redemptive actions of the film star some six years earlier. He returned to the East Coast looking for an exalted art symbol that was not a counterfeit but an authentic image of stability and humanistic community.

(The contrast of Hollywood Babylon and the homiletic "Chap-

linesque" could not be more poignant—except for the example of
Chaplin's own career, which accumulated a weight of sexual scandal
during the 1920s. When Crane had met Chaplin five years earlier, he
had remarked in a letter to his mother, "You cannot imagine a more
perfect and natural gentleman," and "We (just Charlie & I) are to
have dinner together some night next week. He remembered my
poem very well & is very interested in my work." One wonders
whether the publicity surrounding Chaplin's brief marriage to Lita
Grey and the coarse gossip about his adulteries weakened the sense
of solidarity expressed in the "we" of poem and letter alike.)

We can find a hint of Crane's emerging mythology by glancing
at an anecdote related by Susan Jenkins Brown, wife of Slater Brown,
both friends of Crane's for many years. Brown remembers an eve-
ning of good fun when Crane read aloud from a newspaper an item
reporting that carbon monoxide in automobile exhaust tended to
make women sterile and men impotent. Susan Brown remarked, "So
now our culture calls upon us to sacrifice our virility on the altar of
motion."

> Hart put down his paper and slapped his knees, laughing.
> "Sue, you're wonderful! So neat—so apt! On the altar of mo-
> tion." He spread my small *mot* everywhere.[17]

The remark would have intrigued Crane because it combined some-
thing so unmoving as an altar with the concept of motion. But more
than that, it crystallized in a phrase his own doubts about the fluidity
and transience of human experience, the movement of time, which
like the Mississippi River in *The Bridge* obeys an irresistible law:
"Tortured with history, its one will—flow!" or the movement of the
Twentieth Century Limited as it roars through a landscape remade
by technology into the garbled hieroglyphs of advertising lingo.
Everywhere the word in modern America had been sacrificed or
degraded on the altar of motion; it was in need of some redemptive
image, some figure of virility that would serve as a "harp and altar,
of the fury fused"—precisely what he later calls the Brooklyn Bridge.
White Buildings. The Bridge. "The Broken Tower." Crane's master-
pieces praise what is stationary and durable, not in motion but ser-
viceable to the masses, who need some solid stay against the ephem-
eral confusions of passing time and popular culture.

That Crane designed "Chaplinesque" so that it not only paid tribute to the comedian and his films but also implicitly indicated the limitations of cinema as a medium can be inferred by noting how the dandyist style of the early poem makes way for the heightened eloquence—indeed, the baroque elevation—of *The Bridge*. In that poem Crane pays homage to an engineering marvel that can stand against the humdrum, hurried, and mechanical tenor of modern American life, and it is explicitly film that is cast as the antagonist of the bridge in the opening section, "Proem: To Brooklyn Bridge." The poem begins with Crane watching the seagulls glide around the Statue of Liberty, then "with inviolate curve, forsake our eyes" as they fly away. Clearly this is the Romantic bird that like the nightingale of Keats taunts humankind as an apparition of the infinite but passes in flight beyond our holding and enjoying. The third stanza brings this fugitive Romantic image into association with film:

I think of cinemas, panoramic sleights
With multitudes bent toward some flashing scene
Never disclosed, but hastened to again,
Foretold to other eyes on the same screen.

The key term here is "panoramic sleights." Crane has chosen the word "sleights" with obvious care. The first definition given in the *Oxford Universal Dictionary* is "craft or cunning employed so as to deceive; deceitful, subtle, or wily dealing or policy; artifice, strategy, trickery." This is where the most familiar use of the word, "sleight-of-hand," comes from. Five other definitions tease out the implications of the word: it is skill, dexterity, nimbleness. Macaulay is quoted: "A new sleight of tongue to make fools clap."

A poem too is a sleight, a panoramic sleight, like *The Bridge*, which shifts scenes with skillful dexterity. But a distinction must be made. First, there are multitudes watching at the cinema, and what they watch is "flashing"—it is hurrying by too fast to be held stationary, secured in mind, comprehended. Like the seagulls, the cinematic scenes abandon the viewers, they do not "disclose." This latter word is defined as "to open up to the knowledge of others, to reveal." By using words like "sleights" and "never disclosed" Crane is obviously turning upon film the accusations leveled against poetry, and especially against the poetry he liked to write. Film is too accelerated and

too various in its swiftly passing scenes to impress itself deeply upon
an audience, and the proof is that the audience hastens to the theater
again, rewinding cinematic shots through their imaginations but
never making intimate and palpable contact with their objects of
enjoyment. The cinematic cannot nourish the authentic desire for
knowledge that sends people to movie houses. Film, finally, is an
enigma, a Futurist rush of violent motion, luring multitudes in suc-
cession, "other eyes on the same screen," but with no deep wisdom
of the kind language possesses because of its coeval origins with
consciousness. Without the full range of discursive possibilities af-
forded by a diction attentive to the profundity and density of human
experience, knowledge is superficial, apparitional, fragmentary.

In such a passage we find the first of many allusions in movie
poems to the cave of unknowing in Plato's *Republic* as an analogy to
filmgoing. In that dialogue, Socrates tells of mankind being chained
in a cave, their eyes gazing forward at a wall across which move
shadows projected from behind the spectators. If these people lived
all their life in that cave, Socrates says, they would assume that such
shadows are indeed reality, and their knowledge of two-dimensional
life a rational apprehension of the totality of existence. But if one
were to break the chains and walk out of the cave, one would per-
ceive, at first blinded and then accustoming one's eyes to its glorious
existence, the sun of true reason that illuminates the actual dimen-
sions of the world. Since Plato's time, and partly because of his cri-
tique, artists have taken as their task the distinguishing and valorizing
of two kinds of human experience set in opposition. *Illusion* and
reality is the Platonic way of naming these opposed realms, but as
we shall see, poets do not erect such hard and fast boundaries between
the two states of being. When we read any poem about the movies,
we need to measure the value given to the film medium versus the
value given to phenomena outside the theater. Devotion to one or the
other constitutes an essential guideline of the poet's vision.

As a context for Crane's critique of movies in *The Bridge* we
might consider a brief poem, adaptable to Plato's parable, that Crane
probably read: Carl Sandburg's "In a Breath" (1916).

High noon. White sun flashes on the Michigan Avenue asphalt.
Drum of hoofs and whirr of motors. Women trapesing along in
flimsy clothes catching play of sun-fire to their skin and eyes.

Inside the playhouse are movies from under the sea. From the heat of pavements and the dust of sidewalks, passers-by go in a breath to be witnesses of huge cool sponges, large cool fishes, large cool valleys and ridges of coral spread silent in the soak of the ocean floor thousands of years.

A naked swimmer dives. A knife in his right hand shoots a streak at the throat of a shark. The tail of the shark lashes. One swing would kill the swimmer. . . . Soon the knife goes into the soft underneck of the veering fish. . . . Its mouthful of teeth, each tooth a dagger itself, set row on row, glistens when the shuddering, yawning cadaver is hauled up by the brothers of the swimmer.

Outside in the street is the murmur and singing of life in the sun—horses, motors, women trapesing along in flimsy clothes, play of sun-fire in their blood.[18]

The poem constructs a large-scale binary division similar to Florence Kiper Frank's "The Movies," discussed in the Introduction. It opens on high noon, the middle of the day. The framing first and fourth stanzas describe the streets, the two middle stanzas take us into the theater and "in a breath" submerge us in some cinematic otherworld where the heat and noise of Chicago dissolve to the coolness and quiet of an underwater realm, and in another breath to the furious activity of the shark fight.

Reading this prose poem quickly, as one of the 147 vignettes of the volume *Chicago,* we might register the opposition as Sandburg's way of saying that the movies offer city dwellers a means of imaginative escape from the hectic life of the streets. This was (and perhaps still is) the conventional view of the function of popular film in an urban environment. The poem requires a closer look, however. From the heat of sun on asphalt we leap to the women compelled by the same heat to loosen their attire and their gait. The sultry women are figures of erotic appetite (certainly not of Platonic reason), and when the reader, especially the male reader, takes a second look at them, the voice of the street turns into a lyric "singing of life" that contrasts to the mute violence of the shark fight between the naked swimmer and his prey. Sandburg seems to be suggesting that the streets look and feel more desirable after immersion in the destructive element

afforded by the movies. The swimmer has done something heroic
and has made life sweeter, more lyrically charged, to the "witnesses"
who withdraw from the theater into a world imbued with enhanced
instinctual possibilities. "In a Breath" must be compared to the next
poem in the volume, "Bath," in which a man who "saw the whole
world as a grinning skull and cross-bones" enters a theater to hear
Mischa Elman play his violin. Afterward, "He was the same man in
the same world as before. Only there was a singing fire and a climb
of roses everlastingly over the world he looked on."

In his poem on the bridge, Crane does not tell us about the *content*
of those "panoramic sleights" that flash by the audience, and so the
reader receives no durable impression of the world elsewhere they
represent. (If we think of them as Chaplin films, for example, the
whole effect of the poem would change.) Crane wants to preserve the
Plato's cave effect mimicked by Sandburg of rising from the theater
into a more satisfying sunlit reality. Crane finds his trope for that
superior perception in the stanza that follows the one about the mov-
ies:

> And Thee, across the harbor, silver-paced
> As though the sun took step of thee, yet left
> Some motion ever unspent in thy stride,—
> Implicitly thy freedom staying thee!

The Brooklyn Bridge has dynamic movement expressive of spirit
but it also has stability, staying power. And it has *proximity;* it is not
a secondhand apparition of an exotic elsewhere. Or rather, it contains
the antipodes, it reconciles all contraries because it is the purest and
most capacious expression of God's creation. Thus it comprises all
variety of human utterance: "Terrific threshold of the prophet's
pledge, / Prayer of pariah, and the lover's cry." It is an "unfractioned
idiom" derived from God's Word, what Crane calls in the final poem
of the sequence a "multitudinous Verb the suns / And synergy of
waters ever cast, recast / In myriad syllables." Crane continually
addresses the bridge as a poem in steel, and by reflexive action makes
his high diction a mimetic structure participating in its exaltation.
Crane's rhapsodic idiom thus insists upon a distinction between the
limited power of cinema—which Sandburg treated in appropriately
prosaic diction and typography—and the exalted godhead that is ap-

prehensible only in the golden style derived from the most sublime poets. No other medium of transport in *The Bridge*—not the train or flying machine, not radio or film—is deified in this way. Brooklyn Bridge is the radiant realization of Whitman's dream of unity and spiritual resurrection in America. Vachel Lindsay had attributed this power to film in his apocalyptic poem, but Crane discredits that association and proffers his own claim, mingling his song with the "harp and altar" of his unmoving mover.

The Bridge, then, chronicles the triumph of poetry over all of its rivals, including the movies. In a letter written during his brief stay in Hollywood Crane lamented the fact that he lives in an "age of celluloid."[19] Vachel Lindsay's notion that silent movies were a likely successor to written literature would have offended a verbal sensibility as richly endowed as Crane's. Though Crane was not a technophobe he probably would have sympathized with the satire on machinery in Chaplin's *Modern Times* but with the proviso that Chaplin's medium had to share the blame for remaking twentieth-century society into a speeded-up assembly line of goods and services. He had praised Chaplin for converting an ash can into "a grail of laughter," but by 1933 he no longer looked to Hollywood for a redemptive transformation. The bridge had been his grail, but after an unhappy spell in Mexico even the memory of Whitman's city turned to ashes in his imagination. Like Lindsay, Hart Crane took his own life in the early years of the Depression, another member of the visionary company fated to end his quest with a silent gesture, some "final smirk" before bowing out.

Umbo (Otto Umbehr), *Der Rassende Reporter*, 1926. "The Rov-ing Reporter," a photocollage prepared for Walther Ruttmann's film of 1927, *Berlin, die Symphonie einer Grosstadt.* The modern artist is just such a collector of images, assembling materials into discontinuous and random aggregations. "The time of the Image has come," said filmmaker Abel Gance. Poets agreed. (From *Dada: Photographie und Photocollage,* ed. Carl-Albrecht Haenlin [Hanover: Kestern, 1979].)

Chapter 3

Cut on Movement: Archibald MacLeish and the Temptations of Cinematic Form

CINEMA OF A MAN

The earth is bright through the boughs of the moon like a dead planet
It is silent it has no sound the sun is on it
It shines in the dark like a white stone in a deep meadow
It is round above it is flattened under with shadow
      *   *   *   *

He sits in the rue St. Jacques at the iron table
It is dusk it is growing cold the roof stone glitters on the gable
The taxis turn in the rue du Pot de Fer
The gas jets brighten one by one behind the windows of the stair
      *   *   *   *

This is his face the chin long the eyes looking
      *   *   *   *

Now he sits on the porch of the Villa Serbelloni
He is eating white bread and brown honey
The sun is hot on the lake there are boats rowing
It is spring the rhododendrons are out the. wind is blowing
      *   *   *   *

Above Bordeaux by the canal
His shadow passes on the evening wall
His legs are crooked at the knee he has one shoulder
His arms are long he vanishes among the shadows of the alder
      *   *   *   *

He wakes in the Grand Hotel Vierjahreszeiten
It is dawn the carts go by the curtains whiten

59

He sees her yellow hair she has neither father nor mother
Her name is Ann she has had him now and before another
*   *   *   *

This is his face in the light of the full moon
His skin is white and grey like the skin of a quadroon
His head is raised to the sky he stands staring
His mouth is still his face is still his eyes are staring
*   *   *   *

He walks with Ernest in the streets in Saragossa
They are drunk their mouths are hard they say *qué cosa*
They say the cruel words they hurt each other
Their elbows touch their shoulders touch their feet go on and on
   together
*   *   *   *

Now he is by the sea at St.-Tropez
The pines roar in the wind it is hot it is noonday
He is naked he swims in the blue under the sea water
His limbs are drowned in the dapple of sun like the limbs of the
   sea's daughter
*   *   *   *

Now he is in Chicago he is sleeping
The footstep passes on the stone the roofs are dripping
The door is closed the walls are dark the shadows deepen
His head is motionless upon his arm his hand is open
*   *   *   *

Those are the cranes above the Karun River
They fly across the night their wings go over
They cross Orion and the south star of the Wain
A wave has broken in the sea beyond the coast of Spain[1]

—1930

By the time Archibald MacLeish won the second of three Pulitzer prizes for his *Poems 1924–1933,* he was esteemed by many critics as being among the finest poets of his generation. The volume demonstrated that MacLeish could write engagingly in a variety of lyric and narrative styles. His long poem "Einstein" brought up to date the philosophical skepticism explored earlier by Edwin Arlington Robinson in "The Man Against the Sky." His even longer poem *Conquistador,* about Cortés's conquest and exploitation of Mexico, carried forward the insights about the American experience initiated in the 1920s by William Carlos Williams in *In the American Grain* and Hart Crane in *The Bridge.* And MacLeish had sounded the contemporary note as well in imagistic poems shaded just far enough from the practice of his contemporaries that they escaped the charge of being *too* derivative. Like his friends Ernest Hemingway and John Dos Passos, MacLeish had fought in World War I and lived the expatriate life in France and Italy, participating in the heady European experiments of the modernist movement. He would be a famous poet and man of letters for another fifty years till his death in 1982. And yet, in the everyday ongoing conversation of poets and readers, and in recent literary criticism, his reputation seems to have shriveled to the didactic couplet that closes his poem "Ars Poetica": "A poem should not mean / But be."

Any effort to rehabilitate MacLeish will probably have to begin with that couplet and move outward circumspectly toward the epic intentions of *Conquistador,* a poem that will sit better with readers persuaded by the polemics of neonarrative theory than with those raised on the New Criticism and deconstruction. "Ars Poetica" is one of many poems from that period that skillfully moves from image to image in the modernist manner, offering self-contained "shots" in quick succession without the connective tissue of exposition, impressionistic rumination, or logical argument—all the verbiage that poets have quarreled with since Verlaine in *his* ars poetica ("Art poétique") vowed to strangle rhetoric by the neck in order to purify verse of everything that was not poetry. It hardly needs demonstrating that this method became the dominant structural form for verse in this century. Workshop instructors still recommend cinematic form as an antidote to the sluggish meditation or the protracted description. Poetry as the dance of the intellect, the swiftly moving scenario of consciousness, eliding and crosscutting in order to draw the reader into the dynamic act of imagination—this is the dogma of our century's poetics and should make us more sympathetic to the author of exemplary lyrics like "Way-Station," "Signature for Tempo," and "Nocturne," as well as extended Poundian experiments like "Elpenor."

When Sergei Eisenstein canonized the technique of montage in his theoretical books *Film Form* and *The Film Sense,* he demonstrated how D. W. Griffith had adapted his technique not only from novelists like Dickens but from poets like Milton and Shelley. Griffith, who wrote poetry himself, no doubt had read these poets, though it's unlikely he pored over *Paradise Lost* and "Julian and Maddalo" to aid him in preparing the shooting script of *Intolerance.* But modernist poets had no use for Milton and Shelley; indeed, Hulme, Pound, and Eliot developed their poetics as a deliberate rebellion against the rhetoric of those two masters of the grand manner. Rather than the baroque or the Romantic, they appreciated the neoclassical mode of couplet structure, in which each unit holds for a vivid moment a precisely described objective "idea" (in the Lockean sense) before the poem moves quickly to another unit of perception, depending on the alert reader to follow along with growing pleasure in the quick acquisition of new information. The accelerated and disjunctive mode belonged to the first discovery of the modern city as a subject, a discovery congenial also to the modernists, who restored urbanity as a central topic after a century of what they considered decadent pastoralism (the much-detested "Georgian" mode being the last straw). Here is the opening of Jonathan Swift's "A Description of the Morning":

> Now hardly here and there a hackney-coach
> Appearing, showed the ruddy morn's approach.
> Now Betty from her master's bed had flown,
> And softly stole to discompose her own;
> The slip-shod 'prentice from his master's door
> Had pared the dirt and sprinkled round the floor.
> Now Moll had whirled her mop with dex'trous airs,
> Prepared to scrub the entry and the stairs.

And so forth. It is a poem that could go on forever, as one perception is added to another, all contributing to a highly particularized sense of the eighteenth-century city as a place full of masters and servants, dirt and noise, and ubiquitous activity apprehensible only in discrete units as the eye darts from scene to scene. Because of its condensation and maneuverability, couplet structure aspired to include more reality, more of the contemporary world, within its asyntactic units. Eliot would imitate this structure in his imagistic poems about the modern city, "Preludes" and "Rhapsody on a Windy Night," where the implied "Here... There... Now... Now..." structure of the empirical mode directs the reader's attention and fills her sensorium. The succession of dreary images enumerated in a dour tone has been given the term *Eliotic* but it is highly conventional and comes from the first discovery that London, the metropolitan city, could be best represented as a diversity of phenomena, using an additive structure in which each line or couplet rubs against others to produce that peculiar friction of the montage.

Eliot and Pound would advance from the Imagist school to the obvious next step, poems of self-portraiture that manifested a fragmented consciousness. "The Love Song of J. Alfred Prufrock," "Gerontion," and *Hugh Selwyn Mauberley* in their different ways are cinemas of a man. While a poet like Robinson doggedly went on composing immensely long blank-verse story poems about Tristram, Merlin, Lancelot, Roman Bartholow, Cavender, Matthias, Talifer, and King Jasper, modernist poets composed tightly wrought poems in the shape of a psyche, with all the jump cuts that characterize a mind working at maximum efficiency, or—to reverse values—a mind disordered by the vexations of internal and external stimuli. Past and present are brought into juxtaposition, hesitations and repressions are enacted in the elliptical structure, obsessive scenes are smothered in the jarring emotional responses they provoke. Such rhetorical movement had always been part of the dramatic monologue, but the modernists—and one must include Joyce as a chief model—foregrounded the technique of (seemingly) disconnected units laid side by side for the duration of the text, a technique that resembled the condition of cinematic form outlined by Eisenstein, though shed of his Hegelian dialectics.

Filmmakers developed the art of the film by two comparable innovations. Rather than continuing to present a story acted out in a single shot, they remade the film strip into a skein of multiple shots spliced together, sometimes to bring distant places into surprising association. And they began to move the camera, which had formerly remained stationary in front of a stage where exits and entrances followed the theatrical pattern. The great leap forward was the discovery of the fluidity of cinematic time and space, and the limitless play available to the editor in the cutting room. Montage brought into fascinating proximity a variety of points of view, eliminating the tedious panning and traveling shots that (sometimes) slow down a film's tempo for a superfluous chronology or causality. What the movies gained in the process was the effect and celebrity of a unique *acceleration,* especially as shots of shorter duration were used to speed up a narrative. By the time Griffith made *Birth of a Nation* in 1914, the speed of films had become their most distinguishing characteristic. The car chases and slapstick of the Keystone Kops, and Mack Sennett's other comedies, established a frenzied pace that brought films into figural association with Fordist industrial practices, as well as trains, cars, planes, and other swiftly moving vehicles of the modern imagination.

Though Eisenstein is usually credited with refining and perfecting montage form in his great films *Strike* and *Battleship Potemkin,* the development most pertinent to the practice of MacLeish and his contemporaries is that of *absolute film,* the term given by Bela Balazs to avant-garde works that featured the filmmaker's imaginative reconstruction of external reality. The term covers a variety of representational and nonrepresentational films, but it is the former that suggested to poets, including MacLeish, how a disintegrative structure might best reproduce a mind confronted with and subdivided by the plenitude and ambiguity of contemporary visual experience. Using trick-montage photography in his self-reflexive *The Man with the Movie Camera* (1929), Dziga Vertov created a cinema of a man contemporary with MacLeish's own experiment. Alberto Cavalcanti's *Rien que les heures* (1926) presented a multitude of images to document twenty-four hours of Paris life. The masterpiece of the 1920s in this mode, Walther Ruttmann's *Berlin, die Symphonie einer Grosstadt* (1927), likewise offered an overwhelming mélange of images as a way of making its point about the modern citizen's inability to see the city whole, to subdue it—or any reality—to intellectual order. (Joyce invited Ruttmann to make a film of *Ulysses.*) The fragmentation of consciousness here taken to its radical extreme was part of the nature of all film, however, and as film became the preeminent art by means of worldwide endorsement, cinematic or spatial form established itself as the paradigm for the other arts, which were compelled to derive their prestige from similarities with the dominant model. Hence the irony of Pound, in *Hugh Selwyn Mauberley,* a poem full of ellipses and leaps in time and space, denouncing the demand for an "accelerated grimace" by the hoi polloi. What was *Mauberley* if not a sequence of grimaces?

"Cinema of a Man" displays many of the characteristics that link MacLeish both to the Augustan tradition and to his innovative contemporaries. First, it uses the rhymed couplet to frame discrete images of the person it depicts, though these are not the strict decasyllabic units of Swift. The couplets not only divide up the man's appearance in cubist fashion—his legs, his arms, his shadow, his head—but even these fragments of physical being are torn out of their spatiotemporal contexts and rearranged next to one another without logical copulas. Gathered into quatrains, the poem is further subdivided by rows of asterisks. The effect is of an enforced randomness. For example, in stanza 4 we get a shot of the man:

> Now he sits on the porch of the Villa Serbelloni
> He is eating white bread and brown honey

And then, still without any punctuation to obstruct the fluidity of the phrases, our gaze is quickly jerked away from him:

> The sun is hot on the lake there are boats rowing
> It is spring the rhododendrons are out the wind is blowing

This is the mind's eye's restless shifting, a fast-motion derangement of the usual Imagist practice of holding a scene stationary within a stable frame. MacLeish's phrases are like strips of celluloid, some only two or three frames in length ("boats rowing"), which compose a tonal sequence of different tempos. These pictures are moving with a vengeance, and moving in arbitrary fashion into combinations that violate the conventional rules of pictorial representation.

As Wendy Steiner points out in a study of Gertrude Stein's word portraits, however, the arbitrary is far from a modern invention. The Senecan style of the seventeenth century followed a logic defined by one of its scholars in this way: "every period, every sentence almost, is independent, and may be taken asunder, transposed, postponed, anticipated, or set in any new order, as you fancy."[2] Steiner argues that such a style tends to universalize rather than personalize or individualize. The notion of an essential unconscious or buried self worthy of prolonged investigation seemed less interesting to modernist authors in the late 1920s than the linguistic structures they could erect in defiance of psychoanalysis, Freudian or otherwise. MacLeish denies a coherent personality to his man; he defines him in terms of his environments, by discrete evidences rather than from some ruling passion or nexus of distinguishing psychological characteristics or identity formation by social companions. Nor does history exert any influence on his personality. Perhaps man is nothing but a congeries of miscellaneous attributes and features that resists conceptual definition. This man is like Wallace Stevens's blackbird that can be imagined 13 or 113 different ways so long as ingenuity can invent paratactic episodes featuring the same figure. "Cinema of a Man" is a postsymbolist realm of free play empowered by interartistic techniques. Every aspect can be "taken asunder" or given meaning by its arbitrary context, like the experiments of the film director Lev Kuleshov, who rendered a static face alternately sad and happy depending on what shots were provided as prelude. The final effect is of a dizzyingly indeterminate human image, subdivided and multiplied in deliberate violation of reader expectations. When Robert Penn Warren complained in a review that the parts of "Cinema of a Man" could be rearranged without disturbing the effect, he was testifying to MacLeish's intentions.[3] Just as John Locke had defined the percipient mind as a "bundle of sensations," so MacLeish had understood Einstein, in his poem of that title, to argue that personal experiences cannot be unified nor truth ever conceptualized without summoning arbitrary principles of organization. His poem is a melancholy exhibition of the mind's limits as modern science and philosophy had described them.

MacLeish clearly means for us to "watch" the cinema poem according to the conventions of film technique. First, we have the wide-angle establishing shot, in italics, of the earth as seen from outer space, with a jump cut to "a white stone in a deep meadow" to freshen our perception: as above, so below. The poem then proceeds by an imaginary sequence of dissolves or wipes as a succession of different locations ensues. Stanza 2 locates the subject sitting in the rue St. Jacques at an iron table. Iron will recur in the Pot de *Fer* as a linguistic repetition of image, just as the word "sits" links together the rue St. Jacques and the Villa Serbelloni in stanza 4. The gas jets that "brighten" in stanza 2 look back to "The earth is bright," a play of light meant to create a chiaroscuro effect when "shadow" crosses the screen intermittently; the "dapple of sun" on dark water has the animistic aura of all objects in the poem, including the objectified "He." Recurring words and images provide the color key for the poem's composition, teasing us with patterns as the poem proceeds to vex us with its figural abstraction. In the midst of pastoral imagery a woman is introduced, Ann, a woman with a past ("She has had him now and before another"). But we don't see the man from her point of view, as one might in the reverse angle cutting (or shot-counter-shot) of narrative cinema. We cannot suture them together as a real couple. The man is entirely isolated before the camera eye, situated against different backdrops. The wealthy milieus suggest people of means, deracinated, able to move from place to place, lover to lover, the milieus not only of Eliot's *The Waste Land* but of the equally enigmatic visual landscapes of European film, from the silent *Fantomas* to *Last Year at Marienbad*. (An interesting comparison would be Sylvia Plath's more recent couplet poem, "The Munich Mannequins.") "He" is barely glimpsed amidst the "sea at St. Tropez, the roaring pines." "His limbs" fade into "the limbs of the sea's daughter" as once again the pretense of identity in what MacLeish elsewhere called "dismembered universes" is mocked by the jerky splicings of the experimental auteur.[4]

Is this man a real person? Is it Archibald MacLeish? The reference to walking with Ernest in the streets of Saragossa would seem to refer to Hemingway, MacLeish's close friend during the Paris years. The drunknenness and cruel words would not be out of character, needless to say. (MacLeish would quarrel bitterly with Hemingway in the 1930s, and they would drift apart into different worlds. His memorial poem following Hemingway's suicide employs one of the very few cinematic metaphors in his poetry: "Death . . . rewinds remembrance / backward like a film track.") Likewise the reference to Chicago reminds us that MacLeish's poem "You, Andrew Marvell" is an account of his trip from Persia, where he had served in 1926 on a League of Nations committee, to Glencoe, Illinois, where his parents lived, and it too moves from one spatial image to another in quick succession, though the whole poem is a single sentence. "Cinema of a Man" reverses the direction, taking the reader from Chicago to the Karun River in Persia, where the flight of the cranes serves as a metaphorical cut for the migration of the camera eye; the last line returns to Spain to enforce the arbitrary picaresque of its roving reporter. One might say, then, that MacLeish piques his reader's interest in himself but resists the temptation to personalize coherently in the autobiographical mode. He eschews narrative depth by constructing a floating identity, and flaunting the seams in his rhetorical fabric.

MacLeish began his career with the blithe assumption that he would carry on in the Romantic manner by being autobiographical, if not like Wordsworth, then like Swinburne or Robinson or Bridges—key influences he candidly acknowledged. *Tower of Ivory* (1917) and *The Happy Marriage* (1924) are books in this traditional mode. To read MacLeish's letters of the 1920s, however, is to see him reel under the pounding force of new poetics in the foundry of Paris. First, there was Imagism. MacLeish constantly disclaims the Imagists—whom he persistently associates with minor figures like John Gould Fletcher and Joseph Auslander in order to keep his distance more confidently. "I am not a convert," he proclaims. "I cannot express myself in vignettes," he writes later, and in a poem of the early 1930s he inquires, "Who recalls the address now of the Imagists?"[5] And yet he was attracted to the lapidary beauty and structural suppleness of Imagist verse, especially in Amy Lowell's case— indeed, her poem "East, West, North, and South of a Man" is one model for his "Cinema of a Man." Cubist form, already canonized as a contemporary style in painting, became a popular mode for the often enigmatic poems MacLeish sampled in the little magazines of the period. In one letter he mentions that Donald Ogden Stewart has come to Paris and has begun using "Joycian technique" which he defines as "idea suggesting idea without logical or reasonable sequence."[6] Later, in 1924, he claims the method for himself. The following year he praises the "tempo" of John Dos Passos's aleatoric symphony of a city, *Manhattan Transfer,* though he complains that it never really comes to anything as a story.

And then there is the example of Eliot, whose *Waste Land* is the triumph of "the Mosaic School" as MacLeish calls it.[7] MacLeish felt himself forever in the shadow of Eliot and made his belatedness a constant theme in his letters. "After Eliot nothing except more Eliot" was his appraisal of the decade. "The fact is," he writes to John Peale Bishop, "that Eliot has opened to a few people like you and myself a world which we recognize at once as our own and from which we can no more retire than we can go back to the nursing size."[8] Eliot had realized the full potential of cinematic form, or, if one prefers, the principle of juxtaposition or superposition of which cinema became the paradigm for the age. In constructing *The Waste Land,* and historicizing it with a sophistication that made, say, Griffith's cross-cutting technique in *Intolerance* look elementary, Eliot had rescued poetry from secondary status in the hierarchy of the arts. Eliot had written no mere mimetic exercise, like Crane's "Chaplinesque," but a work of transcendent significance, as Crane, with both eyes on Eliot's masterpiece, would likewise attempt in *The Bridge.*

MacLeish's response to the achievements of his modernist contemporaries was twofold and contradictory. First, he drank (too) deeply the lesson of the masters and imitated their experimental structures in the way we have noted. He constrained himself to be a poet of his time, working successfully against the grain of his first allegiances in order to strike the dandyist pose and mimic the heterogeneity and opacity of modern experience in his antirealistic constructions. Even as he did so, however, he published poems undermining and critiquing the aestheticist assumptions of such experiments. "The Hamlet of Archibald MacLeish" (1928) asserted that the modern poet was ineffectual, Chaplinesque, a Prufrockian clown. A few years later, in "Invocation to the Social Muse" (1932), MacLeish would compare poets to whores, the kept pets of an active and purposeful society. The necessity for a less narcissistic poetics is implied in such metaphors of the poet's condition and function.

By the early 1930s MacLeish was in full rout from the implications of modernism. As a public-spirited citizen returning to the United States during a time of Depression he looked back on the cult of discontinuity, incoherence, rupture, and fragmentation as a self-indulgent moment in the history of the literary imagination. Did he include cinematic form in his indictment? He makes no explicit statement about the subject, but we can infer his attitude from remarks on literature in general. First, MacLeish begins to move away from the kind of cinematic form implied in Gertrude Stein's celebration of "the continuous present" as a rhetorical mode. Stein never showed as much sympathy for the cinema as for painting, and she often speaks of it condescendingly. For example, in "How Writing is Written" (1935) she remarked, "I listened to people. I condensed it in about three words. There again, if you read those later *Portraits,* you will see that I used three or four words instead of making a cinema of it."[9] Here "cinema" is a term for continuity, for verisimilitude in the representation of reality. Stein wished to achieve a flattened, abstract effect in her highly reiterative sentences, as if she were setting the nearly identical photographs in a film strip side by side on the page without any persistence of vision to elide them into a fluid, developmental sequence. It is the photography of Muybridge rather than the sound films of Hollywood that informs her practice, and though he claimed that he had not read her work with any degree of care, MacLeish never approached closer to her practice than in the present-tense and word-repetitive structure of "Cinema of a Man." This doctrine of a pure cinema, artifactual rather than mimetic, began to feel dated to him when he left his Paris apartment and reentered the world of business and politics as a staff writer for *Fortune* magazine and, later, Librarian of Congress.

But Stein's patronizing remark allows us to see the kind of loyalty MacLeish could and did retain for film form. He was not averse to "making a cinema of it" if the movie was not some subjective abstraction that reduced the human image to type but had instead a realistic, even documentary, quality. A poetry that reassembled the human image and re-placed it in an historical context, but also moved with the accelerated tempo of a modernist novel or a good nonfiction film, that was MacLeish's ideal. His manifestos began to assert the connection of art and reality more forcefully; for example, "art is an organization of experience in terms of experience, the purpose of which is the recognition of experience. It is an interpreter between ourselves and that which has happened to us, the purpose of which is to make legible what it is that has happened."[10] This practical-minded, Deweyesque statement would not sit comfortably with poems like "Cinema of a Man" nor some of the most widely admired poems of the 1920s. Poetry, MacLeish would tell Mark Van Doren in 1962, "does make things happen. . . . [It] is one of the ways things are brought to happen in the world, to bring a living generation to a knowledge of its dangers, a knowledge of its hopes, of its aspirations, a knowledge of what the world really is in all its potentialities."[11]

MacLeish needed a new hero to succeed the great Eliot, whose faithfulness to experience was indisputable but whose "knowledge of what the world really is in all its potentialities" was too limited, in MacLeish's view. The poet who came to embody MacLeish's need for a public poet in the mid-1930s was Carl Sandburg. When *The People, Yes* appeared, he wrote a review for *The New Masses* which he described as "one long halloo of delight."[12] For many readers Sandburg's book-length poem achieved the task of uniting the montage form in poetry with the ensemble portraiture of documentary. More than a collection of anecdotes, it is an oral history of contemporary America, an attempt to revive the Augustan strain of modernism for Whitmanian purposes. And yet MacLeish distinguished the Whitmanian and Sandburgian modes: "Out of the book comes for the first time in our literature the people of America. Whitman's men were Man. Sandburg's are men of this earth."[13] Implied in this distinction is a critique of the anonymous "Man" of "Cinema of a Man"—man as the mere occasion for an arbitrary juxtaposition of qualities, a hook to hang images on. And the limpidity of Sandburg's content put him on a collision course with the Eliotic assumption that poetry in the century had to be difficult in order to serve its function of purifying the idiom of the tribe. When MacLeish in his review asserted that anyone calling himself a revolutionary had to read *The People, Yes*, he was mounting the same challenge to Pound and Eliot as they had made to the decadent romanticism of the Victorian era; he was saying that the modernist poets had lost contact with the people and the living tongue.

Defenders of modernism, then and now, dismissed Sandburg as vulgar. The New Criticism found nothing to admire in his low-angle carnival of the everyday, and since the 1930s critics have effectively narrowed his reputation in the way MacLeish's has been whittled: the latter to "Ars Poetica" and the former to the few imagist poems one finds in most anthologies: "Fog," "Cool Tombs," "Grass." It may be time to take another look at *The People, Yes*. No poet of the first half of the century so programmatically embodied the "I am a camera" technique in verse as Carl Sandburg. Wandering the streets of Chicago or the farms of the Midwest—or anywhere else—he recorded with epistemological precision the lives and speech of Americans. His work is reminiscent of the cityscapes of Swift and John Gay as well as the obsessive spectatorial efforts of Wordsworth and Whitman. Like the bard of Manhattan, Sandburg claims for himself

the authority of an exemplary watcher: "I am the people—the mob—
the crowd—the mass," he writes in an early poem, "I am the audience
that witnesses history" (71). Sandburg is the ultimate *bricoleur,* the
gatherer of bits and pieces of data that he assembles into larger com-
posites for the purpose of revelation. His collective readers see not
just themselves but the entirety of themselves as agents in a clearly
defined social context, the hopes and aspirations as well as the fierce
and shameful hungers that lie behind the superficial appearances of
city life. The enduring value of Sandburg's poems, and especially *The
People, Yes,* is in the presentation of tableaus that bring his vast sub-
ject into view, where it can be recognized as information vital to the
wellbeing of a society in the process of radical change.

One of Sandburg's principal techniques is borrowed from the
modernist masters: the interpolation of scenes of dialogue from the
street. The conversation of the women in the pub in part 2 of *The
Waste Land* ("You *are* a proper fool, I said. / Well, if Albert won't
leave you alone, there it is, I said.") had become by the 1930s a
much-imitated mode of transcription or found material, and the
ubiquity of radio and sound film further popularized the device.
Sandburg listens to the people and choreographs an immense quan-
tity of the speech acts that define their understanding of their condi-
tion. These include memorable sayings that exhibit a special kind of
cultural knowing with affinities to the wit and compression of poetic
discourse:

> "I had such a good time," said the woman leaving a movie
>   theater with tears in her eyes. "It was a swell picture."
> "A divorced man goes and marries the same kind of woman he is
>   just rid of," said the lawyer.
> "Life is a gigantic fake," read the farewell note of the high school
>   boy who killed himself.
> "I pick jurors with nonconvicting faces,"
>   said the lawyer who usually cleared his man.
> "We earn and we earn and all that we earn goes into the grave,"
>   said the basement-dwelling mother who had lost six of her
>   eight children from the white plague.
> "Don't mourn for me but organize," said the Utah I.W.W.
>   before a firing squad executed sentence of death on him, his
>   last words running: "Let her go!" (463–64)

Sandburg does the same with exchanges of dialogue, and with the same democratic intentions. Unlike Eliot's critique of his lower-class subjects, Sandburg passes along with his obvious endorsement the gentle satire of the folk who see through the pretensions of those who claim a position as superiors:

> "I am John Jones."
> "Take a chair."
> "Yes, and I am the son of John
> Throckmorton Jones."
> "Is that possible? Take two chairs." (529)

The dialogue could be taken from a film by Frank Capra or Preston Sturges. (One glimpses Sandburg's persona in the idealistic poet Longfellow Deeds of Capra's 1936 film, *Mr. Deeds Goes to Town.*) Like their exuberant comedies, his book is an anatomy, a compendium of the country's resourceful language habits.

The elaborate documentary quality of Sandburg's writing allowed him to claim a genuine function for the poet in American society. The poet was not just another con man of the kind treated so abundantly in Sandburg's poems, and certainly not the prostitute of MacLeish's complaint, but a witness who offers to people hungry for truth an authentic and comprehensive representation of their individual and collective experience. Just as patriotic filmmakers in the Soviet Union and the United States invited each viewer to project him- or herself into their stories, and thereby become part of the ideological subject, so the poet breaks down the solitary reader's sense of isolation and gathers him or her into the parade of fellow Americans pictured in the poem. It is crucial that a poem of this kind have a large sale, be widely distributed and reviewed, be welcomed into households that have very little poetry on the shelves. For a civilization devoted to speed Sandburg forged a supple form that did what it intended and captured the audience it sought. The montage form mimicked the movement of film, the arbitrary arrangements of newspaper layout, the shifts in register on the radio as commercials and programming competed for attention. For this reason, if for no other, *The People, Yes* was welcomed by MacLeish as a public poem of enormous importance to the life of poetry in a time of Depression.

It provided not just the elite but the majority with a mirror of their recognizable presence in history.

When in 1937 MacLeish joined John Dos Passos, director Joris Ivens, and an organization called Contemporary Historians in making *The Spanish Earth,* a film protesting Franco's challenge to the Spanish Republic, he characteristically defended his screenplay by distinguishing it from debased models of cinematic form. He began an article for *Cinema Arts* magazine by critiquing the rote imagism of popular media:

> If you look at Spain as an excuse for making a picture, you do not look at Spain at all. You look at the lace mantillas which mean Spain at the box office and you look at the stark shots of shell explosions which mean Spain on the front page, and the rest you do not look at. Particularly you do not look at the people under the shawls—lace or no lace—and the gun crews back of the explosion.[14]

The passage shows MacLeish's newly engendered discomfort with the art of surfaces. He vows to drive beneath appearances, to disclose the truth so easily obscured by the photographic media. And yet film *is* his medium in this case, and the best that he can promise is to "present the world as it really looks." The ambition of *The Spanish Earth,* like his verse plays for radio of the period, and like *The People, Yes,* is to integrate the techniques of cinematic form with the continuous, coherent, naturalistic, expository forms of premodern literature in order to create a sustained and credible commentary on a complex event. Like the Italian neorealists who documented the end of the fascist terror a few years later, MacLeish and Sandburg elected to "look at the people" from the proximity of camera range, and by assembling an abundance of shots rather than privileging a conventional few, make a cinema of it with as much objectivity as documentary style allowed.

The previous year Pare Lorentz had produced a film from a *Fortune* essay by MacLeish titled "The Plow That Broke the Plains." In 1938 MacLeish published *Land of the Free,* an assemblage of Farm Security Administration photographs by Dorothea Lange and others for which he composed a long poem as what he called a "Sound Track." MacLeish was obviously pleased by the "individual case study" format of the photographs, as opposed to the European montage style represented in 1930s America principally by inventive magazine advertisements. The naturalistic photographs favored by Lange, Walker Evans, and other roving reporters of the native scene deliberately eschewed the shock effects of experimental forms. In theory and in practice, MacLeish joined eminent spokesmen like Paul Strand and Lewis Mumford in resisting the claims of the modernist mode in visual construction. "The Plow That Broke the Plains" and *Land of the Free* are exemplary testimonies to MacLeish's liberal vision of America, his attempt to forge a democratic art by means of a cooperating partnership with visual media. Such a partnership realized the ideal of community he proposed for the alienated artist at a time when European fascism threatened the entire society of nations.

As MacLeish was attracted from Axel's castle to the public sphere—to films, radio, and the stage—so W. H. Auden in the mid-1930s turned from his difficult early poems to the composition of verse texts for British documentary films like *Coal Face* and *Night Mail,* and provided verse subtitles for a London Film Society screening of Dziga Vertov's *Three Songs of Lenin.* Such films were shown not just in theaters but in public forums of all kinds in order to lessen the gap between modern art and the masses. Likewise James Agee gravitated from his first vocation as poet to the world of cinema. Agee won the Yale Series of Younger Poets prize for his modernist volume *Permit Me Voyage* in 1934, and then worked with Walker Evans on their documentary book about Alabama sharecroppers, *Let Us Now Praise Famous Men* (1941). Because Agee came to believe that "most of the really good popular art produced anywhere comes from Hollywood" and that movies were "the greatest art medium of [t]his century,"[15] he devoted his career from 1940 on principally to film criticism, for the *Nation, Life,* and *Time,* and to screenplays for Hollywood production. Other poets on the Left continued to work in the field of modernist montage, such as Sol Funaroff, whose 1938 pastiche of *The Waste Land,* titled "What the Thunder Said: A Fire Sermon," and subtitled "*A Cinematic Poem,*" subversively translates Eliot's vision of hooded hordes overrunning unreal cities into an affirmative endorsement of revolutionary action. Noticing that the Sanskrit word "da" also means "yes" in Russian, Funaroff hears in the Eliotic thunder the message, "All Power to the Soviets!"[16] Like Sandburg and Agee, Funaroff, in this and other poems, uses an art of assemblage to shine a moving spotlight on dispossessed people in the American landscape.

The other direction taken by the montage (or more precisely, collage) method was Pound's in *The Cantos,* a poem MacLeish respected at a distance but increasingly deplored in the 1930s for its anti-Semitism, fascist sympathies, and obscurantism. Though deferential to Pound in his letters to the master, and as the person who did as much as anyone to secure Pound's release from St. Elizabeth's Hospital after the war, MacLeish acted as something of a disciple. But his remark that Pound "was a very silly man who had some remarkable gifts" better represents his opinion of the 1930s; he would later claim that Pound had never written a single good poem.[17] The year Sandburg published *The People, Yes,* Pound was writing poems like Canto 46, which opens:

And if you will say that this tale teaches . . .
a lesson, or that the Reverend Eliot
has found a more natural language . . . you who think you will
get through hell in a hurry . . .
That day there was cloud over Zoagli
And for three days snow cloud over the sea
Banked like a line of mountains.
Snow fell. Or rain fell stolid, a wall of lines
So that you could see where the air stopped open
and where the rain fell beside it
Or the snow fell beside it. Seventeen
Years on this case, nineteen years, ninety years
            on this case
An' the fuzzy bloke sez (legs no pants ever wd. fit) 'IF
that is so, any government worth a damn can
pay dividends?'
The major chewed it a bit and sez: 'Y—es, eh . . .
You mean instead of collecting taxes?'
'Instead of collectin' taxes?' That office?
Didja see the Decennio?
?
Decennio exposition, reconstructed office of Il Popolo,
Waal, ours waz like that, minus the Mills bomb an' the teapot . . .

This canto, which follows the famous one on "usura," joins together an immense variety of materials, but unlike Sandburg's collage there is no interest in constructing a discourse comprehensible to the majority of modern readers. Can such verse be called "cinematic" at all? Marshall McLuhan wrote Pound in 1948, "Your Cantos I now judge to be the first and only serious use of the great technical possibilities of the cinematograph."[18] But there has been no rush to endorse such a view, not from Pound scholars and certainly not from most moviegoing readers. Pound's splicings of quotations and voices qualify as "a montage of *personae*," as McLuhan calls them, but their nonnarrative character prevents them from initiating the kind of rapprochement with popular culture McLuhan seems to suggest. Rather, the order of Pound's units is esoteric, disorienting, even whimsical, in the spirit of "Cinema of a Man." Strictly speaking, the poem has more resemblance to the private textures of underground film, an artifice of personal sensibility rather than a camera eye with its shutter open. If Sandburg aspired to the status of quintessential American by inscribing a cinemalike portrait of his people, Pound cultivated a style of social marginality. That is why MacLeish and others looked upon the *Cantos* with such suspicion.

The section quoted above begins by affirming that the poem will not simplify itself in the manner of Eliot's more recent verse, which had retreated from the severe fragmentation of *The Waste Land*. "Burnt Norton," Eliot's most recent important poem before Canto 46, is challenging in its rhetoric but is lucidity itself compared to Pound's practice at this time. No, the reader cannot "get through hell in a hurry," says Pound, who then idles for a while describing a snowfall near Rapallo and then leaps to some matters arising from the eccentric schemes of Major Clifford Douglas to reform the economic system. Pound affects slang, but his poem is the furthest thing from "the language really used by men," for the slang is clearly meant as a patronizing parody of the vernacular, not an example of it, as in Sandburg. Pound's preferred style is the golden one on display across the page: "Usura slayeth the child in the womb / It stayeth the young man's courting." Never feeling at home in his native country or his century, driven by his restless intellect into the archaisms of one speech and the affectations of folk idiom in another, Pound borrows from the menu of styles supplied by literary history; and using the ideogramic method he jumps from one voice to another, defying the contemporary as poets on the Left defined it by making all historical voices contemporary. Like Eliot's practice in *The Waste Land,* Pound assembled what he called "Luminous Details" in a variety of historical and literary voices, but whereas Eliot secured the reader's interest by extended scenes like those of the woman at the mirror and the typist with the clerk, Pound's "snippets" became increasingly fragmentary and hermetic. MacLeish saw Pound this way, in any case. And he noted how inevitably Pound was drawn to a political figure like Mussolini—"Decennio" is the tenth anniversary of Italian fascism in 1932, and "Il Popolo" refers to the newspaper founded by Mussolini in 1914. A violent disorder yearns for a violent order, and Pound's idiosyncratic method of composition, the furthest thing from public speech and rational organization, evoked constantly the ideal of a strongman who would exert single-minded control over the populace. Pound referred repeatedly to Mussolini as an "artist" whose plastic medium was the masses he commanded in his policy directives. A few years later Pound was signing his letters, "Heil Hitler."[19]

Verse montage, then, will have its most important successes when it returns to the notion of moving pictures, a scrapbook, album, or gallery of recognizable figures or vignettes. Langston Hughes's "Montage of a Dream Deferred" intends to put the reader in mind not only of jazz structure but of the fluidity of film, as the poet turns his attention to one scene after another without transition or argument. Likewise Melvin B. Tolson's "Harlem Gallery" and Robert Hayden's "Middle Passage" reveal to readers the neglected times and places of black history in documentary style. Just as Hayden mixes voices and documents describing the slave trade, and Muriel Rukeyser in *U. S. 1* (1938) offers voices and documents about the effects of silicosis in miners, so William Carlos Williams in *Paterson* (1946–58) will welcome into his study of the New Jersey city whatever materials in whatever form he can use to represent with didactic energy the topography of a modern American metropolis. These are all poems motivated by a sense of citizenship rooted in local history, however much they open out onto cosmopolitan topics. "You and I have a considerable responsibility," MacLeish wrote Sandburg. "We cannot escape our duty as political animals."[20] That duty was to put verse into the service of a humane social vision that film form could effectively and judiciously serve if the poet did not make the process of scrutiny too recondite, the associations too obscure. There would be nothing like "Cinema of a Man" in MacLeish's later work. Radio and theater would provide avenues of growth for him after the 1930s, culminating in his popular adaptation of the Book of Job, *J. B.: A Play in Verse* (1957), but film would never engage him again, not as subject, not as a model for poetic structure. The guardians of modernist ideology have never forgiven him the apostasy.

The Mutoscope, or "peep machine," available in Mutoscope Parlors everywhere in America before the rise of theaters. A penny would show you "What the Butler Saw" or what happened "In the Maid's Dressing Room." A primitive form of the projector, it became a metaphor of access to primal desire for more than one poet. (From C. W. Ceram, *Archaeology of the Cinema* [New York: Harcourt, Brace & World, 1965].)

Chapter 4

Winfield Townley Scott and Delmore Schwartz: Halving Reality and Watching It Too

DREAM PENNY IN THE SLOT AT 6 A.M.

Dreaming, he turns the crank to wind her
Through his own eyes that he looks into, and
The girl moves toward him through going mist
Nearer and clearer as though through unwound days and hours
Slowly; and veil after veil slides apart and behind her,
Veils moving over and away from her, ankle and wrist
Breaking the dark dominion. Then the spotlights find her,
Traman sees the long aisle of crushed flowers behind her,
How even now she stands in trampled flowers.

But then he looks again through the small
Slot; keeps busy with the crank's turning (tired)
And sees that it is not flowers at all:
Running in flickers of light at him (not
Tired) she kicks the fallen leaves in the road hollows:
Hot against him now, laughing (this is fun),
Her hair sweet like grass that lies a day in the sun.
She runs away from him. He follows

We will lie in the sun, Traman yells at her. He shouts
We will lie a long time in the sun. But then he sees
The sun going down between his knees: so he props
Her, very solemn, against a haystack and whispers
That the sun isn't going at all down now, anytime ever down;
    and the sun, sure enough, stops.

Something plops.
Light flares. Traman is alone, blind,
And will not remember how he got out of the place.
Nor clearly what happened; nor will he greatly mind,
Being stunned and bewildered, his ears ringing with the terrible
    thunder of all those suddenly collected veils fallen between
    him and her beautiful face.[1]

—1936

E ver since Vachel Lindsay in *Art of the Moving Picture* called attention to Paleolithic art as a model for the film medium, there has been a persistent but unstudied use of cave painting as a metaphor for what Lindsay called "the original poetry of the eye."[2] The comparison summons to mind a scene of the primeval tribe sitting in wonder before the gigantic forms of bison and deer rendered on the cave walls by shaman or artisan. As interpretive stories were offered the tribe to enhance the aura of the pictures, a visual culture began to take form, culminating, according to Lindsay, in the "folk-imagination" on display at the nickelodeon. "The kinetoscope [is] bringing back the primitive in a big rich way," Lindsay asserted in the penultimate chapter of his treatise; "the cave-man longs with an incurable homesickness for his ancient day." The metaphor linking cave art and the movies depends for its effect on a consensus of opinion about the purpose of those cave paintings, but until recently no such consensus existed, either among scholars or the general public. It may be that the habit of moviegoing and television watching in our own century has helped to sponsor such a consensus, for we like to think that our own ritual acts of spectatorship bond us to our ancestors from prehistorical eras. In any case, poets like Lindsay and Winfield Townley Scott may be said to have foreseen the neo-Romantic terms of the comparison.

When Alexander Marshack in the 1960s and 1970s flashed an ultrapowerful raking sidelight on the painted figures of Pech Merle and other caves in southern Europe, he discovered that the colored surfaces were thickly layered, having been retouched a multitude of times by tribal members, presumably for many generations. Likewise, statuettes and stone figurines were commonly overengraved as new inflections were given to basic designs. Marshack identifies this ritual need to retrace and reconstruct visual images as a prime example of civilized behavior. "Cro-Magnon man's way of thinking was fully modern," Marshack believes; "he was using symbols the way we do today." The paintings and other artifacts can be identified as what anthropologists call *extrinsic symbols* or reifications of internal concepts.[3] Cave art was not simply a training guide for young hunters, as some scholars first hypothesized, but primitive peoples' way of discovering and articulating the mystery of their own being. The cave was a theater of the psyche, a brain space, where salient figures of fear and desire would be represented for spectatorial apprehension and enlightenment. People of a hunting tribe in a wilderness environment would understandably be most fascinated by the reproduced forms of animals, their daily preocccupation and no doubt the stuff of their dreams at night.

Because domestic implements have not been found in the caves where the great paintings were done, it can be assumed that these were not living areas, but sacred places set apart for the ceremonial appreciation of the images—"a sanctuary for specialized rites and stories," as Marshack says of the cave called Les Trois Freres.[4] Early humankind's participation with these images implied a special mode of consciousness we would call aesthetic. No doubt the repetitive behavior of revisiting and retracing became a principle of order in this primal world, closely akin to chants and dances and other ceremonial activities of these tribes. In this dreamtime of the species, picture art bridged the gap between the day self and the night self, the impulses of instinct and the mediations of consciousness. The site of the gradual evolution of the human type, then, might fairly be located in the cave. Marshack remarks that along with the regularity and dependability of the coded pictures, cave images changed over time as the wall face was used for different figures, as seasonal vegetation was added to animal presence, as, in some caves, human figures, such as the Aurignacian "Venuses," appeared as goddess symbols. The fascination with female figures in European prehistoric art cannot be simplified as erotic but involved symbolic opportunities for meditating on natural cycles of all kinds. These are records of "thinking in time," Marshack insists, and their location indicates the importance of the sacred cave as a theatrical space where humans came to learn the iconography of the imagination.

From its inception, however, the film medium was vulnerable to comparisons with another cave image, that of Plato's allegory in book 7 of *The Republic*. In that dialogue humanity sits enchained in semidarkness, spellbound by the illusory shadows of material existence cast upon the wall in front of them and ignorant of the sun of truth shining aboveground. The images they witness with their "bodily eyes" are those Plato denounces in preceding sections of his dialogue as the inflammatory nonsense of the false educator: "nothing else than the opinions and beliefs expressed by the public itself." Plato's sophistic cave master clearly resembles the demonized figure of the Hollywood filmmaker, of whom it may also be said, "not in the least knowing which of [the public's] humors and desires is good or bad, right or wrong, he will fit all these terms to the fancies of the great beast and call what it enjoys good and what vexes it bad."[5] The great beast, of course, enjoys most what is bestial, and that soon becomes the unjust standard of taste in the culture served by visual images.

For Plato, it is precisely because the psychic cave is inhabited by creatures shaped from appetite that the free play of narrative can be described as a danger to the community. An art that represents volatile dream images feeds back into the psyche the brutish fantasies engendered by irrational states of feeling. Humans who consume these ghostly forms of desire are stimulated to give them freer rei(g)n in the imagination, and thus to demand more abundant representations of them as the essence of their aesthetic—and moral—life. Instead of cultivating the rational self, human beings are driven by the culture's privileged artifacts to submerge themselves incessantly in the shadow world of unresisted fantasy. Rather than the "cathedral mood" that Lindsay praised, the neighborhood theater could be imagined as a Gothic castle in which viewers hungrily embrace the dead world of their primitive ancestors or infantile selves buried under years of acculturation. "Movie audiences are made up of sentimental necrophiles," Norman Mailer remarks in *The Deer Park*.[6]

In his poem "Dream Penny in the Slot at 6 A.M." Winfield Townley Scott assumes in his choice of metaphor that film represents a total experience of in-sight. Not the insight of rational understanding—the mode of his own poetry—but the more elemental viewing-into that uncovers the crude instincts boarded up in humanity's primordial being. Film, by nature an expressive medium, can uniquely serve as a magic lantern and project concealed images into public view. It can mimic the masturbatory fantasy, as in "Dream Penny," or fantasies of omnipotence and destruction, or any lonely dream that releases the observer from social training. In the private reverie *others* do not really exist; as in Scott's poem the self-absorbed gazes into the eyepiece of the Mutoscope and sees first his own voyeurist gaze.

Traman is the central character of Scott's first book of poems, *Biography for Traman* (1936), and by Scott's own account a portrait of himself as an impressionable young man. In "Dream Penny" Scott preserves his memories of regular visits to the Colonial Theatre in Newport, Rhode Island, where, he wrote in a memoir, he was "in heaven" as he watched the big screen. Traman is Scott's dream self (in German, *träumen* means "to dream"); he enacts the Romantic longing for ecstasy that the cave dweller feels most exuberantly in the experience of gazing at images. As he peers into the eyepiece and turns the crank, the cards that hold the experience (the Mutoscope stills, the personal fantasy) bring the golden girl closer and closer. "Veil after veil slides apart" and she stands revealed in what appears to be flowers. Of this female presence, a constant in Scott's poetry, Scott's wife remarked, "[She] contains the Eden garden, a time of sufficient and abundant love, and physical as well as poetic potency."[7] Her beguiling image offers the promise of sensual joy to which everyman responds: "We will lie in the sun . . . . We will lie a long time in the sun."

But, that inevitable conjunction, opens the second stanza and collapses Traman's hopes in the third. He discovers that she does not emerge from real flowers but merely "flickers of light." Nor will she abide with him; she flees and he follows, turning the crank, though by doing so he murders the pleasure he pursues. The sun is not for them, in "the dark dominion," but for those who hold to the immutable truth of reality. Scott dramatizes the vision moment by moment, sustaining the tension between excited participation and forebodings of failure. In the third stanza Traman's desperation forces a plea from him ("The sun isn't going at all down") contradicted in the same plaintively lengthened line. The sun *stops* when "Something *plops*," a rhyme as rude as Traman's awakening and one that matches the pairing of his *blind* eyes and his absence of *mind* in the same stanza. The narcissist at his machine finds himself alone, "stunned and bewil-

dered," the victim of his unsatisfied craving. Lindsay escaped this fate
by observing the radiant actress sub specie aeternitatis. His desire to
make sweeping historical claims for the "myriad artist clan" kept his
tribute public, ecclesiastical. Scott confronts the female image on a
visceral level, removing even the audience by his choice of the free-
standing peep machine (as it was called), which admits only one
patron at a time.

The movie has not failed Traman; it has been all too successful
in arousing his fundamental desires. But his hope for self-satisfaction
or self-fulfillment based on a joyful union with the dream girl has
suffered another defeat. In a single fatal moment the film's cessation
exiles Traman into the absolute solitude he has in fact been undergo-
ing throughout the duration of the film experience and discloses the
film imagery as a realm of shadows. And what are the alternatives
now that he has been so cheated? The trauma of subsiding back into
a small independent being after such empathy with his soul mate is
not easily healed by social concern, by future-directed activity. Nor
does the reader, especially the male reader, wish for self-sacrifice in
favor of the superego's demands. The reader too is a voyant and
voyeur, watching Traman watch the unveiling female body. Scott
has involved the reader scene by scene in Traman's erotic pleasure,
and so the aftermath of vacancy weighs upon him as another partici-
pant. The reader ought to recognize, if the poem has done its evoca-
tive work, that commitment to a world less absolute in its pleasure
than the world of art would amount to an impoverishment of instinc-
tual life. There is only one alternative and that is the eventual return
to art: another penny in the slot, another turn of the page.

I have been discussing the poem as if it records an activity of
watching a movie. In fact the movie is clearly an extended metaphor
of Traman's dream. The title signals this fact by locating the period
of the viewing as six A.M., an unlikely time to be standing before a
Mutoscope but a likely hour to be indulging an erotic fantasy just
before rising with the sun to meet the day. That the dream is so
entirely expressed in movie imagery testifies to Scott's conviction
that the inner life of American culture cannot be represented except
through the mediation of serial photography. Photography has
trained us to frame all of the visual environment, and especially the
erotic, as the camera eye mandates. We see reality as photographs
teach us to see, and oneiric reality likewise conforms to the way our

movie-nourished imaginations picture objects of desire. The poem
of desire in the twentieth century, then, can be expected to increas-
ingly feature its object with a cinematographer's techniques of posi-
tioning, lighting, and editing, not only in poems about movie stars
but in poems about other real or imaginary personalities whose limi-
nal presence has been appropriated from repeated exhibition in the
cave of primal appearances.

Scott's moralistic poem describes an addiction to fantasy, and
belongs in the tradition of poems like Tennyson's "The Palace of
Art," W. B. Yeats's "The Circus Animals' Desertion," D. H. Law-
rence's "When I Went to the Film—," and Muriel Rukeyser's
"Movie," in which secondary worlds are deprived of their legiti-
macy. "The reality of the dream is not to be equated with the reality
of experience," Scott reminded himself in his notebooks. "At best,
the dream halves such reality."[8] Scott looks upon even the fantasists
he admires—such as E. A. Robinson and H. P. Lovecraft—as crip-
pled by addiction to their inner demons. In the poem "Film-Maker,"
written some thirty years after "Dream Penny," Scott again drama-
tized the helpless incapacity of the fantasist:

> He lay unable to move, unable to waken,
> Pinned by his own preference for dream,
> Unchallenged by the flesh and blood of day.
> Within these films all could be acted out
> As he directed, although even here
> Sometimes his star refused and froze with fright.
> Yet here he clung to what he could not help:
> If wakened by it, crawled toward sleep again,
> Back to alleys of moonlight, into rooms
> Shadowed with shapes of women who received him
> With nude complicities.[9]

The consumer/producer of erotic fantasy has become the denying
critic who interposes his knowledge of past failures between his desire
and his art. Prosodically this later poem enacts the loss of energy it
describes, exchanging the rhythmic inventiveness of "Dream Penny"
for a form in which the stresses are more regular, the relation of line
to sentence less varied, the witty rhyme replaced by a halting blank
verse, and the diction drained of the vitality given the earlier poem

by immersion in mysterious experience. This is a poem about impotence, about the inability to successfully complete an act of erotic engagement with a desired other. It lacks the song quality of the self's willed union with some figurative *belle dame*. Like Prufrock avoiding the siren call of "one" or many female images whom he nevertheless must summon from the deep to torture him with longing, this filmmaker remains "pinned" (the word recalls Eliot's antihero "pinned and wriggling on the wall") by his preference for dream.

Scott's whole oeuvre displays an attempt to willfully restrain his tendencies to addiction. This addiction began in childhood when the Traman part of himself succumbed to the allurements of fantasy. In his memoirs Scott recalled that he and his friends "lived a great deal of the time in a dream world." He was easily "trapped in romance" whenever he opened a book of adventures.[10] The creation of Traman helped him to objectify and purge his spirit of this susceptibility. But he remained uncertain whether his externalizing of the dream self was a creative triumph or a failure of will. Like the American public Scott persisted in fantasies "unchallenged by the flesh and blood of day," wielding control over the the lurid world—the whorish women's "nude complicities"—that shamed his New England conscience. He smoked too much, he drank too much—these were habits he could and did genuinely disapprove. But can an artist regret that he dreams too much? Isn't fantasy the lamia that he destroys at the expense of his own creative life?

Scott believed it his moral duty to pronounce judgment upon the unbridled fantasies he associated with film, and to do so not only for the benefit of a general public but for the diminishing pool of poetry readers tempted like him by the allurements of visual spectacle. And yet he could not resist competing with film and fiction alike by writing book-length narrative poems replete with exciting events, memorable characters, and fundamental passions. *The Sword on the Table* was an account of the Dorr Rebellion, and *The Dark Sister* a Viking romance. Scott's obvious models are the long historical poems of the 1920s and 1930s that reacted against the more condensed subjective mode of modernist practice. Joseph Moncure March's narrative poems *The Wild Party* and *The Set-Up* (both 1928) deserve special notice as two of the very few twentieth-century poems adapted into movies. Archibald MacLeish's *Conquistador*, Stephen Vincent Benét's *John Brown's Body*, Robinson Jeffers's *Cawdor* and *Thurso's Landing*, and a vast number of now-forgotten novels in verse—all of these testify to the desire of many modern poets *not* to relinquish the Homeric mantle to other media. But Scott knew in his heart—and perhaps the knowledge infected his practice—that such poems would not reestablish the ancient claims of the poet to centrality in the culture. The lyric moment of insight, not the protracted immersion in story, was the preferred rhetorical mode of modern poetry, and Scott labored too in this cul-de-sac, as he saw it, with diminishing confidence as he grew older. Finally, Scott retired to New Mexico, where he found in the rigors and resistances of wilderness nature a spiritual alternative to the umbrageous offerings of picture show and poetry alike.

In the 1930s the questions about film raised metaphorically by Scott's poem became ubiquitous in the entire society. They were formulated in the Paleolithic/Platonic terms already outlined. What was actually occurring in those caves of representation to which some eighty million of the tribe resorted each week? Were movies safe sublimations that enhanced the light of consciousness? Or were movies better characterized, as Scott suggests, as addictive surrogates for genuine experience, halving reality rather than having reality, so that the American population was in danger of irrationality on a national scale? I would like to pursue this latter viewpoint a little ways, as an enlargement of my commentary on Scott's poem, before turning to the more positive reading.

"Dream Penny" could not have been written without the context of a national debate on the psychological impact of film on American society. In the 1930s, a period when the temptations to escape reality were especially strong, an immense number of popular books, as well as innumerable newspaper and magazine articles, debated whether film was manipulating and circumscribing the consciousness of audiences by its presentation of inflammatory imagery. The Payne Fund sponsored a series of alarmist reports throughout the decade that prompted national soul-searching about the possible danger to innocent imaginations. Sample titles just from 1933 include *Our Movie-Made Children; Movies, Delinquency and Crime; Motion Pictures and Standards of Morality; Movies and Conduct; The Social Conduct and Attitudes of Movie Fans;* and *Getting Ideas from the Movies.* The social-science methodology of such works was untrustworthy, as Raymond Moley documented in his debunking book of 1938, *Are We Movie-*

Made? But their vigorous warnings about the potency of screen imagery affected literary discourse for a generation; one hears not-so-faint echoes of their admonitions in the controversy over television and popular music in the 1990s.

Our Movie-Made Children, by Henry James Forman, is typical of many tracts of the time that argued not against film per se but against the misuse of the medium to stimulate antisocial thought and behavior. "The writing of the movies upon children's minds appears to be fairly indelible," Forman remarks, and locates the effects of such massive and prolonged inscription in new codes of conduct, especially as regards sex and violence.[11] Forman's book claims to see through the rationalization that "it's only a movie" and ask precisely how such visual "distractions" shape our visceral imperatives and the imaginative reconstruction of reality outside the privileged realm of the theater.

Forman draws heavily upon interviews with children and adolescents. He finds in these interviews testimonies about the full surrender to fantasy in the spectatorial act. "When I saw Ruth Chatterton in 'The Right to Love,' I craved nothing but love and wild party" is a typical remark (216). Another girl has this to say:

> I always put myself in the place of the heroine. If the hero was some man by whom I should enjoy being kissed (as he invariably was), my evening was a success, and I went home in a dreamy frame of mind, my heart beating rather fast and my usually pale cheeks brilliantly flushed. I used to look in the mirror somewhat admiringly and try to imagine Wallace Reid or John Barrymore kissing that face. (153)

The reaction recorded here is the mirror image of Scott's: in both cases the other gender represented in the film is an attractive "type" whose performative function—no matter what the details of the narrative—is to arouse sexual desire in the spectator by a masquerade of provocative gestures. Traman has no male actor within the film to mimic, no safe surrogate to mediate between his lust and the dramatic presentation; hence his severe frustration when the narrative leaves his libidinal demands abruptly unconsummated. The girl in the interview is allowed a fuller participation in the erotic world of the film because the unnamed actresses offer her vicarious access to the fantasy on screen. She brings the movie home with her and lives for a time as its agent, duplicating its effects whenever she looks into the mirror, and presumably on other occasions including her own courtship rituals when she enacts the screened object of masculine attentions. The effect of repeated, indeed addictive recourse to art models of this kind, Forman warns, is an inaptitude at social adjustment, as real romance again and again falls short of the erotic promise of the movies. And once again the crucial point is that the insufficiency of reality to match the excitement of the movies mandates a return to the source of intense pleasure: another dream penny in the slot.

Forman uses a quotation from William James's text *Psychology* to develop this point:

> The drunken Rip Van Winkle, in Jefferson's play, excuses himself for every fresh dereliction by saying, "I won't count this time!" Well! he may not count it, and a kind Heaven may not count it; but it is being counted none the less. Down among his nerve-cells and fibres the molecules are counting it, registering and storing it up to be used against him when the next temptation comes. (35)

Every act of picture watching, by Forman's measurement, contributes to a nervous network of encoded desire. The dream content is constantly retraced in memory by daydreaming and by the repeated and intensely pleasurable experience of formula films that reinforce the original fantasies. By this reading of the filmgoing experience, people can be turned into virtual automatons, as filmmakers program each spectator to be dependent on the pleasures provided by the unique technology of film. The solution to this problem cannot be what Forman recommends, more films that model benevolent conduct, nor the Hays Office to police film content, but rather a distancing from cinematic effects by the interposing power of some demystifying rhetoric. Scott's poem is a perfect example of such a corrosive exposé, one that writers of the 1930s, who saw a relation between Hollywood producers and fascist dictators, offered as an antidote to the addictive attractions of the charismatic.

But if some writers, moralists and poets alike, believed that the theater and the street ought to be kept in wholesome separation, others saw film as a positive model for poetic production and social redemption. Freud had laid the groundwork for such a view by treating dreams, especially daydreams, as the raw material for poetic composition, paradigms of the revelatory practice of contemporary artists. In part because of Freud's influence, films that deliberately mimicked the enigmas and distortions of dream would be termed poetic no matter how often poets protested that they were also transcribers of actuality, every bit as alert to social reality as . . . filmmakers. The central figure in this visionary camp was Jean Cocteau, the French man of letters whose experimental films *Le Sang d'un poète* (1930) and *La Belle et la bête* (1946), culminating in what is arguably the best film ever made about poetry, *Orphée* (1950), showed how fruitfully an artist can employ poetic conventions, private myths, and interartistic techniques in the art of the film. Cocteau's films have a structure of regression and condensation informed by Freudian ideas about childhood, and by expressionist European cinema. These films did not provide easy access to fantasy situations, but constructed idiosyncratic narratives that intrigued viewers by their strangeness not their familiarity. One champion of this practice in the 1930s was the English poet and critic Herbert Read, whose essay "The Poet and the Film" draws upon Coleridge to praise the "strange dream-like fertility of images" in movies like Cocteau's.[12] Read's experience in World War I persuaded him that art must accommodate itself to new technology, and to the forms of experience new technology enforced. Read drew upon psychoanalysis as well to formulate an aesthetic hospitable to film as the paradigmatic work of "Imagination" in the modern era. As a champion of the surrealist movement, Read argued that a rational work of art is a contradiction in terms.

Gabriela Mistral, in a lengthy essay, "The Poet's Attitude Toward the Movies," went further. The Chilean poet, who would receive the Nobel Prize for literature in 1945, contributed her essay to an anthology of 1936, *The Movies on Trial*. The book is a response to "the storm of protest," as the editor calls it, about the immorality and antisocial effects of films, not only from conservative groups like The Payne Fund that feared the undermining of social norms, but from writers on the Left who assailed Hollywood films as propaganda for capitalism and a narrowly defined nationalism. Amidst such polemics as Seymour Stern's "The Bankruptcy of Cinema as Art" and Wolf W. Moss's "The Movies and the Social Revolution," Mistral's commentary must have struck readers as wholly bizarre.

She writes ardently about the apocalyptic impact of movies upon the modern imagination. Film is invaluable to the extent it can offer images "transformed into phosphorescent myths, fashioned by truth and dreaming in collaboration." Mistral argues for a cinema that causes regression to the primitive consciousness enjoyed by each moviegoer before being "cast . . . headlong into the blackest slime, into the foulest cloaca of the real."[13] With such neo-Romantic sentiments, what films would Mistral be likely to enjoy? She mentions only the "Mickeys, Felixes, and Betty Boops" of animated film and *The Invisible Man* as standards of excellence; but she would have been able to construct a large canon from the fantasist Hollywood fare of the Depression period.

(Parenthetically, one might note how routinely the movies themselves argued Mistral's point. *Sullivan's Travels* [1941] depicts a successful director of comic films who wants to try his hand at the social problem genre. He learns by traveling in disguise among the lower classes, and especially in a prison scene when the convicts respond enthusiastically to a Mickey Mouse cartoon, how much more important fancy is than reality in the movies. And *The Wizard of Oz* [1939] brilliantly contrasts the drabness of workaday American experience in the black-and-white Kansas sequences with the technicolor world Dorothy enters in her dream. The film is a parable of magical entertainment's resuscitative power in a time of depression.)

Mistral's essay maintains a running argument with the naturalism of Zola and what she sees as the institutional extension of naturalism into the social system: the network of churches, schools, governments, and families that colonizes the realm of wonder. She is able to turn to her purposes the common charge that movies infantilize the public, for this is precisely their liberating mission: "We poets ask of the movies this thing which we have given up asking . . . that they should reproduce a state of childhood in the adult and prolong it in the child by means of the story of pure imagination."[14] By positing a common parent for the two arts, Imagination, Mistral and Read joined the visionary company of neo-Romantic poets in the twentieth century whose mystical tendencies made them sympathetic to a "poetic" new medium able to popularize magical effects, *and* made them contemptuous of the realism enforced on film by its photographic nature. Their antirational essays justified their own pursuit of the transcendent, but provided no useful guide to American poets of the

1930s who wished to engage the "cloaca of the real" as they found it in their surroundings or in their hearts.

Possibly no poet during the 1930s was so addicted to movies as Delmore Schwartz, who sought to appease his urgent egoistic needs throughout his youth and mature years in the experience of the cinema. As a poet who persisted in this obsession at the same time he perfected his craft, Schwartz was destined to write the century's most famous short story on the subject, "In Dreams Begin Responsibilities," the title work of his 1938 volume that included his best poems as well. This story, written at age twenty-two and published two years afterward to universal acclaim in the first number of *Partisan Review*, can usefully be considered as a preface to Schwartz's own lyrical efforts, as he acknowledged when he placed it first in his first book of poems. Required reading for all young writers who followed the twists and turns of the New York intellectuals during the next three decades, the story has probably had as much influence on poets as any poem about the movies.

The story is as compressed as a poem; it occupies just eight pages in the 1978 collection of Schwartz's short fiction that bears its name. As the title tells us, the narrative is that of a dream, but this is definitely a Freudian dream, a symptom of neurosis. "I think it is the year 1909," the story begins. "I feel as if I were in a motion picture theatre, the long arm of light crossing the darkness and spinning, my eyes fixed on the screen." The dream projected on the screen of the narrator's inner mind is one of happy wooing as his father-to-be visits his fiancée and her parents and takes her on an outing at Coney Island. The present-tense declarative sentences laid end to end make the story sound like a shooting script, as the narrator directs his characters, who are also his procreators. The narrator/spectator begins to weep as he imagines his prospective parents' courtship. "The determined old lady who sits next to me in the theatre is annoyed and looks at me with an angry face, and being intimidated, I stop." This same old lady will comfort him in the next section of the story: "There, there, all of this is only a movie, young man, only a movie." He goes to the men's room and when he returns to his seat the tone changes as the inevitability of the proposal, and its declaration, produce astonishing effects. The fiancée begins to weep and says, "It's all I've wanted from the moment I saw you," causing the father his first of many misgivings, and the narrator, as if to arrest the action at this critical stage, rises in his seat and shouts, "Don't do it. It's not too late to change your minds, both of you. Nothing good will come of it, only remorse, hatred, scandal, and two children whose characters are monstrous."

Two final sections follow this outburst. In the first the newly engaged couple have their picture taken, the father very impatient, the mother nervous, and finally both "become quite depressed." In the final section the couple passes a fortune-teller's booth; the mother wants to go in, the father resists. They argue, and shortly after they enter the father gets up angrily and stalks out, while the fortune-teller holds the mother's arm so that she will stay and hear what anyone could predict for their future. The narrator once again begins to shout and protest that these actors ought to have more sense, the mother should go after the father, the father should show more sympathy. An usher arrives and reprimands the young man, using many of the same words he used to reprove his parents: "What are you doing? Don't you know that you can't do whatever you want to do? Why should a young man like you, with your whole life before you, get hysterical like this?... you will find out soon enough, everything you do matters too much." The usher's intervention—like the old lady's, a response of the superego to the narrator's egoism—signals the end of this Kafkaesque fiction. The narrator awakens on the morning of his twenty-first birthday, time for him to begin his adult life, both informed and burdened by the revelations of the dream offered to him in the movie house of his imagination.

The story compels the reader to undertake the task of dream interpretation. The starting point is the central metaphor of the mind as a picture house, to use a term popular in the 1930s. The mind is a "gallery of memory," as Schwartz writes elsewhere, which holds the portraits and events of the past for constant "reprojecting" in reverie and dream. Life, Schwartz wrote in an essay of 1939, is "purified in and reprojected from the human imagination."[15] All through our lives we retrace the memories that inform our identity, fondling and caressing them like the Paleolithic people who passed their hands continually over the painted surfaces of their caves in order to participate more intimately with the figures that haunted them. A more modern, and Freudian, way of saying "haunted" is "disturbed." In his long autobiographical poem *Genesis,* Schwartz reminds himself that "Like Oedipus / No one can go away from genesis, / From parents, early crime, and character, / Guilty or innocent!"[16] The poet's oedipal conflict ensures that the dominating forms of his imagination will be the progenitors of his consciousness and therefore the obsessive content of his art. Once again, the specular metaphor points outward to the world shared by a tribe of readers. Schwartz intends his trope of the movies to have all the power of a central cultural metaphor, like the city as hive, God as watchmaker, or wilderness as Eden. It registers the insight that in a media culture the individual must henceforth apprehend his or her own life as one of passive spectatorship. For the moviegoer the actual is to be experienced at one remove, as the narrator watches himself watch the movie of what was formerly unmediated experience.

The scenes in Schwartz's story are not dreamlike or symbolic but straightforward and sequential, in keeping with Freud's observation that "*distortion is not essential to the nature of the dream.*"[17] Children frequently have such dreams, Freud insisted, and if so the choice of technique is an appropriate one because Schwartz wants us to see the events with the child's eye—the child whose consciousness of the present has been nourished by parental recollections of the courtship period. Schwartz's story, one might say, locates the origins of the celebrity culture in the child's awe of the parents. They are the first giant forms that impose their irresistible potency upon his or her consciousness. A simile in *Genesis* makes this connection explicitly:

> As from the shadows on the silver screen, the audience
> Takes home the Hollywood stars, admits their influence
> Which dwells in them then, and enters, look, gesture, and love,
> So did the notions of the parents impress the child,
> And will impress him forever![18]

Because the child is the father of the man, it is inevitable that the narrator/spectator of "In Dreams Begin Responsibilities" is condemned to repeat this dreamwork forever; it is the sign of his passage into adult life. Though it can (and must) be retraced, it cannot be changed; precisely because it is the donnée of his existence, he is the product of the archetypal family romance that continues to provoke him into rescreening it. (All persons have parents; this is the common tale of the tribe.) He would not have to shout his futile instructions to his parents if their unhappiness had not made him the alienated and unhappy (indeed, "monstrous") person he is. The knowledge of his condition, as it is refracted by the comments of the old woman in the audience and the usher, represents the only chance he has to gain some distance upon his enslavement to the inescapable forms of his imagination. Such knowledge is in turn transferred to readers by the dreamer, in his role as narrator. Like the Ancient Mariner, the artist rids himself of his neurotic disturbance by making his dream experience public.

The dreamer awakens at the end of Schwartz's story to what seems to be "reality," figured as the lip of snow he sees outside the window. In Scott's poem the awakening dreamer is "stunned and bewildered" upon being dispossessed of his wished-for companion. Schwartz's closure holds a more delicate balance between the two realms. As with Scott's poem, the dream has more actuality than the external world, for the snow will strike most readers as a literary convention, whereas the dream will appear to be grounded—the more so as we learn more of Schwartz's biography—in credible and verifiable events. Schwartz is reprojecting his mother's stories of how and why the father abandoned the family when Schwartz was nine into the dream narrative. That the unconscious or dream life is the *true* life, and the external world is seemingly a fictive shadow, an artful simulation derived from the iconography of the artistic tradition—this insight inverts the Platonic parable with a vengeance. In the modern century only the photographed simulacra of experience will carry the conviction that formerly belonged to actuality. Just as dreams allow the dreamer to go on sleeping, in Freud's view, so the culture at large now requires dream stories to remain awake, to cope, to comprehend, to live with the past that comprises the near totality, the grounds and condition, of its contingent existence.

Schwartz's seminal story is a rebuke of the imagination to the kind of reality orientation one finds in, say, *Partisan Review,* with its rational analyses of social and political events. Just as Schwartz cast the Trojan War as a movie in his verse play "Paris and Helen" (1941), with Robert Montgomery as Paris and Madeleine Carroll as Helen, and as Venus "Greta Garbo, Myrna Loy, Hedy Lamarr, Dame May Whitty, alternately," so the tragic struggle of World War II and the cold war yielded in his mind to the greater reality of poetry and film.[19] As one who took pains to avoid conscription in the war and

avoided the political controversies that absorbed his colleagues on the
Partisan Review staff, Schwartz settled gladly for spectatorial status
on world events, not without kibbitzing friends like Dwight
Macdonald who actively entered every political debate. Schwartz
maintained his freedom as a poet by keeping his distance . . . or did
he? It could be argued that Schwartz increasingly locked himself into
the role of passive spectator as firmly as movie stars became locked
into type. Perhaps one can read his comments in 1955 on Mary
Pickford (in a review of her autobiography) as self-reflexive. "The
star becomes the prisoner of her own stardom forever," he writes,
and notes "Miss Pickford's intense feeling that the reality of selfhood
was given to her by the parts she played: appearance is the supreme
reality and the actuality of the individual merely the nondescript soil
out of which it has grown."[20] To the narcissistic artist like Schwartz,
such an imprisonment must have come to seem the very image of his
own enchainment in the dream cave of his ego, closed off from the
full apprehension of reality by the personal history he transcribed in
the manner of Cocteau's vain Orpheus.

It has now become so commonplace to think of life as a movie
that the radical originality of "In Dreams Begin Responsibilities" has
been compromised by promiscuous usage. The story is in danger of
becoming banal, a victim of its own success. We can recover some
of its originality by noting how Schwartz struggled against the impli-
cations of his self-portrayal as spellbound voyeur at the spectacle of
his own prehistory. Schwartz's work offers us a running critique of
addiction to moviegoing. As a college student Schwartz enjoined his
followers, "To see no moving pictures" but rather to read inces-
santly. In a journal entry of 1939 he notes, "At the movie, I suffered
from the sense of guilt and shame which often comes at that enter-
tainment."[21] In his essays he would warn against the seductions of
mass and middlebrow culture. He considered moviegoing to be a
sign of his weakness, of his defeat as an artist—and, we surmise from
"In Dreams Begin Responsibilities," as a man. The forum of escape
from this self-hypnosis was poetry. Modernist poetry, he constantly
argued in his essays, permitted the active intelligence to become the
subject, not the spectatorial object, of experience. His poems were
the means by which he could achieve control over his addiction by
submitting it to analysis. If phenomenal life was nothing but a movie,
poetry was the real and authentic soul of temporal existence, the

medium that witnesses and resists the constraints of imprisonment inside Plato's cave.

As in his story, so in his poems, we confront the paradox that a cinematic imagination is displayed for the purpose of defeating the totalizing power of spectatorial passivity. The perfect example is Schwartz's most frequently anthologized poem, "In the Naked Bed, In Plato's Cave," written at the same time as "In Dreams Begin Responsibilities." One could break down the opening into shots, in the manner of Eisenstein on Pushkin:

1. In the naked bed, in Plato's cave,
2. Reflected headlights slowly slid the wall,
3. Carpenters hammered under the shaded window,
4. Wind troubled the window curtains all night long,
5. A fleet of trucks strained uphill, grinding,
   Their freights covered, as usual.
6. The ceiling lightened again, the slanting diagram
   Slid slowly forth.

The entire poem assembles impressions of this kind in a montage form. The leaping structure makes the essential point about the I or ego who speaks the poem. The room is a dark cave of unknowing where the only intimations of real life lie outside, audible but not visible until the speaker walks to the window to identify the source of reflected sensations. Windows, shadows, mirrors, photographs, paintings, films—these are all important images in Schwartz's poems and testify to the claustrophobic sense of self-enclosure for which media offer a window into the other world, but only as a looser boundary of subjective self-regard. Worthy of notice in the poem is how Schwartz masochistically catalogs the purposeful life of the outer world—the cars, the trucks with their freight, the carpenters (getting a *very* early start in this predawn period)—in marked contrast to the speaker who seems enervated by the activity that excludes him. Here is the dulled spectator of other people's desires, the *symboliste* dandy whose poetry of ennui is an ironic response to the world's serious business.

Another poem from the same period assumes the same pose, though with a hint of protest. The poem's title, "Metro-Goldwyn-Mayer," recalls the dedication of Schwartz's verse play "Paris and

Helen" to the same studio. As the largest and wealthiest studio, and the one that put the shiniest production gloss on its movies, M-G-M was a conventional metonym for the whole of the Hollywood glamour industry. The fact that it was a studio founded and controlled by Jews, the putative outsiders of American society, would have made it more attractive to Schwartz as a symbol of the triumph of the fantasy industry over reality in modern America.

> I looked toward the movie, the common dream,
> The he and she in close-ups, nearer than life,
> And I accepted such things as they seem,
>
> The easy poise, the absence of the knife,
> The near summer happily ever after,
> The understood question, the immediate strife,
>
> Not dangerous, nor mortal, but the fadeout
> Enormously kissing amid warm laughter,
> As if such things were not always played out
>
> By an ignorant arm, which crosses the dark
> And lights up a thin sheet with a shadow's mark.[22]

The near-sonnet form allows Schwartz to first immerse himself empathetically in the romantic scene on the screen and then reject it in the final couplet as a deceit, a sleight. The closure enacts the awakening of the poet from his trance into a consciousness of being overpowered by the erotic "common dream." Like "Dream Penny" the poem is the therapeutic act of withdrawal from the cave of unknowing ("an *ignorant* arm"), and by that critical act it places itself into a literary tradition effective at exploding illusions now that its power to foster them has diminished.

The text by Schwartz most relevant to our purposes, and one that gathers all of the significant motifs noted in his other work, is his short story "Screeno," written in the late 1930s but like his poem "Metro-Goldwyn-Mayer" published posthumously.[23] The story begins with a poet figure in a typical Schwartz situation: "For three hours, Cornelius Schmidt attempted to raise himself from the willlessness and despondency which had overcome him." Restless and bored, even with his own verse, he decides by the end of the first paragraph to seek escape from his condition: "There was only one refuge, one sanctuary: the movies."

He is pleased to see that the neighborhood theater is showing a film with Spencer Tracy, whose "absolute unself-consciousness" he has always envied. But his desire to give himself up to the dream of being Spencer Tracy rather than a relentlessly self-regarding poet is thwarted by the theater's featured entertainment before the movie, a version of lotto (or bingo) called Screeno. What could be further from the experience of romantic dreaming represented by the picture house than this microcosm of the acquisitive society that has driven Schmidt first to poetry and this night to film?

The game quickly becomes dreamlike, however, as Schmidt finds to his amazement that he has all the numbers needed to win a prize of $425, a sum large enough to let him purchase, at last, the complete Loeb Library. Schmidt comes to the stage, and the master of ceremonies, interrupted continually by a heckler in the balcony, asks Schmidt what he does for a living and, when Schmidt timorously announces he is a poet, asks him to recite some of his poetry. First the master of ceremonies recites a poem himself: "He's a poet, / His feet show it, / They're Longfellow's!" With this cruel burlesque of verse hovering in the theater, Schmidt bravely steps forward and recites a section of T. S. Eliot's "Gerontion," beginning "Think now, / History has many cunning passages . . ." The ensuing exchange is a significant one:

> He ended appalled at himself, as if he had made a shocking confession. But he saw that his effort was a failure for his tone had been false, too serious. The audience had been silenced and puzzled by the verses, but the young man [the emcee] curiously enough had been impressed.
>
> "Are those your own verses?" he asked.
>
> "No, I wish they were," said Cornelius. The audience wakened at this and laughed.
>
> "Those verses were written by the best of modern poets," said Cornelius, "a man named T. S. Eliot, whom all of you ought to read." Even in saying this, Cornelius knew that this advertisement was a foolish thing.

And then an usher arrives with the money; soon after, another man claims that he has won the jackpot as well, and the story takes several turns before Cornelius gives the pathetic rival his prize money and goes home still poor but blessed in spirit, recalling to himself a fourteenth-century Scottish poem about the virtues of charity and good cheer.

What is remarkable about the story is that the poet goes to the movies and no movie is shown. Rather, the poet becomes the star performer of the scenario constructed by the owners of the movie house, and manages to act with grace and generosity just when we would expect him (as we might expect ourselves in the same situation) to take advantage of a financial opportunity. But even this comfortable fantasy is resisted in the story. As a young poet Schmidt naturally desires fame, if not his name in lights like Spencer Tracy's, at least respectful recognition of his effort by a captive audience like the one in the theater. Yet when given a chance to publicize his work he defers to the acknowledged star of the poetry scene. The history of Delmore Schwartz's one-sided rivalry with T. S. Eliot would fill a book in itself, and can be read in his well-known essays, "T. S. Eliot as the International Hero," "T. S. Eliot's Voice and His Voices," and "The Literary Dictatorship of T. S. Eliot," not to mention his wisecracks about Eliot, often scurrilous, in his letters, journals, and reported conversation. The presence of such a figure in the literary firmament haunted Schwartz as the idols of the cave did the cave dwellers. Eliot, who advocated extinction of personality, and Spencer Tracy, the model of unself-consciousness, are the polestars by which the egoistic Schwartz/Schmidt sets his course and comes to understand his condition.

The displacement of Tracy by Eliot in the story is a gesture of faith in poetry on Schwartz's part. But as we see in the passage quoted above, the displacement is unsuccessful. The audience is "silenced and puzzled" by Eliot's verses and laughs in relief when told that the performer on the stage feels inferior to them. Like the "Longfellow" mockery of verse, this audience response is yet another reminder that serious lyric poetry has no hope of interesting a mass public. But Schmidt does not back down; he insists from his platform that Eliot is a poet "whom all of you ought to read." Eliot *is* the truth; his remarks on history in "Gerontion" never made more sense than in the prewar period of the story's composition. The audience, especially as figured demonically in the heckler, is no less despondent than Schmidt; it is desperate for some prize money in the Screeno competition, desperate to escape its empty and aimless lives for a couple of hours at the movies. If these people could appreciate Eliot, they would have some apprehension of a transcendent truth that allows them aesthetic and spiritual distance from their condition.

But no sooner does Schmidt make his admiring statement about Eliot than he knows "that this advertisement was a foolish thing." He is driven by his own gesture back into the self-consciousness he had hoped to escape by fleeing to this "refuge" or "sanctuary." The highbrow mediator between truth and unknowing can only be perceived as a fool, a clown who is out of place in a society suspicious of his "puzzling" proclamations on great subjects. Here the figure of Chaplin comes to mind, as Hart Crane offered him in "Chaplinesque," and as Schwartz repeatedly alluded to him in his poems. In *Genesis* Schwartz uses *The Kid* repeatedly as a mirror of his own experience. In "Prothalamion" he summons the isolato to his wedding:

> You too, Crusoe, to utter the emotion
> Of finding Friday, no longer alone;
> You too, Chaplin, muse of the curbstone,
> Mummer of hope, you understand!

And in "Time's Dedication" Schwartz imagines himself and his wife traveling life's road like the tramp with his good fortune:

> Walking together on the receding road
> Like Chaplin and his orphan sister,
> Moving together through time to all good.[24]

The persistent identification of poet and clown speaks both to the limits of the poet's self-image and to the resilience and resourcefulness endowed upon them by their marginal status in a world of getting and spending.

The title of the film featuring Spencer Tracy in "Screeno" is "Freedom." Tracy never made such a film, but the title is useful for Schwartz's purposes because the freedom of the poet is precisely what is affirmed in this story. Schmidt achieves freedom from necessity in several ways. First, he triumphs over the movies by becoming the star of the show and doing what poets long to do, publicizing the greatness of poetry and truth. Though the old man to whom he gives the money remains to watch the movie, Schmidt does not and walks home in an ecstatic mood, which only the Scottish poem can articulate. For by giving away the money he has repudiated the power over him both of an acquisitive society and a spellbinding art form, and affirmed, if only for an evening, the superior value of spending his talents for the benefit of others. Though Eliot is more free, perhaps, having removed himself from the entrapment of history by means of his poetic vision, Schmidt, and Schwartz, have won an existential victory over the ruder fantasy that threatened to degrade them. The victory is hardly a permanent one: walking home from the theater, the isolation and fog of the evening settle once more around him, but the tone of the story seems to guarantee a lingering sense of wellbeing. If, in reading the earlier story, we ask "What responsibilities are engendered in dreams?" then "Screeno" offers us, not without irony, a scenario for poetry's unlikely defeat of its twentieth-century rival.

In the film version of *The Day of the Locust* (1975), as in the novel, the kiss of the culprit Faye enchants Tod Hackett and subjects him to the glamour of cinema make-believe.

The Day of the Locust as a Rite of Passage

I believed for a long time that "character is fate" before it occurred to me that in cases like mine character consists so much in the accidental destiny of place that the maxim should read "location is fate." I was fated to grow up in Culver City, an offshoot of Los Angeles favored by movie companies in the early years of the industry. Hal Roach built his studio on Washington Boulevard and filmed there some of his best slapstick comedies. The ramshackle studios Thomas Ince erected in Culver City during the silent era were appropriated and vastly extended by Metro-Goldwyn-Mayer, and some of them by David O. Selznick in the 1930s. M-G-M, part of my newspaper route in the mid-1950s, made Culver City the "Heart of Screenland" it once proclaimed itself. Although my family never had any association with the movies, what dreamy kid would not be influenced by the presence and prestige, the mystique, of this century's dominant art, as it shaped his city's growth and nourished local conversations and local pride?

At the same time that I grew into my teens with a sense of privilege in this film capital, the cynosure, as I imagined it, of envious regard everywhere on earth, I became conscious of the fact that Los Angeles and Hollywood were held in contempt by not only the intelligentsia but even the popular media of the East. Poring over back issues of *Life, Look, Colliers,* and the *Saturday Evening Post* at Stanley Brile's secondhand bookstore, I was sensitive to the routinely condescending treatment of nearby landscapes I was visiting with more and more pleasure. One *Life* photo essay proclaimed the region "Cuckooland" (21 November 1938). "This lovely place is corrupted with an odd community giddiness," the text asserted amid shots of an orange stand in the form of a pagoda, a nudist camp, and Aimée Semple MacPherson hugging a large white cross. "Such giddiness infects all of America," *Life* allowed, but "in Southern California it has erupted most wildly. Nowhere else do eccentrics flourish in such close abundance. Nowhere do spiritual or economic panaceas grow so lushly. Nowhere is undisciplined gullibility so widespread." Though my mother and father, who had fled the frozen wastes of Iowa and Saskatchewan respectively, never spoke of their new home with anything less than grateful relief for its warm climate and job opportunities during the Depression, and my beach- and desert-going friends at school continued to blithely enjoy the good life shortly to be immortalized in the films and television shows of the 1960s, I was increasingly disturbed by the notion that Southern California was a kind of laughingstock in civilized regions east of the Rockies.

The effect on me was a cognitive dissonance that I have spent my life trying to resolve. I possessed both a pride of place derived from the glamour and inventiveness of the area's preeminent industry, counterbalanced by hostile appraisals I gradually incorporated into my consciousness, my sense of identity. I understood intuitively that criticism of "screwy California" was directed in large part at its chief product, movies themselves, which had been condemned from their inception for deforming the moral backbone of the nation. After a half century of influence, the movies I cherished in the Meralta and Culver theaters every weekend still appeared to intellectuals—and I had already begun to aspire in this direction—as, well, eccentric. For them, with some notable exceptions, Hollywood was what Diana Trilling called it in her essay on Marilyn Monroe, "a madness in our culture."[1] Wasn't it inevitable, these critics asked, that at the seat of empire "queer people" would assemble to mass-produce the formula fantasies craved by sensation-seeking audiences of all ages? If in Hollywood, as Oscar Levant memorably remarked, behind the fake tinself lies . . . real tinsel, might not the same be true of homegrown movie lovers like myself, fostered by the all-powerful genius loci, the studios? On restless nights I would stroll up Venice Boulevard, kicking the rubble of the Coliseum erected in the 1920s for *Ben Hur,* or climb the fence of a nearby M-G-M lot and wander through old sets, as if to test my susceptibility to their enchantment. I would sit down at the facade of Tara and wonder which coast, which realm of discourse, really owned my soul.

At the same time I read feverishly the long novels of the nineteenth century, a literature seemingly directed at teenagers. Scott,

Stevenson, Hugo, Dickens, Cooper, Dumas, Twain, Verne, the Brontës, H. Rider Haggard—I devoured the full texts I knew in abstract from Classics Illustrated comics and the movie versions on Channel 9. Indeed, these fictions ran through my imagination like movies, so that my idea of a good time in those juvenile years was daydreaming in solitude or nocturnal reveries in which I enacted the roles of D'Artagnan, Deerslayer, Heathcliff. I became accustomed to authorizing composite versions of these tales and began to plan on writing them myself. First, I thought of sequels or rewrites, and then of new fictions as redolent of passionate life as these. I was not the only dreamer around, not the only playactor of inner scenarios, but nearly the only one conversant with so many literary master-pieces. The exigencies of real life saved me from the Quixotism threatening my imagination, real life in the form of parents, teach-ers, sports, and girls who had nothing in common with fictive hero-ines except their ability to make me daydream about them. I contin-ued to be confused about the great question of puberty: how to live in a world I had divided radically into competing spheres of illusion and fact.

Of course I see now that these nineteenth-century novels are not the straightforward romances I willed them to be. They always offer internal resistance to the formulaic dreamwork they present as a basic plot. Doubtless I misread them as I needed to, and doubtless some measure of their psychological and narratological complexity over-came my desire to keep them within the comic-book constraints of my adolescent imagination. If not, I could not have recognized the ironics of Nathanael West's *The Day of the Locust,* which I first read in those years as a racy novel about nearby Hollywood. West's novel struck me at once, as it has on all subsequent readings, as a stringent antidote to the illusions engendered in me by movies, the movie capital, and the novels I had remade as movies to suit my needs. If, as environmental psychologists tell us, we require art to help redraft the "cognitive map" designed in our minds by experience in familiar locales, *The Day of the Locust* effectively fulfilled that revisionary function. It compelled me to rechart the imaginative territory I had hyperbolically stored, indeed *crammed* into my brain, by challenging the seductive archetypes to which I had half-wittingly committed myself. I suspect that West wrote the novel to liberate himself from the same engrossments. His achievement inspired me, for better or worse, to think of disillusionment as an honorable task for the writer, even for myself.

At the center of the novel, as I then read it, was the antiromantic couple Tod Hackett and Faye Greener. The would-be actress Faye was recognizable to me as a descendant of those sirens I had savored in so many nineteenth-century novels: Milady, She-Who-Must-Be-Obeyed, and more than a touch of Cathy Earnshaw who tormented and then betrayed her cohabitant of Wuthering Heights. On the mythic plane, Faye, as her name suggests, is one of those idealized fairy creatures who cannot consummate what they constantly offer to mortal man, a life of ceaseless sensual gratification. (West had previously burlesqued the rituals of enticement in the figure of Fay Doyle in *Miss Lonelyhearts*.) Herman Melville dared to possess the alien creature he called "Fayaway" in *Typee*, before losing her, and then he turned her into the archetype of the unattainable feminine soul in *Mardi*, where she is called Yillah and pursued across hundreds of pages by the lovelorn male narrator Taji. In the 1890s Yeats named this alluring temptress Niamh, queen of the fays, who calls to her mortal lover in one poem:

> Away, come away:
> Empty your heart of its mortal dream.
> The winds awaken, the leaves whirl round,
> Our cheeks are pale, our hair is unbound,
> Our breasts are heaving, our eyes are agleam,
> Our arms are waving, our lips are apart;
> And, if any gaze on our rushing band,
> We come between him and the deed of his hand,
> We come between him and the hope of his heart.[2]

The motion pictures brought this fairy queen down to earth and called her the vamp, a Romantic image borrowed from Decadent practice, and popularized in West's teenage years by the likes of Pola Negri and Lya de Putti. West's brother-in-law, S. J. Perelman, would later skewer this figure, and his own nostalgia for it, in one of his Cloudland Revisited satires, "The Wickedest Woman in Larchmont" (Theda Bara).

In Tod's painting *The Burning of Los Angeles* "Faye is the naked girl in the left foreground being chased by the group of men and women who have separated from the main body of the mob. . . . She is running with her eyes closed and a strange half-smile on her lips."[3] What West calls "the dreamy repose of her face" belongs to the iconography of the femme fatale in late Victorian culture. That Faye flaunts her sexuality carelessly, indeed ostentatiously, but never satisfies the lustful cravings of Tod and her more pathetic admirer Homer Simpson struck me as not only in keeping with the habits of her foremothers in romantic fiction but true to my own experience with the fickle and teasing girls I knew in secondary schools. Years later I would write in a poem about my youthful fascination with *The Three Musketeers:*

> Wicked Milady! of course other names
> proved worse: Natalie, Rosanne—
> these would break your dumb heart
> a century's-length of junior high.
> In songs you sent them to execution;
> in thoughts no engraving could render
> you cast them from Eden, cast yourself.[4]

Tod is Faye's inevitable victim, but also, as his depiction of her in his art suggests, her vindictive tormentor as well. As a way of justifying his rape fantasies, he persuades himself that "her invitation wasn't to pleasure, but to struggle, hard and sharp, closer to murder than to love" (34). As Hollywood's version of Death and the Maiden (in German, *tod* means "death"), Tod and Faye enact a struggle neither can win. Faye is *fey* in this sense, both doomed and otherworldly in her indifference to Tod's violent libidinous fantasies.

Tod's sadism derives in some degree from the frustrations of his professional life. As his name suggests, Tod has chosen to hack it, to undergo the purgatorial rite of the hack in American culture, in order to ultimately astonish his public with a visionary depiction of the lower depths he has witnessed in Hollywood. In his three-month experience in California, after graduation from Yale, where he had developed a comely style of illustration, Tod has begun to scavenge and thrive upon the degraded subject matter of offscreen Hollywood, drafting cartoons for the apocalyptic painting that the authorial voice assures us has brought him fame. Faye is part of the raw material he will alchemize into high art, and it is his relentless and hard-earned aestheticism that keeps him sane, and human, until the novel's last page, when the riot at Kahn's Persian Palace snaps his tightly pulled nerves and he howls dismally along with a police siren.

It was important to me, after first reading the novel, to learn that West had created Tod from the voyeurist compulsion of his own Hollywood experience. During the 1930s, while writing ridiculous movies for Republic Studios, he cruised among the riffraff of the underworld, achieving by sympathetic osmosis a sense of the grotesque dreams and ambitions of marginal Hollywood types. A friend of West remarked that the novelist was "a keen observer, always looking for bizarre backgrounds, and always attempting to improve his knowledge of the human race. . . . He was very interested in . . . the really seamy side of life."[5] We know from West's manuscripts that Tod Hackett emerged only in the final draft as an organizing principle of the novel's episodic structure. Originally the screenwriter Claude Estee served as guide through Heartbreak Town, as it was popularly known in the 1930s. But the sardonic and parodic Claude clearly would not do; he lacks both the ethical rigor and the emotional vulnerability of the Jeremiah figure Tod aspires to be. Tod is an effective stand-in for West's own perspective, and the reader's, precisely because he embodies any likely reader's puritanical fascination with this dystopian frontier of American social experience.

Like so many of his subjects, Nathanael West had migrated in spirit as in body to Los Angeles, ready to construct a new self in this supreme place of ready-made identities. As a teenager he had emptied himself of his Jewish heritage by changing his name from Weinstein to West, leaving himself naked to the cultural instrumentality that would shape his X-ray vision. What he saw in Southern California was a landscape and populace eager to be seen. In its theatricality, its obsessive cult of appearances, the city so often called Wonderland mimicked the two-dimensional reality of its ubiquitous product. If John Grierson could define the art of documentaries as "decent seeing," Hollywood magnified itself by a perverse principle of indecent seeing and compelled each of its citizens, architects no less than extras, to act in conformity with the masquerades fostered by the local commerce.[6] With his artist's eye—and it is important that the central intelligence of the novel is a painter, not a writer—Tod sees both the tinsel *and* sees through it to the primal reality beneath the disguise. Of Faye, for example:

> She appeared a moment later in a new flower print dress and
> picture hat and it was [Tod's] turn to sigh. She was much more
> than pretty. She posed, quivering and balanced, on the doorstep
> and looked down at the two men in the patio. She was smiling,
> a subtle, half-smile uncontaminated by thought. She looked just
> born, everything moist and fresh, volatile and perfumed. Tod
> suddenly became very conscious of his dull, insensitive feet
> bound in dead skin and of his hands, sticky and thick, holding a
> heavy, rough felt hat. (140)

Seen in the right light, in the right pose, this fairy incarnation has the
"egg-like self-sufficiency" Tod notices elsewhere, an unearthly charm
that makes him, poor mortal, want to kiss her and also crush her in
revenge. The dwarf Abe sees Faye only as a "quiff," and others see
her as a "bitch." Tod's view of her as a kind of Persephone, a being
of the underworld but somehow ethereal as well, represents the dou-
ble vision of person and place required of the artist, not the caricatur-
ist or the illustrator, but the artist.

Decent seeing, I learned from *The Day of the Locust,* can be
defined as accurate and sympathetic observation of the indecent. No
fiction I had previously read anatomized the morality of fine discrimi-
nations so self-consciously and persuasively. *Life* magazine might
feature photos of food stands trumped up as oriental temples or pri-
vate homes disguised as castles—this was the conventional satirical
stance toward the unreality of Los Angeles. But of a similar neighbor-
hood West humanely remarks: "Both houses were comic, but [Tod]
didn't laugh. Their desire to startle was so eager and guileless" (24).
The same could be said, and West says it, about the iconic Faye, with
her mechanical gestures and her trashy dreams of success, and about
her father Harry Greener, whose years in vaudeville have made him
incapable of uttering a single authentic sentence. The spirit of exhibi-
tion is upon them so strongly that they have recreated their normal
behavior for the benefit (if that's the word) of spectators, and all the
world to them is nothing but spectators. The catastrophic effects of
succumbing to preexisting fictions at a formative stage of life were
depicted in this novel at just the time when I needed to be saved from
the solipsism of a romantic imagination. The negative examples of
Faye and Harry, and the windup toy of a child Adore Loomis, and
all the others, warned me to keep my personality at a healthy remove

from the incendiary influence of fantasy-inflating cultural artifacts. West's cool style and caustic imagery modeled for me the double take appropriate for what came to be called the Southern California lifestyle. I began to appreciate the forensic art that laid bare both the visceral power and banality of Faye-images in my experience.

Ironically, West's novel and others like it (*The Great Gatsby,* for example) permitted me to return to nineteenth-century fiction and recognize how assiduously those authors defined the aesthetic distance for decent seeing. How Walter Scott keeps his protagonist Edward Waverley from the attractions of Fergus and Flora MacIvor and their romantic surroundings in the Scottish Highlands. How Emily Brontë mortifies our fondness for Cathy and the allurements of Thrushcross Grange by filtering her story through the knowing eyes of Nelly Dean. Or how Balzac, to name a writer with more than a passing resemblance to West, portrays the corruption of Paris by first exposing some young man from the provinces to its fatal lure, and then bringing him through a myriad of glittering social and sexual triumphs to a recognition of the kind Eugène de Rastignac imparts to Bianchon at the conclusion of *Le Père Goriot:* "I am in hell, and must stay there. Believe whatever evil you may hear about the world, it's all true! No Juvenal could adequately paint its gilded and bejewelled horror." Perceptions of this kind do not require that their authors—Juvenal, Balzac, or West—abandon their adopted cities; on the contrary, they must continue to reside in the City of Fame as witnesses-in-residence. I may have intuited then, what I can formulate more clearly now, how a writer no less than a connoisseur of novels like *The Day of the Locust* must consume urban melodramas as an analysand both suffers from and scrutinizes the memories that feed his or her neurosis.

Although Faye disappears from the novel once she has slept with the cockfighter Miguel, her symbolic function thereby neutralized, the demonic relation of Tod and his bewitcher is displaced immediately onto the Hollywood Boulevard crowd that hungers for a glimpse or touch of a movie star at a premiere. This is the book's most famous scene, and justly so. West's clinical style shifts to a different register as he renders the push and shove of the mob in accelerated cinematic shots of increasing grotesqueness and horror. If Hollywood had been praised a generation earlier by Vachel Lindsay in *The Art of the Moving Picture* for engendering "crowd splendor" equivalent to the religious ceremonies of the Middle Ages, West uses his vantage point as one of the hacks, one of The Cheated (the novel's original title) to measure the frenzy of frustrated desire characteristic of the moviegoer. James T. Farrell had remarked in the 1930s that "film enervates rather than energizes," and Jean-Paul Sartre noted that after seeing a movie, "in the street I found myself superfluous."[7] West engineers the narrative so that our final take on Hollywood is of an archetypal mass of superfluous and enervated souls testifying in "demoniac" fashion to their hopeless condition.

The people assembled at Kahn's Persian Palace—a reference to Grauman's (now Mann's) Chinese Theatre—are not simply movie-goers, as I would have described myself, but fans, the short term for fanatics. They desire to wholly inhabit the world of make-believe evoked by the allusion to Coleridge's poem "Kubla Khan" jokingly inscribed in the novel: "MR. KAHN A PLEASURE DOME DE-CREED." Just as the spectators of a pornographic film at Mrs. Jennings's brothel, earlier in the novel, performed a mock riot when deprived of the film's lewd conclusion, so these pleasure seekers rage against their loss of fulfillment, their unremitting status as "civilians"—to cite the Hollywood term for people outside the movie-making process. The crowd transforms itself in a conscious if unpremeditated manner into a spectacle that will outmatch the artificial creation within the pleasure dome. By doing so it achieves the unconscious motive for its collective presence, to seize an active role in the Hollywood culture. It will be the headline story in the next day's newspaper, eclipsing the movie that it has rendered merely the occasion for its own celebrity. The high spirits of the crowd, even as it becomes a rough-and-tumble mob threatening bodily damage, comes from this ecstatic sense of pure existence formerly denied its members as spectators.

This implied view of themselves is different, however, from the author's view of them. West's description of this deracinated and desperate agglomeration of bodies is a famous one, but so brilliant and prophetic it must be quoted here again:

> New groups, whole families, kept arriving. He could see a
> change come over them as soon as they had become part of the
> crowd. Until they reached the line, they looked diffident, almost
> furtive, but the moment they had become part of it, they turned

arrogant and pugnacious. It was a mistake to think them harmless curiosity seekers. They were savage and bitter, especially the middle-aged and the old, and had been made so by boredom and disappointment.

All their lives they had slaved at some kind of dull, heavy labor, behind desks and counters, in the fields and at tedious machines of all sorts, saving their pennies and dreaming of the leisure that would be theirs when they had enough. Finally that day came. They could draw a weekly income of ten or fifteen dollars. Where else should they go but California, the land of sunshine and oranges?

Once there, they discover that sunshine isn't enough. They get tired of oranges, even of avocado pears and passion fruit. Nothing happens. They don't know what to do with their time. They haven't the mental equipment for leisure, the money nor the physical equipment for pleasure. Did they slave so long just to go to an occasional Iowa picnic? What else is there? They watch the waves come in at Venice. There wasn't any ocean where most of them came from, but after you've seen one wave, you've seen them all. The same is true of the airplanes at Glendale. If only a plane would crash once in a while so that they could watch the passengers being consumed in a "holocaust of flame," as the newspapers put it. But the planes never crash.

Their boredom becomes more and more terrible. They realize that they've been tricked and burn with resentment. Every day of their lives they read the newspapers and went to the movies. Both fed them on lynchings, murder, sex crimes, explosions, wrecks, love nests, fires, miracles, revolutions, wars. This daily diet made sophisticates of them. The sun is a joke. Oranges can't titillate their jaded palates. Nothing can ever be violent enough to make taut their slack minds and bodies. They have been cheated and betrayed. They have slaved and saved for nothing. (191–93)

What is the grievance of this crowd? It has been cheated, not out of wages but out of the opportunity for decent seeing. Its oppressors (note how West refers to the workers as slaves) are not railroads or the federal government, but something more sinister, the fantasy-inflaming media that have kept these people from becoming the free agents of their own destiny. The media have gradually raised the pleasure threshold in their sensibilities until hardly anything in everyday reality satisfies them except moments of violence. Thus they are driven to enact Tod's fantasy rape of Faye by performing sexual violations upon each other in the course of their lewd *frottage,* and by killing Homer Simpson, who has assaulted the teasing boy Adore with similar intent and for similar cause—all achieving orgasmic release from the repression of a lifetime.

In this "bedlam," as the radio announcer calls it, the inmates take over the institution, in what is now a familiar convention of modern literature. These dispossessed insist on being players, if only bit players, in melodramas of their own staging, though no Coleridgean creative imagination shapes their actions. No doubt West, an ardent leftist, here conceived the pliable *Massenproletariat* on the model of the crowds then being worked by those media idols Hitler and Mussolini. One recalls Frank Capra's film *Meet John Doe* and Sinclair Lewis's novel *It Can't Happen Here* as contemporary warnings of an American-style fascism founded on the cult of the charismatic personality fostered by Hollywood public relations. The social ramifications of such star worship are suggested by the religious and political figures mentioned in the novel, such as Dr. Know-All Pierce-All, whose appeal owes much to the émigré condition West anatomizes.

The truth I first glimpsed in West's novel is that the entire population of the United States can be fruitfully perceived and described in terms of its affection for and its addiction to the forms and discourses of the popular media and those persons who embody them. If this is now a trite observation, it is because artists have, in my lifetime, devoted their craft in so many ways to the alienation of our affections from the enormous power of media promises and media presence. In my own politics, and in my professional life as a teacher and writer, I have committed myself reactively to that detached "criticism of life" that Matthew Arnold offered as a grim definition of culture. This has taken the form of deconstructing the fantasy rhetoric, the indecent seeing, that Hollywood so often propagates in order to weld the public into an uncritical mass.

Now something further needs to be said about the frenzied climax of *The Day of the Locust.* No one can read it, I think, without sensing an affinity between the author's highly charged rhetoric ("If only a plane would crash. . . . The sun is a joke") and the extremity of mob behavior. That West is venting his own bitterness about the falsity of the American Dream by recourse to a Jeremiah-like, indeed "demoniac" prose, struck me on first reading the novel, and does so on each rereading. Then my objection took a naive form: *Who are all these people? I've been to Iowa picnics. I've visited Venice and Hollywood. This is all imaginary, all make-believe!* Now I see better how West deliberately acknowledges, by means of his riotous prose style and his stand-in Tod Hackett, how he is bonded to the turbulent character of the crowd. Tod not only engages in the same kicking and shoving behavior but, in the midst of all the turmoil, is able to think clearly about his vindictive painting *The Burning of Los Angeles,* an obvious trope for *The Day of the Locust.* (West had once written a poem titled "Burn the Cities.") In the painting Tod picks up a stone to throw at the advancing mob. The artwork, in both cases, represents West's vengeance upon the benighted masses who would not buy his masterpieces—*Miss Lonelyhearts* sold fewer than eight hundred copies—but rushed by the millions to watch him hack it in movies like *Jim Hanvey, Detective* and *Let's Make Music.*

The perception that being one of the cheated can drive an artist mad, and that his rage can take a verbal form as mannered and nonmimetic as anything in Dumas or Verne allowed me to retract credulous belief from *The Day of the Locust* as well. And not only from West's novel, but from latter-day infernal visions of Los Angeles in the same spirit: Joan Didion's *Play It As It Lays* or Bret Easton Ellis's *Less Than Zero.* Recognizing through West's good agency that antiromance has no more cachet than romance in the "criticism of life" that constitutes literary culture put me back where I started as a reader. With one exception: I saw how the conventional consummations of romantic love might be more realistic than twentieth-century writers allowed. (West made the same discovery, in his brief happy marriage to Eileen McKenny in 1940.) Knowing that disillusionment is a literary device, and not a privileged act of absolute truth, has liberated my imagination into a higher innocence, one that discerns in my adolescence its soul-making origin.

Do kids in Culver City still struggle with these great questions of culture and identity? I have revisited my hometown often to walk the locales where I underwent successive immersions into and withdrawals from popular culture. To my nostalgic eye Culver City seems to be a ruin of its former self. The Meralta and Culver theatres and Stanley Brile's bookstore are gone; the Hal Roach studios have been replaced by offices and warehouses; and M-G-M, even before its acquisition by a shady Italian financier, sold off most of its lot for lucrative real estate developments. Yet even as I lament such loss and change, I concede the elegiac conventions determining my expressions; indeed, I have written a scholarly book on just this subject. I have learned to gauge the authenticity of my responses to almost everything by recognitions that the architectonics of my imagination, like West's bizarre Hollywood neighborhoods, are composed from bits and pieces of verbal and visual texts. Without such recognitions, I could not write or teach with any hope of originality. Perhaps I could not remain sane in a society where one is bombarded by so many stimuli calling for stock response. I think gratefully of *The Day of the Locust* for helping me get my bearings on the significant space of my first twenty years. Reminding myself that the "Heart of Screenland" is located as much in the pathways of memory as in the streets of Culver City has become a wry mental reflex I practice in the spirit of Nathanael West, whom I salute in this book he helped to make possible.

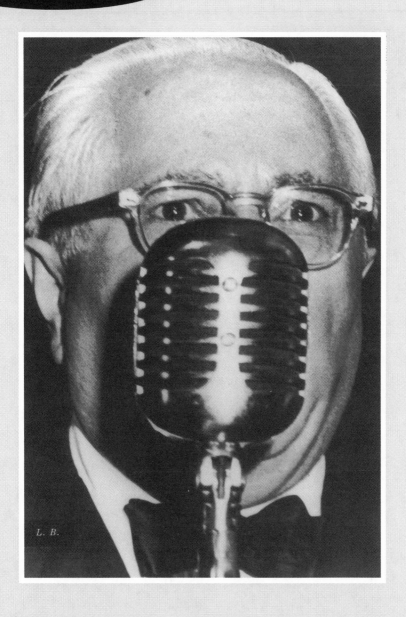

L. B.

In this photo by Weegee, M-G-M producer Louis B. Mayer broadcasts his vision of life with imperious authority. His grandson declared of the Jewish tycoon, "The one part of life in Communist Russia he would have admired if he had stayed behind was the way in which art is forced to shape society." (From the book *Naked Hollywood* by Weegee and Mel Harris [New York: Pellegrini & Cudahy, 1953].)

Chapter 5

Karl Shapiro, "An American Jew and a Poet": Looking toward New Zion in the Golden State

HOLLYWOOD

Farthest from any war, unique in time
Like Athens or Baghdad, this city lies
Between dry purple mountains and the sea.
The air is clear and famous, every day
Bright as a postcard, bringing bungalows
    And sights. The broad nights advertise
For love and music and astronomy.

Heart of a continent, the hearts converge
On open boulevards where palms are nursed
With flare-pots like a grove, on villa roads
Where castles cultivated like a style
Breed fabulous metaphors in foreign stone,
    And on enormous movie lots
Where history repeats its vivid blunders.

Alice and Cinderella are most real.
Here may the tourist, quite sincere at last,
Rest from his dream of travels. All is new,
No ruins claim his awe, and permanence,
Despised like customs, fails at every turn.
    Here where the eccentric thrives,
Laughter and love are leading industries.

125

Luck is another. Here the body-guard,
The parasite, the scholar are well paid,
The quack erects his alabaster office,
The moron and the genius are enshrined,
And the mystic makes a fortune quietly;
    Here all superlatives come true
And beauty is marketed like a basic food.

O can we understand it? Is it ours,
A crude whim of a beginning people,
A private orgy in a secluded spot?
Or alien like the word *harem,* or true
Like hideous Pittsburgh or depraved Atlanta?
    Is adolescence just as vile
As this its architecture and its talk?

Or are they parvenus, like boys and girls?
Or ours and happy, cleverest of all?
Yes. Yes. Though glamorous to the ignorant
This is the simplest city, a new school.
What is more nearly ours? If soul can mean
    The civilization of the brain,
This is a soul, a possibly proud Florence.[1]

—1942

K arl Shapiro visited Los Angeles and Hollywood in the late 1930s en route to Tahiti, where he and his lover hoped to live the fantasy of *luxe, calme, et volupté* evoked by Shapiro's favorite author, Charles Baudelaire, as the birthright of the poet. Before this time, Shapiro tells us in his autobiography, he had sampled and rejected the customary alternatives. He had turned first to the past, writing "archaic tragedies" about historical figures as "an exit to the present." He had considered the expatriate careers of poets in the previous decade and concluded that in a period of gathering war clouds, "to go to Europe was to go the wrong way."[2] Marxism attracted him briefly, but he sensed too close an affinity between its austere orthodoxy and the Jewish prohibitions from which he wished to break free. Nor did academia satisfy his craving for more intense experience; it strengthened the critic in him, whereas he was most happy and most creative when he partook of the extracurricular. Shapiro believed himself to be, like his favorite contemporary, William Carlos Williams, "a thing poet"; his education demanded an amplification of sensual experience, a wider opening of the doors of perception. Tahiti beckoned as a paradise of new sensations.

In this frame of mind he was understandably susceptible to the allurements of the coastal cities of California. Young and in love, beginning an adventure modeled after the fantasies of many modern artists, including filmmakers, Shapiro was intoxicated by the "fabulous metaphors" he found in the climate, flora, and eccentric architecture of Hollywood. In his poem the site is evoked almost entirely by hyperbolical comparisons in the manner of travel brochures or movie advertisements: "Here all superlatives come true." Shapiro's westward crossing from Baltimore, "the Actual City" as he calls it in his autobiography, to the acknowledged paradise of the public imagination represents an eruption of counterhistorical desire into the orderly life mandated by his father and by the society his father spoke for. Hollywood, as a way station or gateway to the gardens of Tahiti, is not only "farthest from any war," but farthest from the Hebraic moralism of a nation preparing for war.

"This is a soul," he asserts, after calling Hollywood "Heart of a continent." "Soul" is qualified, however, by the conditional phrasing of the preceding clause, "If soul can mean / The civilization of the brain." This word choice would never satisfy a philosopher, but the essential point seems clear. Hollywood is still the redemptive city Vachel Lindsay said it was in *The Art of the Moving Picture*. Lindsay had asserted that

> it is possible for Los Angeles to lay hold of the motion picture as our national text-book in Art as Boston appropriated to herself the guardianship of the national text-books of Literature. If California has a shining soul and not merely a golden body, let her forget her seventeen-year-old melodramatics, and turn to her poets who understand the heart underneath the glory. (251)

By telling filmmakers to turn to the poets, Lindsay conscripts poets to collaborate with filmmakers in the creation of a new national mythology. Implicit in Shapiro's poem, which uses the same language of heart and soul as Lindsay's prose, is the campaign to shift not just the locus of art production but the whole spirit of American civilization westward, toward that frontier realm of Romantic consciousness in which the imaginary becomes the actual.

If Shapiro's poem is hyperbolical, it may be that pro-Hollywood writing had to be extreme in order to counteract the hyperbole of anti-Hollywood prejudice in works like Nathanael West's *The Day of the Locust*. There seems to be a clear allusion to West's novel in the lines, "And on enormous movie lots / Where history repeats its vivid blunders." In one of West's most admired scenes actors dressed as Napoleon's soldiers storm Mont St. Jean but collapse through the set because struts have not been placed under the fake mountain. "It was the classic mistake, Tod realized, the same one Napoleon had made. Then it had been wrong for a different reason."[3] For West, the movie lots are a "Sargasso of the imagination," a "final dumping ground" for history's mad ambitions. Tod Hackett has gone to the lot to find Faye Greener, who is playing a *vivandière* in the movie *Waterloo*. But film consciousness keeps her forever divided from him, as we have seen, stimulating the murderous rage of frustration he shares with the deracinated populace of Los Angeles. In Shapiro's poem the streets are places where "hearts converge," but the riotous convergence on Hollywood Boulevard that ends West's novel represents a state of rage, not love. In *The Day of the Locust*, Hollywood is no "possibly proud Florence," but a terminal stage in the decline of the humanistic tradition.

One might say that Shapiro's poem performs a lyric revision of West's novel, keeping the exotic character of place but offering a radically different evaluation of it. The allusions to Athens, Baghdad, palms, villa roads, castles, Alice, and Cinderella preserve the faux-international atmosphere West recreated, but Shapiro rejects the prophetic anger of the novel in favor of a playful fondness for this bygone world turned by time into the stuff of dreams. The nonpresence of "the cheated" is one of many absences that becomes noticeable when the poem is set in the context of contemporary literary discourse about Hollywood. "Farthest from any war," Hollywood is dehistoricized, not only from the fascist menace and the Depression, but from Lindsay's millennialist hopes as well. We hear of no "prophet-wizards," and no utopian workers' paradise. Indeed, the clear air testifies to Hollywood's lucky evasion of the Industrial Revolution. "Laughter and love are leading industries," not steel or chemicals. Shapiro revels in discovering a mythic landscape that mirrors his own raffish and hedonistic values. Just as he recalls in *The Bourgeois Poet* that when he reached Tahiti he found the natives fascinated by Murnau's *Tabu*, a film about themselves, so in Hollywood he seemed to discover a moving picture of the youthful sensibility he shared with Southern Californians.[4]

The playwright and screenwriter Robert E. Sherwood remarked in 1938 that Hollywood was "the most loudly advertised and the most thoroughly misunderstood of the communities in creation."[5] Whatever else one says about Hollywood of this period, it's certainly true that it was a dynamic success story of the kind it would recreate persistently in its own narratives. In the prewar period movies were the nation's eleventh largest industry, manufacturing four hundred new products every year, attracting more than eighty million people to the theaters every week. The decade of the talkies had brought movies to a sheen and texture of the highest artistry, producing not just profitable merchandise but artistic masterpieces that would increasingly form an essential part of the cultural heritage of every living American. *Gone with the Wind, The Wizard of Oz, A Star Is Born, Stagecoach, The Philadelphia Story, Mr. Smith Goes to Washington, Citizen Kane, Casablanca*—whatever examples one chooses, such films could not be treated, even by novelists, as simply the accidental by-product of a corrupt system. Poets might ignore or deplore it, but the industry was generating imitations of life that in their own way were perfect. *Perfect* is the word that recurs in Kenneth Fearing's poems whenever the movies are summoned, as in this one from 1935:

Magic film, unwind, unroll, unfold in silver on that million mile
    screen, take us all, bear us again to the perfect denouement—

Where everything lost, needed, each forgotten thing, all that
    never happens,
Gathers at last into a dynamite triumph, a rainbow peace, a
    thunderbolt kiss,
For you, the invincible, and I, grown older, and he, the shipping
    clerk, and she, an underweight blonde journeying home in the
    last express.[6]

Even if the film is sorrowful, he says in another poem, "the movie heroine smiles once more through perfect tears." Fearing's point is that the democratic art requites the needs of the lowliest shipping clerk. Shapiro adds that even the parasite, the quack, and the moron, heaped into the same stanza as the scholar and the genius, find a perfect place to exercise their confidence games. Such a land of opportunity may even have a spot for the poet, especially a poet as critical of contemporary elite culture as Karl Shapiro.

Fearing is obviously being facetious in his praise of cinematic effects as perfect. Is Shapiro? Is there skepticism in his encomiastic poem? I think that it flaunts a counterskeptical attitude based on Shapiro's need for a standpoint removed from the cultural establishment of the late 1930s and early 1940s. Hollywood is a microcosm of the redskin America that the neoprimitive Shapiro feels comfortable in praising. Though one of the constant themes of Shapiro's criticism is the undesirability of making America a subject—he takes Sandburg and MacLeish to task for this in *Essay on Rime*—Shapiro is clearly as mythopoetic as anyone else in the 1930s when it comes to organizing a history, character, and destiny for his native land. In his poem "Jefferson" Shapiro hails the founder of American democracy as one who constituted Virginia as a "Florence of your soul." But Hollywood is a "possibly proud Florence" as well. Which is the true and which is the false *locus amoenus,* the redemptive source of genuinely American culture?

For a poet like Shapiro, who embraced the Whitmanian example, the question translates into a different kind of question: Which reality deserves greater loyalty, the historical or the ahistorical? In a period of wartime, when Jews were the principal victims of a messianic and utopian ideology, the question took on a political cast that Shaprio highlighted in his poems of the 1930s and 1940s. In "Hollywood" he endorses the fantasy site where "permanence" is "despised at every turn" in order to deploy his energy against the perdurable political forces that threaten to constrain or annihilate his freedom, forces he first encountered at Jefferson's own university, where, as he puts it in a much-anthologized poem, "To hurt the Negro and avoid the Jew / Is our curriculum" ("University"). His strategy is to create an alternative and subversive history, a poet's history. Hollywood is perfect for his purposes because it was already undertaking the reimagining not only of the American experience but the European as well, as

Delmore Schwartz humorously acknowledged when he cast movie actors for his verse play "Paris and Helen," and when he addressed the city in *Genesis* as a terminal product of the Judeo-Christian civilization: "O Hollywood! new Milky Way! and last / Capital of the Western mind!"[7] Nathanael West, too, offered a tongue-in-cheek prophecy of the American triumph over Hitler's mad ambitions in his send-up of Napoleon's failure to conquer the world.

West (né Weinstein) and Schwartz and Shapiro. These authors born with unmistakably Jewish names represent points along the spectrum of opinion ranging from the severest critique of the new medium, to a mixed attitude about its claims upon a literary imagination, to an enthusiastic endorsement of its hegemonic power. Is there something about the rise of the movies to a central position in the culture that challenged Jews especially and called forth a response from them? Shapiro can help us to engage this question more fully. Early in his autobiography, while describing his developing sense of beauty, he asks, "Who chose the ladies whose close-ups in the movies made the watchers dissolve?" (18). Shapiro had answered the question in his poem of 1944, "Movie Actress," which begins:

> She is young and lies curved on the velvety floor of her fame
> Like a prize-winning cat on a mirror of fire and oak,
> And her dreams are as black as the Jew who uncovered
>   her name.

This poem identifies the Jew as the maker of the seductive film images that tantalize the audience. He refers of course to the fact that the chief producers of the major Hollywood studios, as well as writers, directors, agents, and other personnel, were Jews. They were the star-makers, the star-namers, the begetters of erotic fantasies throughout the world centered on the temptress. In mimicking this power, West had invented a shikse vamp in Faye Greener, whose teasing or cheating nature was fully exposed in the course of the narrative. Shapiro does something similar in his poem, where he creates special effects of wardrobe, lighting, and miking to highlight his star:

> She is folded in magic and hushed in the pride of her cloak
> Which is woven of worship like silk for the hollows of eyes

That are raised in the dark to her image that shimmered
  and spoke . . .[8]

As in Vachel Lindsay's poem on Mae Marsh the imagery is ostenta-
tiously Pre-Raphaelite and seems to follow Lindsay in its details.
"Folded in magic" and "worship like silk" certainly recall Lindsay's
"Rare silk the fine director's hand / May weave for magic if he will."
The anapestic meter and mannered diction suggest Swinburne or
Shapiro's fellow Baltimore symbolist, Edgar Allan Poe. But Shapiro
is not so evangelical as Lindsay; his vision of the actress, and of the
Jew who names and exhibits her, is crossed with the moral misgiv-
ings of a Baudelaire. "Her dreams are *black* as the Jew." What does
this mean? Perhaps only that the Jew is dark-skinned, as when
Shapiro in another poem refers to Moses's "black wife." Or that the
modern Jew is dabbling in black magic, a Svengali as potent as
George du Maurier's Semitic dominator in the fin de siècle romance
Trilby? That he has violated the Mosaic injunction against idolatry in
order to show his dark-dreaming woman, his whore of Babylon, to
an unregenerate public? Shapiro concludes his sonnet, "She is coarse
with the honors of power, the duties of fun /And amazed at the
regions of pleasure where skill is begun." Here is the heathen deity
as clinically described by a Jewish producer of texts who seems in-
fatuated with the forbidden presence he has "uncovered" for his read-
ers.

The movies were a Jewish industry. It is impossible to overstate
how much this fact fascinated writers, both Jewish and gentile. For
Jews, the power wielded by the likes of Samuel Goldwyn, Adolph
Zukor, Jesse Lasky, William Fox, B. P. Schulberg, Harry Cohn,
Louis B. Mayer, Irving Thalberg, the Warner brothers, L. J. Selznick
and his son David, Carl Laemmle, and others inevitably provoked a
fantasy of success especially poignant for poets. One hears in Shapiro's
poem on Hollywood the urgent voice of an oppressed minority in
the lines, "Is it ours . . . / Yes. Yes. Though glamorous to the ignorant
/ This is the simplest city, a new school." The poet who would publish
a volume titled *Poems of a Jew* in 1958 and declare of himself in his
autobiography, "He was an American Jew and a poet" (167), presum-
ably in that order, was understandably fascinated with the topos of
Jew as Promethean dream maker in American culture. Like Delmore
Schwartz, Shapiro conspired to seize the poetic tradition from the

grasp of Pound and Eliot, the anti-Semites and cultural dictators. He acknowledges in a later essay that "my quarrel with the Pound-Eliot school was a *Jewish* quarrel."[9] The Hollywood Jews had shown how it might be done, not by filling subordinate positions in corporate bodies closed to Jews in any case (e.g., industries like oil and automobiles), but by constructing culture industries that brought with them the contemporary audience. Poets too could found or sponsor a "new school" and create, in the phrase Neal Gabler has used as the title of his book on the Jewish producers, "An Empire of Their Own."

Gabler's thesis is that the Jewish producers found California's primitive social structure congenial for the establishment of a new Zion in which the civic religion would be the dogma of the movies themselves. They would make the content of Hollywood movies propitiatory to a considerable degree, granting to gentile America a starring role justified by its commanding power as a majority of the population. But paradoxically the success of the movies depended upon the producers' instinct for stories rooted in the Jewish desire for bourgeois stability. Of Louis B. Mayer, for example, Gabler writes:

> What Mayer did in the thirties—what he was situated to do as a Jew yearning to belong—was provide reassurance against the anxieties and disruptions of the time. He did this by fashioning a vast, compelling national fantasy out of his dreams and out of the basic tenets of his own dogmatic faith—a belief in virtue, in the bulwark of the family, in the merits of loyalty, in the soundness of tradition in America itself.
>
> Native born, white, Anglo-Saxon Protestant Americans could share this fantasy with Mayer and even call it their own. But it is unlikely that any of them could have or would have invented it. To do so, one would have needed the same desperate longing for security that Mayer and so many of the other Hollywood Jews felt. One would have had to suffer the same compulsion to merge oneself with the world. One would have had to be so fearful of being outside and alone that one would go to any lengths to fabricate America as a sanctuary, safe and secure, and then promulgate this idealization to other Americans.[10]

Because the Hollywood Jews were deracinated and assimilation minded, there was nothing cynical about their creative project. What they spun out of their fantasies of belonging to a new and hospitable society became the master narratives of a heterogeneous society uncertain about its own identity and its appropriate behavior in the new century. The Hollywood Jews, by this perspective, did not identify with the Christian majority and then reflect back to them their values, but actually created those values out of anxiety about becoming *heimlich* or native to the soil they had chosen for settlement. Mayer considered conversion to Christianity, as did Shapiro, but this very temptation to belong more thoroughly to the majority indicated nothing so much as the essential Jewishness of producer and poet alike. The essential condition of the Diaspora is one of being uprooted, and of escaping alienation by rooting oneself in a hospitable community immune from the antagonistic forces that have tormented the Jews throughout history.

The silent era of filmmaking offered an abundance of films that dramatized the movement of the Jew out of the ghetto and into the mainstream of American life. *The Jazz Singer* is the most famous of these paradigmatic stories. In the play and film versions, Jakie Rabinowitz, the cantor's son, transforms himself into Jack Robin the pop singer, but his assimilation is constantly inhibited by the demands made upon him by his orthodox, immigrant parents. In the theatrical version he returns at the end to his synagogue to sing the Kol Nidre while his father is dying, thereby ruining his big chance to perform opening night of a Broadway musical. In the film version a Hollywood ending is appended where he is given a second chance at fame and fortune. His triumph is the wish fantasy of the Jewish artists who created the movie, and no doubt of the Jewish artists who consumed it. The success story often had its origins in Jewish aspiration for cultural power, as in films like *Humoresque* (1920, remade in 1946), *Make Me a Star* (1932), *Once in a Lifetime* (1932), *A Star Is Born* (1937, remade in 1954 and 1976), and *Golden Boy* (1939). Often such films self-reflexively showed newcomers making it in Hollywood, and usually drew upon Jewish artists for their creation and interpretation: Fannie Hurst, Al Jolson, Samson Raphaelson, Dorothy Parker, George Kaufman and Moss Hart, Gregory Ratoff, Arthur Kober, Rouben Mamoulian, and so on. These films became object lessons for all Jewish artists who sought opportunities in the new society symbolized by the Jewish-owned movie industry itself.

There was in Shapiro a powerful desire to escape the obligations and opportunities of social mobility implied in such success stories. Rivalry with the gentile models of success was the last thing on his mind when he lingered in Southern California on the way to Tahiti, as we have seen. Poised in the early 1940s to enter the greatest military conflict of all time, he yearned to retreat to the site of fancy "unique in time" and "farthest from any war." One thinks of Henry Miller, whom Shapiro would later call "The Greatest Living Author," turning his back on political struggles like the Spanish Civil War in order to indulge his sensual desires in Paris. But Shapiro came to believe that no Jew is free to retreat from history, nor will history allow the Jew to withdraw in good faith into some pleasure dome. In *Poems of a Jew* he will resort to biblical typology and imagine America as "this great Palestine," a trope that commits Shapiro, no less than King David or David Ben-Gurion, to active struggle against powerful enemies.[11] Likewise the Jewish producers, sometimes against their will, felt compelled to engage social problems in the 1930s, including, very discreetly, anti-Semitism and the rise of fascism in Europe and even in America. The Jew, and especially the Jewish poet, had to resist the injustices of historical reality in order to guarantee the new Zion, for poets as well as everyone else.

In 1942, the date of "Hollywood," history threatened the "American Jew and poet" in two forms. The first of course was the mobilization of the Axis powers, and Shapiro put his life on the line in the Pacific theater in order to combat the menace. One does not want to be sanctimonious about Shapiro's military service, since he treats the experience in his autobiography with a considerable lack of solemnity. Nevertheless his poems about the soldier's life in *V-Letter* and elsewhere have been rightly valued for their eyewitness accounts of the achievements as well as the distractions of ordinary people conscripted by history. These poems aspire to give dramatic visibility to those who bravely took arms against antidemocratic and anti-American regimes.

"Antidemocratic and anti-American" is a phrase Shapiro uses in an essay to describe Pound and Eliot, and this usage alerts us to the other historical force Shapiro felt called upon to resist.[12] In Eliot, Shapiro saw a demonic figure who had corrupted both poetic practice and critical discourse by the end of the 1930s. In a later essay Shapiro would write that Eliot "is Modern Literature incarnate and an institution unto himself. . . . [He is] absolute monarch and Archbishop of

Canterbury in one."[13] Eliot had achieved this role in part by his talents, which Shapiro never denied, but also by the advocacy of authors like Archibald MacLeish, F. O. Matthiessen, and Delmore Schwartz, liberals who deferred to his authoritarian pronouncements on the cultural decay of the West. In "Gerontion" the decayed house of Europe is presided over by the Jew, who "squats on the window sill, the owner." In his magazine *The Criterion* Eliot sponsored anti-Semitic commentary, as in an issue of 1925 featuring his own poem "The Hollow Men." At the back of the book a reviewer named I. P. Fassett asserts that "no Jew can ever be a great artist, and . . . the best they can do is to achieve by a fine cleverness, by very hard work, and by great restraint a marvellous imitation of art."[14] The speaker of "Gerontion" is a fictional person, not (necessarily) T. S. Eliot, but the editor and essayist Eliot deployed prejudicial remarks about Jews often enough to invite readers to place him with his admired models Henry Adams and Ezra Pound, not to mention more bigoted voices in the London-Paris literary milieu such as Wyndham Lewis and Charles Maurras. Likewise in *The Sun Also Rises* Hemingway featured the Jewish Robert Cohn as the pseudoartist and phony intellectual, an unwelcome presence in the community presided over by the book's moral center, Jake Barnes. And Aldous Huxley devoted a chapter of his book of essays, *Do What You Will* (1929), to a study of *The Jazz Singer* that ostentatiously denigrated Jewish culture in the manner of Fassett. The closing off of the art world against the Jews by the dominant voices of the modernist establishment forms the context for Shapiro's hypersensitivity to his Jewishness.

Shapiro's chief complaint about modernists like Yeats, Pound, and Eliot is that in trying to effect an anachronistic cultural program by means of highly intellectualized poems they had sacrificed the large reading audience that once appreciated poetry for its sensuality. In *Essay on Rime* he asks, "At what point in the history of art / Has such a cleavage between audience / and poet existed?"[15] He was not the only one to be asking such questions. In *Axel's Castle* (1931) Edmund Wilson had remarked that "for some reason or other, verse as a technique of literary expression is being abandoned by humanity altogether."[16] If what Wilson calls a "futile aestheticism" has alienated the modern audience, where has that audience gone? Some poets, perhaps consulting their own habits, believed that it must have fled to the movie theater. Thomas McGrath would make this comic lament in the 1940s:

> Nobody wants your roundelay, nobody wants your sestina,
> Said the housewife, we want Hedy Lamarr and Gable at the
>   cinema,
> Get out of my technicolor dream with your tragic view and
>   your verses;
> Down with iambic pentameter and hurray for Louella Parsons.[17]

Shapiro does not want to applaud a culture shift in which the poetry audience abandons verse for movies, but as his poem suggests, he sees much in Hollywood that can teach poets how to keep and enlarge that audience. To the extent that he continues to argue for the popular sensibility versus what he calls in his essay on Pound "the obscurities of the pedant and the obscurities of pedantic rhetoric," Shapiro makes common cause with the Jewish producers who based their art entirely on the "technicolor dream" of the ordinary person. By endorsing the dignity of the common viewer, Shapiro seems to be arguing, the movies help to defeat what he called "the fascist coup d'etat" engineered by the critics and poets, some of them Jews, who took their orders from the cultural dictators in London.[18]

One can define the culture shift from East to West, and past to present, by examining a scene from F. Scott Fitzgerald's unfinished novel of 1939, *The Last Tycoon,* in which a profascist and anti-Semitic visitor to Hollywood is confronted with what is "most real" in this place of illusion. The setting for the scene is the commissary of the studio presided over by the novel's idealized hero, Monroe Stahr, a producer based on Irving Thalberg, the Jewish boy genius of M-G-M, whose premature death in 1936 insured his legendary status in the film colony. Fitzgerald had worked with Thalberg and considered him the epitome of creative intelligence in the new medium. "He had an intense respect for learning, a racial memory of the old *schules*," Fitzgerald writes of Stahr. The novel's narrator, an ingenue named Cecelia, describes him earlier in the book as a "proud young shepherd" running "ahead through trackless wastes of perception into fields where very few men were able to follow him."[19] Perception is very much on Cecelia's mind, and on Fitzgerald's, since how to see, and see through

disguises, emerges as the central question of the novel. As the Jewish
boy from the East Coast who initiates a golden age of the movies,
Stahr signifies the fantasy triumph of the Jew in a hostile Christian
environment. (Fitzgerald turns Thalberg's rival, Louis B. Mayer, into
an Irish-American named Patrick Brady.) Stahr's relation to his audi-
ence is measured first by Cecelia, a figure for the moviegoer, who
acknowledges that "some of the pictures Stahr himself conceived had
shaped me into what I was" (18). Another figure for the audience is
the reactionary Prince Agge, who is being shown around the studio
compound by Stahr:

> Coming out of the private dining room, they passed
> through a corner of the commissary proper. Prince Agge drank
> it in—eagerly. It was gay with gypsies and with citizens and
> soldiers, with the sideburns and braided coats of the First Em-
> pire. From a little distance they were men who lived and walked
> a hundred years ago, and Agge wondered how he and the men
> of his time would look as extras in some future costume picture.
>   Then he saw Abraham Lincoln, and his whole feeling sud-
> denly changed. He had been brought up in the dawn of Scandina-
> vian socialism when Nicolay's biography was much read. He had
> been told Lincoln was a great man whom he should admire, and
> he hated him instead, because he was forced upon him. But now
> seeing him sitting here, his legs crossed, his kindly face fixed on
> a forty-cent dinner, including dessert, his shawl wrapped around
> him as if to protect himself from the erratic air-cooling—now
> Prince Agge, who was in America at last, stared as a tourist at
> the mummy of Lenin in the Kremlin. This, then, was Lincoln.
> Stahr had walked on far ahead of him, turned waiting for him—
> but still Agge stared.
>   This, then, he thought, was what they all meant to be.
>   Lincoln suddenly raised a triangle of pie and jammed it in his
> mouth, and, a little frightened, Prince Agge hurried to join
> Stahr. (49)

The passage is an insightful summation of moviegoing psychol-
ogy and an argument for the relocation of cultural power. First of all,
the Prince, devoid of all but ceremonial status in his own country,
identifies instinctively with the movie extras whose costumes are no

less disguises than the Prince's title and regalia. What has devalued the Prince is the democratic forces embodied in America's past as symbolized by Lincoln, and in America's contemporary mythmaker, the movie studio. He is farsighted enough to realize that the European nobility he represents is likely to end up as nothing more than a quaint story, and he himself nothing more than a bit role in future movies. The self-humbling of the Prince is appropriate given the presence of his successor, Stahr, "the last of the princes" (27), the producer of that cinematic form of history humankind will ever afterward consume as truth.

But these whimsical meditations change course when Agge catches sight of Lincoln. Lincoln was a popular figure in the literature and movies of the 1930s, when his example was needed for the crises of Depression and imminent war. Best-selling biographies of Lincoln by, among others, Edgar Lee Masters (1931) and Carl Sandburg (1939) had pointed up the contemporaneity of the embattled president, and filmmakers like D. W. Griffith (*Abraham Lincoln,* 1930), John Ford (*Young Mr. Lincoln,* 1939), and John Cromwell (*Abe Lincoln in Illinois,* 1940) lovingly retold the story, folklore and all. The public's need for Lincoln as a cinematic image is echoed in Agge's sudden spellbound belief in the reality of the figure he sees before him. Lincoln is no mummy like Lenin—this is Fitzgerald's end-of-decade critique of the moribund and already nostalgic condition of Bolshevism—but a living visible presence in the future-oriented storehouse of cultural memory.

When the actor playing Lincoln jams a piece of pie into his mouth, the illusion is broken and Agge retreats to Stahr's side. This denouement can be read as a critique of movie illusion. But Fitzgerald's final irony is that Stahr will be described later in the novel as a personification of Lincoln: "[The English writer] Boxley . . . had been reading Lord Charnwood and he recognized that Stahr like Lincoln was a leader carrying on a long war on many fronts; almost single-handed he had moved pictures sharply forward through a decade, to a point where the content of the 'A' productions was wider and richer than that of the stage" (106). The producer's first name, Monroe, deliberately refers to one of the nation's founding fathers, and another president is summoned in the novel's first scene when Stahr's plane makes an emergency landing in Nashville, and some of the Hollywood personnel visit the Hermitage, Andrew Jackson's home. Stahr is a visionary leader who consults his own taste with confidence because he too is a man of the people. He is "the dream made flesh" (50), specifically the American dream of upward social mobility in an American century. As the soul of the movie industry, Stahr has been charged by history to generate a democratic renaissance for worldwide consumption.

At one point in the novel Prince Agge asks Stahr what makes the unity of elements that compose a movie. Stahr answers, "I'm the unity" (58). Shapiro's question in his early polemical writing on poetry is the same. Who is the unity? Nobody in the literary world is given that role in *Essay on Rime,* though many poets are appreciated. By writing such a work of criticism, however, Shapiro seemed to be making a bid for the position of cultural arbiter then held by Eliot, and like Eliot he made claims for the centrality of a certain way of looking at the world. Indeed, the composition of an essay-poem in the manner of Auden—conversational, witty, discursive—was an attempt to make contact with an audience put off by the demands of modernist literature. In his lyrics, Shapiro likewise adopted Auden's and Williams's habit of incorporating the diversity of modern phenomena. He sought to sensually reclaim the world's body for the large audience Eliot disdained. Shapiro argued for a nativist and populist art, based on the enthusiastic celebration of those vulgar realities that had chased Pound and Eliot from their homeland. Those expatriates with their "provincial snobbery," as Shapiro called it, left the field wide open to some latter-day Whitman who would in Hollywood style hold the mirror—or the camera—up to the land of Lincoln and its people. (Shapiro, disappointed in his own failure to enact that role, would later hail Allen Ginsberg as the "new Hebrew Walt Whitman.")[20]

Shapiro looked upon the body of experience with a hungry eye. He had no desire to reject the symbolists; he learned from poets like Baudelaire how to infuse an urgency of personal need into his thickly textured phrases. From the beginning he saw his task as the synthesizing of Baudelaire and Williams, the rhetorical heightening of emotional responses to everyday imagery. Eliot had started his career by doing this in "Preludes" and "Prufrock" but had progressed, Shapiro would lament at immense length in his essays, to the pontifical abstraction of his later verse. Shapiro located this swerve into abstraction as the vulnerable point of the century's poetics, the wrong turn that his own generation must correct. Shapiro almost programmatically set out to make the art of seeing one of his fundamental subjects, with the confidence that a moviegoing public would find such habits congenial.

In *Person, Place and Thing* Shapiro emphasizes visualizing as a trope of being in one of the first poems, "The Dome of Sunday." What the camera eye picks out in the clarity of a Sunday matinee are "The hard legs of our women, / Our women are one woman, dressed in black," who swagger (in collective form) down the street while the poet's gaze enjoys the moving picture.[21] In his autobiography, Shapiro will say of his early self, "Gazing is his occupation" (64) and that the object of his spectatorial impulse is women. In the poems, however, voyeurism extends to all objects, so that the entire world is eroticized by the caressing touch of his ocular attentions. In the poem following "The Dome of Sunday," we hear of the camera eye again: "I click click the shutter of sight." The moving pictures continue in "Love Poem," where the speaker rushes into a house to look at an attempted suicide: "I was one among the heads / Converged like cameras on your waking." In "Midnight Show," the poet slips into a movie theater, and after the curtains part on the blank screen, he is compelled to see in the accelerated speed of montage the "shattered cities" of world war, and much more, "Byrd at the world's bottom" and "the Unemployed," all created ex nihilo on "the vacant field" of his eye's entire universe by "God the Light." The power is irresistible:

Revulsion cannot rouse our heads for pride or protest.
The eye sees as the camera, a clean moronic gaze,
And to go is not impossible but merely careless.

Movie imagery enters the lens of the camera obscura that is human consciousness like the shower of divine light upon the Creation. The Romantic model for poetic activity conceives the secondary world of verbal imagery as the reprojection of that originary light. How can one persuade an audience to gaze at the page that was once a vacant field before the poet filled it with life? That is the implied question of all these poems fascinated by the picture-making powers of the *caméra-stylo*. Many poems in *Person, Place and Thing* give the reader plenty to look at, just as the popular culture celebrated in poems like "Honkytonk," "Drug Store," and "Emporium" gratifies the bourgeois taste for visual stimulation and abundant merchandise. What spectacles of equivalent attraction can the poet offer? The volume's last poem, "Poet," tries to come to terms with the implications of the camera eye metaphor.

"Poet" is a demystifying portrait that emphasizes not the poet's high intelligence or profound sensibility, as in Romantic and modernist versions, but his vulgarity, which Shapiro brandishes with defiant energy. The poet is not only "childlike," a term of praise, but adolescent, a "conscious fool" who peers at himself in the mirror at the beginning of the poem and peers at his personal history in order to re-collect the parts of himself for public inspection. This is Baudelaire's dandy, the artist who lives always in front of a mirror, and sees his public as another glass for his approval. Because women are most tolerant of such behavior, they are the special audience for this figure who, "erotic as an ape, / Dreamy as puberty," subsists upon their voluptuous gifts. Baudelaire's fable for such postpuberty fantasy is the poem Shapiro translates in this volume, "Giantess," in which the speaker luxuriates amidst the amplitude of an enormous female. Pleasure seeking is the poet's prerogative, we are made to understand, for he is a figure of the repressed who returns to claim the birthright denied by civilization. Shapiro's penultimate stanza of "Poet" is especially interesting in this regard:

> He is the business man, on beauty trades,
> Dealer in arts and thoughts, who, like the Jew,
> Shall rise from slums and hated dialects
> A tower of bitterness. Shall be always strange,
> Hunted and then sought after. . . .

The poet is the subversive in culture, a figure of vengeance for the repressed instincts that a Christian ideology impressed upon the public imagination. Shapiro's poems "Shylock," "Synagogue," and "Jew," in *V-Letter and Other Poems,* make the connection explicit. The Jew's revenge takes the form of denying authentic reality to the genteel codes of the Establishment and offering instead a language of incitements, of desire. "Sentio ergo sum" is the motto of the poet in Shapiro's poem, and it is specifically erotic desire that undermines the militant rationality of a puritanical state. Like the Jewish producer summoned in "Movie Actress," the Jewish poet can captivate an

audience by spotlighting "regions of pleasure" unvisited by modern-
ist rivals. He will be "sought after" by the same audience that for-
merly "hunted" him, now responsive to the guilty enjoyments of a
poetry full of sensations rather than thoughts. The Jew is not custom-
arily evoked as a figure for this kind of romantic subversion, but
Shapiro is able to make the connection because of the Hollywood
associations already outlined.

And so this poem leads us back to "Hollywood," and specifically
to the penultimate stanza of that poem, in which a series of questions
probes the erotic character of the place. Shapiro has given the reader
several stanzas of defamiliarizing rhetoric in which Hollywood is
celebrated for its exotic flavor as a place of "love" and "beauty," a
fairy-tale locale. Now comes a series of questions in the manner of
Keats's feverish interrogations in "Ode on a Grecian Urn." Is the real
Hollywood essentially a site for erotic fantasy, "A private orgy" as
alien to our ordinary lives as the word *harem* with all its voluptuous
connotations? And finally, "Is adolescence just as vile /As this its
architecture and its talk?" Before Shapiro swerves away from this
possibility and closes the poem with his reference to "a soul, a possi-
bly proud Florence," he poses for our consideration the possibility
that Hollywood's appeal is to our visceral obsession with the gigantic
forms of women—or, to extend his male perspective, for the sexual
cornucopia evoked by the word harem, the orgy that is always on the
mind of the randy adolescent. An art based solidly on the pleasure
principle, and produced by the businessman, the bitter Jew who gives
the seductress her name, is thus moved to the center of our civiliza-
tion, if only as the wish-fulfillment of one Jewish poet eager to thumb
his nose at reactionary modernism.

The similarity of Shapiro's crusade to that of some Jewish novel-
ists—Philip Roth and Norman Mailer leap to mind—has never been
satisfactorily described, in part because critics of Jewish fiction neglect
poetry so persistently. Leslie Fiedler has been an exception, and more
recently Mark Shechner has traced a Reichian strain in Jewish litera-
ture that seeks to defeat the power of the superego and the social
superstructure alike by strengthening libidinal instinct and sexual
freedom. Alex Portnoy's battle cry, "Let's Put the Id Back into Yid"
is the reductive but telling commandment in this counter-Mosaic
tradition.[22] When the story of Jewish-American poetry in this century
receives more attention, Shapiro's unique situation will need to be

distinguished from his immediate predecessors, who explored radical
alternatives for a future more secular and sexually fulfilling than the
world of their fathers. For example, Isidor Schneider's poem of 1934
"Harem from a Bus Top" is *like* Shapiro's in the way it tells of the
voyeurist pleasures of watching and mentally undressing women
while riding through the city. Schneider's poems evoke the quasi-
assimilated Jew's envy of the intuitive and passionate life forbidden
by his laws and folkways. But as a committed member of the Com-
munist party Schneider is *unlike* Shapiro in the way he dutifully con-
demns the erotics of movies as capitalist seduction; he fantasizes a
violent disfiguring in the revolutionary poem "Dollars":

> pluck bodices
> of movie queens, the suck of all men's eyes;
> cut carefully the bevelled noses of
> star actors famous for the faultless sneer.[23]

That such stars are the creations of Jewish moviemakers intent on
their own revolution, an egalitarian empire in the Zion of the Golden
State, lends the polemics against Hollywood an almost farcical air of
intratribal rivalry for cultural power.

(Shapiro's endorsement of the poet's libidinous tendencies re-
minds us that many of the writers and directors in Hollywood who
promulgated the gospel of eroticism were Jewish. One thinks of Jules
Furthman and Joseph von Sternberg creating the seductive image of
Marlene Dietrich, Ben Hecht's hot-blooded imagination, the erotic
comedies of Ernst Lubitsch, George Cukor's flattering of female
sexuality, Otto Preminger's showcasing of glamorous actresses, Billy
Wilder's prurient presentation of Barbara Stanwyck and Marilyn
Monroe... down to the Chaplinesque permutations of neurotic de-
sire in the films of Woody Allen.)

Another way of saying this is that Shapiro carries a Freudian
rather than Marxist ideology into the realm of poetry, just as the
Jewish producers had done in their movies. For those under attack,
the two subversive traditions may have seemed indistinguishable and
their ideological differences irrelevant so long as the defiant disturbers
of the peace were imaginable as the long-detested Jew. The demonic
way of imagining this usurpation of the cultural tradition is the
Eliotic view in "Gerontion," "Burbank with a Baedeker: Bleistein

with a Cigar," and *After Strange Gods,* his lectures of 1933 at the University of Virginia, in which Eliot remarked that "reasons of race and religion combine to make any large number of free-thinking Jews undesirable" in a Christian society.[24] Pound's implied linkage of the unforgivable sin of usury with the Jews, and his attacks on "kikery" in his radio broadcasts for the Italian fascists make the same critique of the Jewish presence in modern history. In the Hollywood milieu, Budd Schulberg's novel *What Makes Sammy Run?* made the reactionary case against Jewish opportunist Sammy Glick, who seeks to grasp the ultimate power of the studio (American) system. In his poems and criticism Shapiro proposes a more positive reading of Jewish aspirations as a return of the repressed. Who better than Jews know how powerful the dream life is in a hostile world intolerant of hedonic claims? Shapiro's "Poet" and the Jewish moviemakers and Freud all together are the dreamers and interpreters of dreams for the gentile world, confronting a patriarchal Establishment with their dangerous secret about the polymorphous forms of sexual desire.

When Shapiro went to war, he carried with him an internalized Hollywood, that is, a way of seeing that preserved a spectatorial distance from events. In his autobiography Shapiro reveals at great length, as he could not in poems sent back to his fiancée from the front, how much of his leave time in Australia was taken up with womanizing and lingering affairs. The world evoked in his poem "Movie," from *V-Letter and Other Poems,* draws together the motifs we have studied so far. In the theater the speaker becomes conscious of an attractive woman sitting beside him and compares her to the film image, a tantalizing blonde he calls "Astarte" as he surrenders to her charm. The poem's concluding stanza erases the distance between reality and illusion:

> The world swallows your pill, quack that it is,
> And loves it. Yes, it works a cure,
> It makes us turn our heads, like smelling salts;
> We think, *We'll go slow after this.*
> *It was terrific:* or perhaps more sure
> Of what's unreal, Inside or Out, we sight
> A skirt, and with an intimating cough
> Follow it down the street; or else we light
> A cigarette, and start to walk it off.

The attitude here is again reminiscent of Keats's ambivalence toward the Grecian urn, an object Keats favors with hyperbolic questions and then both praises and criticizes. The urn remains a friend to man in the same sense that the sugar pill offered to the spectator in Shapiro's film is both a quack remedy and a cure: sensual art heightens our consciousness, makes us more alert ("like smelling salts"), and therefore more aware of the continuity between the real and the unreal, as in the way a blond sexpot on the screen will turn our erotic gaze outward, to "sight a skirt" and follow it in order to mimic the pleasure depicted on the screen. Perhaps we need the stimulus of art to express our desires, and if so the poet's honeyed words will remain irreplaceable in the economy of a pleasure-loving society. In any case, the conquest in real life is endorsed and made meaningful by the "Yes" breathed by the artwork. (One recalls the "Yes. Yes." of "Hollywood." Joyce had popularized the word in *Ulysses* as a code for the surrender to erotic yearning.) By endorsing sensual gratification, the Jewish poet achieves full citizenship in a secular society no longer bullied into warfare with the body.

Karl Shapiro's career after the publication of "Hollywood" would mimic the success stories popularized by the movies. He would win the Pulitzer Prize for *V-Letter,* be appointed Consultant in Poetry at the Library of Congress, accept a tenured professorship at Johns Hopkins University, and become editor of *Poetry* magazine, among his other honors. Hollywood did foretell and perhaps enable his meteoric rise from the lowly status of G.I. to the role of cultural arbiter (if not dictator) in the postwar literary world. And World War II itself, subject of so many Hollywood movies during wartime, ultimately took on for Shapiro the semblance of a movie, as he documented his part in it. In his autobiography, *The Younger Son,* where he looks back over a gulf of decades to recreate the life of a person he describes in third person, the movie imagery recurs compulsively:

> But people had stopped glorifying war and the heroics of war long ago, except in the movies. War had become a movie property. (181–82)

> They entered the movie set harbor of Rio de Janeiro. (187)

[In Perth] the Yanks didn't know what to make of these people who treated them like movie stars. (190)

And while the sleeping soldiers were all metamorphosing quietly into Robert Taylors and Gary Coopers the poet was entering his own movie. (196)

In fact, the whole of the poet's experience, screened in thior of his memory, seems in retrospect a sequence of movie moments, great scenes in which he has been the leading man. In *The Bourgeois Poet* he will comment ruefully on how as a middle-aged man he enjoys watching war movies that feature figures like his former self, and how droll it is that while a soldier he so much enjoyed watching movies of some other history, hardly conscious that he, like Prince Agge, would someday be nothing more than a model for costume pictures of the future.[25] Shapiro's wry insight is made possible by the dominance of cinema in our culture. Mallarmé remarked that all of reality exists to end between the pages of a book; likewise, all of Shapiro's personal history, as he predicted in his poem of the "Poet," exists to be absorbed into the ongoing movie produced by the soul of our society, the collective unconscious we call Hollywood. One wonders, who will play the role of Karl Shapiro when his life and work is made into a movie.

Chapter 6

"The best / And brightest screens fade out," wrote John Hollander. The pathos of extinguished movie theaters, including drive-ins, has informed the elegiac poetry about moviegoing since the 1950s. (Photo by John Margolies. Courtesy Esto Photographics.)

Chapter 6

"The Audience Vanishes": Frank O'Hara and the Mythos of Decline

To the Film Industry in Crisis

Not you, lean quarterlies and swarthy periodicals
with your studious incursions toward the pomposity of ants,
nor you, experimental theatre in which Emotive Fruition
is wedding Poetic Insight perpetually, nor you,
promenading Grand Opera, obvious as an ear (though you
are close to my heart), but you, Motion Picture Industry,
it's you I love!

In times of crisis, we must all decide again and again whom we love.
And give credit where it's due: not to my starched nurse, who
     taught me
how to be bad and not bad rather than good (and has lately availed
herself of this information), not to the Catholic Church
which is at best an oversolemn introduction to cosmic entertainment
not to the American Legion, which hates everybody, but to you,
glorious Silver Screen, tragic Technicolor, amorphous Cinemascope,
stretching Vistavision and startling Stereophonic Sound, with all
your heavenly dimensions and reverberations and iconoclasms! To
Richard Barthelmess as the "tol'able" boy barefoot and in pants,
Jeanette MacDonald of the flaming hair and lips and long, long neck,
Sue Carroll as she sits for eternity on the damaged fender of a car
and smiles, Ginger Rogers with her pageboy bob like a sausage
on her shuffling shoulders, peach-melba-voiced Fred Astaire of the
     feet,
Erich von Stroheim, the seducer of mountain-climbers' gasping
     spouses,

the Tarzans, each and every one of you (I cannot bring myself to
    prefer
Johnny Weissmuller to Lex Barker, I cannot!), Mae West in a furry
    sled,
her bordello radiance and bland remarks, Rudolph Valentino of the
    moon,
its crushing passions, and moonlike, too, the gentle Norma Shearer,
Miriam Hopkins dropping her champagne glass off Joel McCrea's
    yacht
and crying into the dappled sea, Clark Gable rescuing Gene Tierney
from Russia and Allan Jones rescuing Kitty Carlisle from Harpo
    Marx,
Cornel Wilde coughing blood on the piano keys while Merle Oberon
    berates,
Marilyn Monroe in her little spike heels reeling through Niagara
    Falls,
Joseph Cotten puzzling and Orson Welles puzzled and Dolores Del
    Rio
eating orchids for lunch and breaking mirrors, Gloria Swanson re-
    clining,
and Jean Harlow reclining and wiggling, and Alice Faye reclining
and wiggling and singing, Myrna Loy being calm and wise, William
    Powell
in his stunning urbanity, Elizabeth Taylor blossoming, yes, to you

and to all you others, the great, the near-great, the featured, the extras
who pass quickly and return in dreams saying your one or two lines,
    my love!
Long may you illumine space with your marvellous appearances,
    delays
and enunciations, and may the money of the world glitteringly cover
    you
as you rest after a long day under the klieg lights with your faces
in packs for our edification, the way the clouds come often at night
but the heavens operate on the star system. It is a divine precedent
you perpetuate! Roll on, reels of celluloid, as the great earth rolls on![1]
                                                                —1957

How many readers, coming across this poem in an anthology or in Frank O'Hara's *Selected Poems,* will ask the obvious question: What crisis? O'Hara characteristically provides no explanation, assuming that readers of the late 1950s will need none, and unwilling to forfeit the advantages of his mock-declamatory tone by remarking at length on the sociohistorical circumstances that inform the poem. O'Hara's instinct is a good one: most readers even two generations later are able to identify the crisis, if only by the single word, television. And yet, as we shall see, this response begs the question more than answers it. Understanding the nature of the crisis is important to understanding the showmanship of the poem as well as its representative character in the 1950s. For "To the Film Industry in Crisis" is not only "O'Hara's best poem on the movies," as Alan Feldman asserts, but the poem with the most powerful influence on his contemporaries and successors.[2] Published in *Meditations in an Emergency* (1957), the first volume by O'Hara to receive wide distribution, it helped a whole school of poets in their rhetorical negotiations with popular culture.

The fact upon which O'Hara's poem stands is succintly stated by Otto Friedrich: "Millions of people suddenly stopped going to the movies. Attendance sank from eighty million per week in 1946 to sixty-seven million in 1948 to sixty million in 1950, and it kept sinking."[3] Theaters began to disappear, along with the secondary studio productions that had made the old movie palaces so attractive, especially to children: B movies, serials, cartoons, and newsreels. The number of feature films Hollywood manufactured dwindled from 500 per year in its heyday to 200 by the late 1960s. This astonishing decline has intrigued film historians during the postwar period. Gilbert Seldes began his section on the movies in *The Great Audience* (1950) with the chapter title, "The Audience Vanishes." While Richard Dyer MacCann hopefully titled his book of 1962 *Hollywood in Transition,* one of the best-selling histories of the period, by Ezra Goodman, bore the more discouraging title, *The Fifty Year Decline and Fall of Hollywood* (1961). Charles Higham's chronicle of 1972, *Hollywood at Sunset,* has the subtitle, *The Decline and Fall of the Most Colorful Empire since Rome.* Otto Friedrich's own portrait of Hollywood in the 1940s, after noting that weekly attendance at the movies declined as low as forty million in the 1950s, quotes Michael Wood's remark apropos of the movie industry's fascination for extravaganzas about doomed empires in this decade, "Hollywood was Egypt, and Rome, and Jerusalem. The ancient world of the epics was a huge, many-faceted metaphor for Hollywood itself."[4] One might suggest other metaphors: the havoc wrought in cities and suburbs by irradiated insects swollen to monstrous size, and the hostile aliens bent on usurpation in movies like *The Beginning of the End* and *Invasion of the Body Snatchers*.

That the film industry remained not only viable but profitable after the problems of midcentury does not discredit in the least the mythos of decline in books of this type. Their authors do not need, like Edward Gibbon, to walk over the actual ruins of empire before summoning their elegiac sentiments. Audiences come and go in variable numbers, but what irreversibly changed in the 1950s, according to these historians, was the habitual attitude of affectionate loyalty toward Hollywood movies, one that O'Hara commits himself to defining and recuperating. Yet even to write such a poem is to acknowledge the truth of such dirgelike chronicles. For the first time in its brief history, part of the charismatic power of the movies is felt to be its condition of being passé, and the poet's stance has correspondingly become one of retrospection. O'Hara observes in himself the chasm opening between some presumed golden age before the audience vanished and his own precarious contemporary period when the emotions invested in classic films begin to feel inauthentic. If O'Hara's persistent association of the movies with a perfect heaven is more than an impious joke, then he must pledge himself to confront the crisis with some of the wisdom he has earned from the sorrows of aging in a media culture.

If movies are the preeminent art of adolescence, as O'Hara seemed to believe, did the disappearing audience point to a maturing of the American public at large? There was a widespread feeling in Hollywood that battle-scarred veterans and their emotionally strained families, transiting from a hot war to a cold one presided over by nuclear weapons, would require a different kind of entertainment than the prewar variety. The change in textures, styles, and attitudes closed off the first full generation of the talkies just as the talkies had closed off the silents into a self-contained historical period. Television, of course, emerged as the principal rival for dollars and attention, but as Douglas Gomery has argued, "suburbanization and the baby boom led to less moviegoing, and would have done so even without the coming of television."⁵ Families strapped by mortgage payments and the demands of new domesticity tended to stay at home rather than travel downtown to the movies. And for those with more disposable income, more options for leisure time became available: the fantasy world of automobiles, the opportunities for travel, especially in Europe where the exchange rate made middle-class Americans rich, the rise of sports as a national obsession, the appeal of popular music, and the burgeoning mass culture from comic books to evangelical churches—all militated against the unique dominance exercised by the movies before 1946. The aging and retirement of the studio bosses became emblematic of the decline of the old industry, as one by one the legends in their lifetime like Louis B. Mayer, Samuel Goldwyn, Harry Cohn, and finally Darryl Zanuck gave up control of their empires to younger counterparts.

For the producers who began during the silent era, as they had to in order to become leaders after 1929, this was the end of the road. For the stars who emerged in the 1930s, usually in their early twenties, this was a time of middle-age yielding to the new generation. For someone like O'Hara, born in 1926 and old enough during World War II to serve on a destroyer in the Pacific, this noticeable shift of generations in the 1950s inevitably divided his sympathies. Should his primary allegiance be to the films he cherished as a child and as an adolescent, the films that shaped his prewar sensibility, or would he wholeheartedly endorse the cultural transformation of which the film industry's crisis was an outward manifestation? This was no easy question for someone as forward-looking in his artistic taste as O'Hara, the champion of experimental ballet and music as well as new American painting in the abstract expressionist mode. As the author of the first important study of Jackson Pollock, and an enthusiast of "the tradition of the new," O'Hara necessarily felt ambivalent about the pull of Hollywood's past upon his affections.

O'Hara's poems on film always involve a psychological crisis for which the film material provides an effective screen. When he can keep his anxiety at a distance by means of humor, the poems tend to be capacious in their thematic negotiations between the self and the world projected apart from the self. O'Hara's abjectness before this overmastering world is one of the subtexts of "To the Film Industry in Crisis." This subtext may be more visible if we consider an earlier poem on the experience of moviegoing that casts a raking light on the later masterpiece. "An Image of Leda" begins in this way:

> The cinema is cruel
> like a miracle. We
> sit in the darkened
> room asking nothing
> of the empty white
> space but that it
> remain pure. And
> suddenly despite us
> it blackens. Not by
> the hand that holds
> the pen. There is
> no message. We our-
> selves appear naked
> on the river bank
> spread-eagled while
> the machine wings
> nearer.

O'Hara compares his situation as moviegoer to that of Leda just before the swan, a disguised Jupiter, king of the gods, assaults her with ravishing attentions. O'Hara is testifying to a common but rarely acknowledged feeling of moviegoers: their defenseless vulnerability before the compelling experience they have volunteered to undergo through desire for the transcendent. One speaks of the vicarious experience of the filmgoer, but there is nothing vicarious about the feelings one has during a movie; they are the more intense for being voluntarily, even desperately, submitted to. To call the cinema "cruel," then, is to project onto it the blame for one's own abject need for its overwhelming power. The cinema takes advantage of that need, and satisfies it; thus it is "like a miracle." For a Catholic, even a lapsed one like O'Hara, the association of Leda and the swan with the annunciation to Mary would be an obvious, indeed a conventional one. In both cases a figure representing the supreme power of the universe interpenetrates the mortal world in order to impregnate a woman. Such an association underlies Yeats's poem, "Leda and the Swan," which O'Hara inevitably has in mind, as well as the theory of gyres Yeats developed in *A Vision* and some of his poems on the subject of the holy incarnation. O'Hara imagines himself as "an image of Leda" the moment before violation, both fearing it— asking that the white space before him remain innocent, pure—but also desiring to be violated by it, or why would he have come to the theater? The screen is nothing that he can write on—he has surrendered his role as creator by coming to the cinema; rather, the screen is an agent for the "machine" that writes its will upon his receptive sensibility, changing him forever by its enduring visual inscription.

The machinery of erotic aggression originates not in some demonic realm but in the heaven that humans hopefully imagine as a source of continuous pleasure for themselves. The poem concludes:

> . . . Is
> it our prayer or
> wish that this
> occur? Oh what is
> this light that
> holds us fast? Our
> limbs quicken even
> to disgrace under
> this white eye as
> if there were real
> pleasure in loving
> a shadow and caress-
> ing a disguise![6]

Light is the physical force that creates the shadow, a paradox familiar from devotional poetry, and common to most writings about the movies. The light "holds us fast" as Jupiter holds Leda in Yeats's poem: "He holds her helpless breast upon his breast." It is part of the myth of Leda that the rape is in some sense her "prayer or / wish" and that she enjoys the ecstatic experience she undergoes. O'Hara certainly feels this way, and the quickening of his limbs—no doubt he is thinking of his favorite romantic movies—is also a "disgrace" for reasons the "as if" clause articulates. The "real pleasure" lies outside the cave of light, where something more physical than shadows can be embraced. It has been the irresistible function of shadows to enforce this recognition upon the speaker.

"An Image of Leda" is an artless poem in O'Hara's typical breathless manner. It is a poem, one feels, that exists only because it had to be written as a defensive filling of white space to ward off the shadows it testifies against. But it is that need to assert the poetic enterprise against the cinematic one that keeps the poem fresh and useful as witness. It also helps us to read O'Hara's notorious poem, "Ave Maria," in which the poet tells the mothers of America to send their kids to the movies, where they may have "their first sexual experience . . . with a pleasant stranger whose apartment is in the Heaven on Earth Bldg. / near the Williamsburg Bridge." Whether or not they get picked up, "they'll have been truly entertained." Clearly some kind of equivalence is being asserted between the experiences of moviegoing and seduction or rape. In part this is another of O'Hara's joking incongruities, as if the two experiences were metaphorically identical. Yet from the perspective of "An Image of Leda" we can see that in his imagination they *are* comparable in effect. Cinema is cruel because it effects a rape of the mind, just as a molester effects a rape of the body. And yet, so goes the poetic logic, however sugared with jocularity, both are desired by the Freudian "tykes" who clamor to be allowed exposure to the surprising thrills of the matinee. Robert Pinsky's uneasy discussion of the poem praises its rhetorical excess, its "exuberant, homosexual *schpritzing*," as a justifiable means of refreshing our sense of "all the grotesque, glorious fantasy life associated with the movies."[7] Jim Elledge, too, has cautioned against focusing on the moral outrageousness of the poem rather than on the stimulating activity of moviegoing, of which the stranger's intervention is an auxiliary metaphor.[8] The experience of lost innocence is the central fact of adolescence, a cruel violation and an exquisite temptation; O'Hara's female role playing in the poem on Leda gives us the consumer's view of forbidden pleasures, while in "Ave Maria" he switches roles to endorse the power of purveyors of sex and fantasy to have their way.

When we turn back to "To the Film Industry in Crisis," we see at once how scrupulously O'Hara has prevented this disturbing thematic material from entering the poem overtly. As befits a public address to an institution, he first establishes the grounds for praise.

The movies are not like "lean quarterlies and swarthy periodicals," for openers. The adjectives are common ones for people, perhaps the kind of people who waylay the innocent and initiate them into adult experience? O'Hara at this time is writing for just such periodicals, if we include journals like *Art News* as well as those that published his poetry. Perhaps O'Hara is warning poetry readers against quarterlies that increasingly published New Critical essays in the 1950s, with all their dry formalist prejudices and terminological posturing, so much at odds with the improvisatory art O'Hara advocated. Though he will conspicuously not mention painting as one of those pompous occupations like "experimental theatre" and "Grand Opera," the categorical praise of the "Motion Picture Industry" would seem to collect together the other arts as subordinate. "It's you I love!" can only be directed at one object in this love poem, though to do so is to critique the arts of poetry and painting and the practice of impressionistic criticism to which he devoted most of his energy and enthusiasm throughout his life. "Love," then, is a gestural locution, not a precise judgment, as one might say, "I love Mexican food" to mean, "Here is something that brings me appetitive pleasure." The high pitch of the exclamation clues us to the rhetorical overinflation, the studied insincerity. The poem begins, in other words, by patronizing its object in the manner of camp.

The next stanza is the heart of the poem. O'Hara pushes off from the Catholic church and the American Legion, as he did from the high-culture models of the first stanza, into a long catalog of movie personalities. This is something new in poetry devoted to cinema, though one can find approximations in the 1940s. Parker Tyler's "Ode to Hollywood," for example, features a series of tercets devoted in turn to Greta Garbo, Lillian Gish, Gloria Swanson, Theda Bara, Marlene Dietrich, Bette Davis, and so forth, culminating, as in O'Hara's poem, in a hyperbolic closure:

> Still, forever from that city of incredibly
> Rapid and beautiful and fragile movement,
>   The kiss in perpetuum mobile![9]

Two things break the convention O'Hara inherits from his predecessors: the length of the list and its diversity of recondite examples. As to the length, the exuberant energy of his enumeration enacts the "love" by testifying to prolific knowledge. Knowledge is what the moviegoer obtains during long exposure to the inseminating power of the movies. Whether there is something inherently comical in profound knowledge of the totality of *movie* history is one of the central questions raised by the poem. No previous poet had made of his submission to the movies such a polemical incitement. A critic may feel trapped into associating this roll call incongruously with sublime models. Alan Feldman writes, "The movies, O'Hara suggests, provide us with a whole array of eternal beings who, like the Greek gods, are not particularly virtuous or admirable, but who have unchanging essences. O'Hara, in one long list like those in Homer's *Iliad*, cites two dozen or so of such beings."[10] One hears O'Hara's giggle from the sidelines. The length of the list cannot help but trivialize the claims made for the "stars," as if one should say, "I love you, and I also love the following twenty acquaintances just as much." The indiscriminate list—Marjorie Perloff calls it a "litany"[11]—is not only mock epic but mock romantic as well.

"I'm so damned literary . . . I'm so damned empty," O'Hara writes in another poem.[12] What fills up this *sammler* of images are the names of people and places and products he encounters in everyday life. The movies are the paradigm of such casual empirical acquaintance with the multitudinous appearances of the modern city. This is one of many poems in which O'Hara, like Whitman, divulges or vomits forth such data. The reader's pleasure in perusing the list of names, each with some epithet or motif like a collection of captioned stills, is the narrow but satisfying pleasure of recognition. One feels part of the poet's, and the culture's, privileged engagement with a secondary world seemingly infinite in its variety. Here is God's plenty, one might think, while reading this list and generating more names from one's private experience of the movies. One might not know Sue Carroll—the most esoteric of the citations—or not know the film referred to in "Clark Gable rescuing Gene Tierney / from Russia" (the film is *Never Let Me Go*, 1953), but paradoxically not recognizing a certain number of references enhances the effect of the poem, for we are made to appreciate how abundant our film heritage really is. And along the way, O'Hara relieves us of the embarrassment of our own guilty pleasures, sure to be no more ridiculous than Sue Carroll and Alice Faye. In general, O'Hara makes the movies more congenial for readers by treating them not as an art form or a symbol of modern technology, but simply as an adolescent pastime like baseball or teenage music. The more he inflates the tone of his poem by reference to the star system as "The divine precedent you perpetuate" the more demystified the subject becomes. Unlike the genuinely reverent tone of Lindsay on Mae Marsh, O'Hara installs the Muse amid the kitchenware and croons an operatic aria at her that winks conspiratorially at the eavesdropper.

In short, O'Hara is working in the same manner as earlier poets who found cinematic form a congenial model for their urban sensibility. O'Hara's long lines may be an homage to Whitman, but for the witty effects of incongruity he harks back even further to Augustan practice. Just as Alexander Pope establishes an equivalence of high and low by running together "Puffs, powders, patches, Bibles, billet-doux" in describing Belinda's dressing table, so O'Hara artfully jams together "Marilyn Monroe in her little spike heels reeling through Niagara Falls, / Joseph Cotten puzzling and Orson Welles puzzled and Dolores Del Rio / eating orchids for lunch and breaking mirrors." The pleasure of reading such lines is a film buff's knowing connection of *Niagara*, in which Joseph Cotten responds murderously to Marilyn Monroe's infidelities, with *Journey into Fear*, in which Cotten plays a confused businessman in Turkey to Orson Welles's detective and Dolores Del Rio's mysterious fellow traveler. But Del Rio does not eat any orchids in this thriller; one must segue to ... what film? Some inane comedy, no doubt. We are inside what O'Hara called his "movie-fed head" on a roller-coaster ride through the accidental conjunctions of spontaneously generated memories. Of poems like this one might say, as O'Hara did about Happenings, "It's supposed to remind you that art is fun and that we're all children and that it's marvelous."[13]

"To the Film Industry in Crisis" is a poem full of *schpritzing*, to adopt Pinsky's term, but is it like "Ave Maria" an example of "homosexual *schpritzing*"? The easy answer to this question would make use of Susan Sontag's classic essay of 1964 on camp to argue that, yes, O'Hara's shower of affectionate praise on subjects he assumes his reader will recognize as infra dig creates the disjuncture between form and content essential to camp sensibility. Since homosexuals are identified as the aristocratic vanguard of camp, the poem falls automatically into the category of "epicene" or "gay." In an essay on John Rechy's novel *City of Night*, O'Hara directs us to another way of thinking about the matter, however. He refers to Rechy's "run-on casual, or hysterical faggoty diction . . . the Exact tone of homosexual bar talk."[14] The poem, too, arguably attempts to mimic the performance characteristics of a subculture crazy about Hollywood movies and eager to talk about them in the theatrical rush of language common to gay locales. Though gay language per se does not exist, a gay or underground manner can signal to the reader certain kinds of emotional investment in the subject that lends a poem more depth. As with his agonized poems on the death of James Dean, O'Hara makes it clear in this comic poem how much his love of the movies is a matter of desperately embracing the icons of popular culture. Devoted to imageless and abstract painting, he reserved one part of his imagination for the glamorous representations with whom he could make the kind of direct, if anonymous, emotional contact he experienced as a lovelorn adolescent. O'Hara's indifference to experimental film, so often the province of the homosexual artist such as Andy Warhol, Jack Smith, and Kenneth Anger, and so often self-consciously hermetic in its narratives, has much to do with his sense of Hollywood movies as a fantasy lifeline to the majority culture. Like most gay moviegoers, O'Hara recognized intuitively that he could appropriate Hollywood movies by acting on their subtextual cues and subversive inflections. (Sometimes not so *sub*textual, as when *Rebel without a Cause* permits the male viewer homoerotic access to James Dean by means of the Sal Mineo character.) Though much has been written about the affinities of O'Hara's poems with Jackson Pollock's improvisatory paintings, the more significant connection between his poems of personal friendship and the animated arts may well be with the "iconoclasms" of Valentino, the Marx Brothers, and Mae West.

"Long may you illumine space with your marvellous appearances," he writes. It is in the last stanza that the "crisis" recurs to mind, as the plangency of O'Hara's appeal makes itself felt in the aftermath of his antic catalog. Time has already finished off the careers of some of his actors—this may be the meaning of "I cannot bring myself to prefer Johnny Weissmuller to Lex Barker, I cannot!" And some of the careers have changed from the romantic to the postromantic, such as Myrna Loy, who is playing "calm and wise" matrons in the mid-1950s rather than the sexy, keen-witted Nora Charles to William Powell's Nick. (Powell's career is finished by

1957.) But Elizabeth Taylor is "blossoming," and so is Marilyn Monroe, though her life will be cut short like James Dean's, and O'Hara's as well. The toll of names in the catalog is accompanied by the tolling of bells in the distance, plainly audible to those who have something of O'Hara's encyclopedic knowledge of the movies. If the poem is partly about O'Hara's powers of articulation and preservation, as all love poems may be said to be about the power of the poet to praise the beloved, it is also about the way adolescent passions are abruptly terminated in a world less immortal than the silver screen. The passion to create from what one has loved and lost is infinitely more endangered than the movie industry, so that by endorsing the projected icons of shared fantasy the poet strengthens his own power by means of appropriate(d) knowledge. The "crisis" is resolved through the imperatives of this representative moviegoer: "Roll on, reels of celluloid, as the great earth rolls on!" The mantric force of his rhapsodic appeal parodies Byron's famous apostrophe in *Childe Harold's Pilgrimage:* "Roll on, thou deep and dark blue Ocean—roll!" O'Hara's peroration may be a needless gesture of support for the movies, which were no more likely to cease their motion than the ocean, but it loudly and successfully signaled a generation of his contemporaries to take up the cultic enumerations where he left off.

Perhaps the unlikeliest poet to engage the subject in O'Hara's spirit was John Hollander, in the title work of his 1962 collection *Movie-Going.* Hollander had just published a critical work of imposing erudition, *The Untuning of the Sky: Ideas of Music in English Poetry, 1500–1700,* and his ongoing attempt to make use of the full range of English topoi and rhetorical forms can be seen in the 1962 volume. The longest poem of the volume, "Upon Apthorp House," obviously nods toward Andrew Marvell's "Upon Appleton House" as a forerunner in the country-house tradition. Likewise, the lengthy "Eclogue" looks back to classical models for its form and thematic argument. To read Hollander is to become reacquainted with Theocritus and Horace, with Milton and Spenser. No other modern American poet has worked so hard to incorporate the traditional manners of Western poetry into his own prolific practice. At first glance he would seem to have little in common with the ostentatiously colloquial O'Hara, whose free-verse extravaganzas pretend to reinvent poetic structures from scratch. But the fan-magazine tone of both poems links them in the common cause of preserving juvenile memory of the movies intact.

Hollander subdues his poem to the classical tradition by making it an elegy for the lost glamour of moviegoing in America. From O'Hara he derives the potent subject matter of the film industry in crisis and the oratorical model, and from the elegiac tradition he takes the tone of high seriousness that lifts this poem out of the category of camp and gives it *dignitas*. One hears the obvious tonal shift from O'Hara's risible repetitions:

> Gloria Swanson reclining,
> and Jean Harlow reclining and wiggling, and Alice Faye reclining
> and wiggling and singing . . .

to Hollander's:

> Remember those who have gone—
> (Where's bat-squeaking Butterfly McQueen? Will we see again
> That ever-anonymous drunk, waxed-moustached, rubber-
>   legged
> Caught in revolving doors?) and think of the light-years logged
> Up in those humbly noble orbits, where no hot
> Spotlight of solar grace consumes some blazing hearts,
> Bestowing the flimsy immortality of stars
> For some great instant.[15]

As Robert von Hallberg remarks of a different passage of the poem, "Hollander has his tongue in his cheek, but not so firmly that he cannot praise."[16] Part of the effect comes from the address to the reader rather than, as in O'Hara's case, to the film industry or the stars themselves. The poem is shaped as an instruction to the public on the protocols of authentic emotion. One notes the directly intoned *ubi sunt* convention in his lament for Butterfly McQueen, best known for her role in the elegiac *Gone with the Wind*, and the refusal to make a joke of the pun on "stars" but rather to refresh the trope by taking it seriously and extending it as a governing conceit. No doubt his work on ideas of harmony in the Renaissance inspired Hollander to imagine not only actors and actresses but later in the poem the whole constellation of movie houses as a kind of Platonic reflection of the perfect order of the heavens. Mars and Venus shine most brightly, he tells us in the lines following the passage quoted above, but one must look beyond their brazen fame toward the "humble" bodies or asteroids that shoot by beyond the spotlights, such as Butterfly McQueen or the anonymous drunk, and regard them as contributing parts of the harmony of the universe.

The list is a powerful device for insisting on the significance of what is otherwise overlooked; it rescues the neglected and makes the point that every life, every place, is worthy of attention and sympathy, and—in the most extreme form—the caressing affection of the poet as he savors the names his speech will preserve from oblivion. O'Hara's speech is inflected toward the phrasing of captions or gossip columns or the patois of the weekly newsmagazine. His epithets may also be a special case of what has been called queertalk, in a register derived from a minority coterie. Hollander seeks a broader music to represent the potential profundity of the topic. Capitalization of the initial letter in each line, as opposed to O'Hara's casual lowercase, sets the tone for Hollander's magisterial adherence to the great tradition. The iambic hexameter couplets offer us a variety of harmonious chimes and off rhymes to please the ear, as in "Will we see a*gain*" recalling "those who have *gone*" or the "immortality of *stars*" counterpointed to "Out of the darkness *stares.*" The nasal m's of "humbly," "consumes," and "immortality" play off against the plosive t's of "hot," "Spotlight," and "hearts." If O'Hara is vaudeville, obvious and zany, Hollander inclines more toward the art movie or opera, flattering the trained ear with recognizable melodies to anchor the indecorous subject matter.

Another way of saying this is that Hollander persuades us that he knows more about movie history than does O'Hara, because he knows more about the history of verse, as if erudition is contagious from one art to the other. O'Hara can match him for epithets, certainly; "peach-melba-voiced Fred Astaire of the feet" is just as vivid as "bat-squeaking Butterfly McQueen." But Hollander can explain precisely *why* we should attend to "bit-players" like Donald Meek or Eugene Pallette who mimic the minor situation of most readers in their own life-scenarios. Hollander sees too that moviegoing has much to do with the sanctity of the theater, the place of revelation:

I remember: the RKO COLONIAL; the cheap
ARDEN and ALDEN both; LOEW'S LINCOLN SQUARE's
  bright shape;
The NEWSREEL; the mandarin BEACON, resplendently ar-
  rayed

and so on for twenty-one more lines. So often the names of the
vanishing theaters suggest the mandarin quality of their wrought
illusion (the Thalia, the Symphony), so that even readers who have
never had contact with them can drink in the romantic associations.
And Hollander's objection to the degradation of theaters into merely
functional markets for fish and vegetables, their marquees blazoned
with sale items, speaks to the "transmogrified" character of 1950s and
1960s America, increasingly unromantic, materialistic, utilitarian. In
the multiplication of TV antennas Hollander sees a sign of the unrav-
eling of the congregational spirit. The special pleasure of taking one's
children to the theaters one was taken to as a child by one's parents—
that great experience of intergenerational bonding has been ruptured
in the postwar era. At the head of the list Hollander places the insis-
tent note of retrospection: "I remember." Here it is much clearer that
the crisis of the movies is a crisis in the life of the aging moviegoer
who increasingly must subsist on shadows of shadows, dimming
recollections detached from the sacred places and icons of the imagi-
nation. Here one finds the urban equivalent of Wordsworth's sorrow
at the gradual desolation of his places of refuge in the Lake District,
and his sorrow at the fading of that unique light he described in the
"Ode: Intimations of Immortality" as the master light of all our days.

  If Hollander's poem derives from O'Hara, it also surpasses any
of O'Hara's fifty-four poems that Jim Elledge counts as relying to a
significant degree upon the movies. One laughs at O'Hara's feigned
horror at the all-caps headline, "LANA TURNER COLLAPSES,"
and at his high-pitched command, "oh Lana Turner we love you get
up." (A gay critic characterizes the line as "one *queen* addressing an-
other."[17]) But Hollander's artful mixture of higher and lower diction
and his supple articulation give "Movie-Going" a unique place in the
tradition of the movie poem. O'Hara's tribute implies elegy without
tapping its enormous reservoir of rhetorical (and thus emotional)
possibilities. By seizing upon the full dimensions of the Hollywood

crisis and internalizing them in the Romantic mode, Hollander con-
structed one of the most artful poems of his generation.

Star- and asteroid-gazing poets who insisted on the reality as well as
the illusion of that "some place wholly elsewhere" Hollander apo-
theosized became fascinated with the pastness of Hollywood, as a
metaphor for their own aging and for the transformation of American
culture. The elegiac mode they adopted to meditate on the deaths of
eminent public figures—for such the stars had become—is a measure
of how intimately these actors and actresses had become involved in
the psychic lives of the poets. The elegies were sometimes whimsical
and mock forms, as in Hollander's "To the Lady Portrayed by Mar-
garet Dumont," from *Movie-Going*, but they could be earnest enough
to serve as the modern equivalent of the pastoral elegy on the death
of a fellow poet. When O'Hara speaks in the voice of James Dean in
one of his three elegies on the actor, he makes it clear that Dean was
so much a part of himself, a love object internalized as a personal
double, that his poems of mourning are testaments of a debrided
identity. A friend of O'Hara's and Hollander's, a fellow flaneur in the
metropolis, Allen Ginsberg adapts their methods in some of his po-
ems that touch on movie figures. It is not just playfulness that gener-
ates a passage like the following:

Where's Stravinsky? Theda Bara? Chaplin? Harpo Marx?
    Where's Laurel and his Hardy?
                        Laughing phantoms
                        going to the grave—
Last time this town   I saw them in movies
    Ending *The Road to Utopia*   'O Carib Isle!'
    Laurel aged & white-haired Hardy
            Hydrogen Comic smoke billowing
                up from their Kingdom[18]

Ginsberg's tribute to Laurel and Hardy in *The Fall of America*
(1973) illustrates the allusive nature of the elegiac sentiment in poetry
after O'Hara. The passage quoted above is immediately preceded by
a section in which Ginsberg is haunted by the ghosts of his previous
visits to Los Angeles, especially the figures of Neal Cassady and

Lawrence Ferlinghetti. These shades of time past are redolent with happy associations. Neal Cassady, the Dean Moriarty of Jack Kerouac's *On the Road,* symbolized the careless freedom of adolescence, the wholehearted acceptance of worldly life that Whitman urged upon Americans in "Song of the Open Road" as the supreme adventure of the spirit. On the road with his friends Ginsberg had found sufficient paradise in the beat of life, its momentary pulsations. In this section of *The Fall of America* his recollection of picnicking in a canyon with his comrades represents the pastoral dream that the Beat movement celebrated. In his camera eye it shines like the glow in Winfield Townley Scott's first peek into the Mutoscope: *We will lie in the sun . . . a long time in the sun.*

But by 1965 all that has passed away. Ginsberg is now, in a phrase he uses elsewhere, "rotting Ginsberg," a ruin of time. Surrounded by shades of his former pleasures he lapses (as Hollander did) into the *ubi sunt* of conventional elegy. François Villon used this formula to recall famous beauties, John Lydgate to lament the fall of princes; Ginsberg turns to modern star presences equally admired by the masses. After listing a few names—Stravinsky presumably set among the stars because he lived in Los Angeles—Ginsberg artfully settles on Laurel and Hardy as a means of linking the ghosts of his personal life with public phantoms. Laurel and Hardy serve his purpose in several ways. First, they represent the happy male fellowship that Ginsberg had just summoned in the references to Cassady and Ferlinghetti. Vito Russo has argued that of all the classic slapstick comedies featuring buddies, Laurel and Hardy films offer the most overtly homoerotic situations and dialogue.[19] The allusion to Hart Crane's Key West poem " 'O Carib Isle' " has as one of its functions the extension of homoerotic sympathies backward into the American poetic tradition. (Crane, in *The Bridge,* had reached his hand back to Whitman.) Though Ginsberg composed this section before Neal Cassady's death in 1968, the elegies about Cassady bound into *The Fall of America* enhance the significance of Ginsberg's cameo memorial of the two comics.

It is important, too, that Ginsberg remembers (or invents) the fact that when he last visited Los Angeles he saw a film in which Laurel and Hardy appeared aged and feeble. In fact, *Utopia* (1951), also called *Atoll K,* is a painful experience for viewers who know the comics only from the athletic mime of their early films. The poet, in his newly adopted persona of "rotting Ginsberg" uses, though he does not exploit, the pathos of their decline to extend a personal obsession.

Utopia serves him in another way. He misquotes the title as *The Road to Utopia,* so that the word road, with its resonant associations with Whitman and Kerouac, will knit together the motifs of the poem. (It recalls as well the Crosby-Hope road movies, including a *Road to Utopia,* models of carefree male fellowship.) *Utopia,* a French-Italian coproduction, depicts how Laurel and Hardy achieve governance of a uranium-rich kingdom but lose it amid revolution, chaos, and exploding bombs that resemble the atomic holocausts that haunted America in the postwar years. The man-made "Hydrogen Comic smoke" billowing up in Ginsberg's poem thus updates the ghastly but wholly natural "tropic death" that Crane imagines at the conclusion of "'O Carib Isle'":

You have given me the shell, Satan—carbonic amulet
Sere of the sun exploded in the sea.

Ginsberg has linked the fall-of-princes convention to his ongoing fears about the cold war. The whole of *The Fall of America* attempts to chart America's decline from a libertarian utopia, conceived in revolution, into an oppressive imperial power whose adventurism in Vietnam threatens not only the lives of young men on the battlefield but just such a holocaust as the comic film dramatizes.

"The forces of darkness spread everywhere now, and the best / And brightest screens fade out," lamented Hollander. The fading of screens and screen actors became the source of a new Graveyard School of poets, whose mordant texts documented the gradual encroachment of the forces of darkness upon themselves and their culture. Robert Frost had originated the mode in his poem of the 1930s, "Provide, Provide," in which "the picture pride of Hollywood," the famous Abishag, has withered in this period of Depression into an impoverished "hag" and washerwoman. Her pathetic fall from high estate startles the poet into a high-pitched defense of ruthless money-grubbing lest he and his readers someday share her fate. In "The Lost World," Randall Jarrell sees the props of a movie about the extinct saurians, and is prompted to memories about his own lost world of childhood, the Eden or dreamtime of fantasy extinguished by the

light of common day. Gregory Corso's lament for Errol Flynn in
Elegiac Feelings American (1978) has a clear affinity with the poems
by O'Hara, Hollander, and Ginsberg. Robert Lowell devotes a com-
memorative sonnet to Harpo Marx in *History;* David R. Slavitt like-
wise memorializes Randolph Scott and Joel McCrea in his poem
"Ride the High Country," a recreation of their pathos-filled film of
that title about aged cowboys and the end of the Old West.[20]

The O'Hara line of poets nourished by the vitality and charm of the
movies culminates in Edward Field's volume, *Variety Photoplays,*
published in 1967. These campy retellings of classic Hollywood genre
pictures—"White Jungle Queen," "The Bride of Frankenstein"—had
two qualities that earned them an enthusiastic audience: they were
easy to understand and they were funny. In reading them and (inevi-
tably) reciting them to friends, one recaptured the pleasure not only
of old movies but of one's adolescent delight in narrative poems—in
"The Raven," for example, or "The Highwayman." *Variety Photo-
plays* rode the rising tide of academic interest in popular culture, and
especially film studies, which had crept into the curriculum without
losing the mystique of its cultic origins. The strong nostalgia running
through pop culture expresses a primitivist regret for our having
exchanged the childhood experiences of storytelling and song for the
fascination of what's difficult. Edward Field was not difficult.
    Indeed, avoiding the difficulty of "highbrow" poems (his term)
was Field's chief ambition as a young poet. "I . . . rebelled against
my generation's poetry of the 'cultivated' man," Field has written,
"and insisted on writing out of what I couldn't deny, that at bottom,
I was still little Eddie Field of Lynbrook, starstruck, fucked up, and
with a language that came out of my immigrant Jewish back-
ground."[21] By removing himself from competition with the line of
poets descended from Eliot through Robert Lowell and Richard
Wilbur—erudite masters of highly-wrought traditional and innova-
tive rhetorical forms—Field backed into the powerful countercultural
movement of the late 1960s, in which his good-humored, movie-
inspired fantasies of sexual release found a congenial home. Like
Shapiro, Field links his Jewishness to his working hypothesis that
movie stars are surrogate agents for the audience's repressed sexual-
ity, even when the films have little to do with romance. Since these
are the primal texts of our postchildhood lives, the stories bear retell-

ing for the same reason the folk cling to their ballads, because of the stories' deep immersion in the libidinous stuff of the unconscious.

The notion that film stories are nothing more than elaborate disguises for psychic needs was popularized in the essays of Parker Tyler, a poet whose overheated prose owed something to the hermeneutics he practiced. (Gore Vidal lampoons Tyler's style throughout *Myra Breckenridge*.) Tyler emphasized the seductive aspects of film, the way movies are shaped to engineer dreamlike liaisons between actor or actress and filmgoers. These fantasy couplings, and not the screen stories (in the Freudian sense as well), constitute the fundamental experience of cinema, he claimed. Tyler's poetics joins together the pantheon of classical legends with the depth analysis of Freudian and Jungian theory to create both a sophisticated American mythology and a sophisticated audience of dark interpreters. Field drilled himself to systematically *see through* the dressed-up plots of old movies to the hedonistic dream play of bodily desires being enacted by the shadows on the screen, abstracting actors—and more often actresses—from the distraction of plots, and featuring plots without the distraction of actors.

O'Hara, Hollander, and Ginsberg might flaunt consumer icons for the titillation of the informed reader, but Field is the first to attempt a *Metamorphoses* to recreate the condition of moviegoing both as homage and critique. His satirical retellings of classic movies mortify his—and our—nostalgic fondness for those hokey plots we drank in at matinees, but they do so in order to effect a heightening of consciousness. From childhood we are trained in movie theaters to recognize artifice in the tension of actor and story, of powerful desire and aesthetic constraint. Literary theory has demonstrated how a cunning poet creates subversive effects for a competent audience. But only recently have academic critics acknowledged that popular art can create the same effects. Perhaps a fool does see the same film that a wise man sees. Field plays the fool by aping the crude contents of old movies, but he intends for us to see through him too, and recognize universal human nature all the better for his comic underlining.

One can write about these dynamics as a moralist—as Tyler did—or reproduce them as an artist. Field's limpid style and unprepossessing good humor allow him to retell his tribal fictions with a faux-naïf flexibility of belief. An ironist who sees only the absurdity of film stories would miss their subliminal impact, their tenacious

purchase upon our adolescent conditioning. By means of a studied
artlessness, Field keeps a precarious balance:

> she is tormented by the knowledge of her tendency:
> That she daren't hug a man
> unless she wants to risk clawing him up.
>
> This puts you both in a difficult position—
> panting lovers who are prevented from touching,
> not by bars but by circumstance:
> You have terrible fights and say cruel things
> for having the hots does not give you a sweet temper.
> ("The Curse of the Cat Woman")

> She sighed, and went off to work in the five and ten
> wearing her made-over dress with little washable collar and
>   cuffs.
> Even with her prole accent and the cheap bag and shoes
> she was a good looker.
> Men used to come by in their flashy suits and big cigars,
> call her tootsie and ask for a date,
> but she knew a poor girl didn't stand a chance with them.
> She wasn't one of those innocents
> who thinks a guy loves you if he gets a hard-on.
> ("The Life of Joan Crawford")

The knowing tone, which alerts the reader by such diction as "hots"
and "hard-on" that we are in the realm of low comedy, nevertheless
accommodates an element of folk wisdom that cannot be laughed
away. The vagaries of sexual desire are so powerful that no formulaic
treatment or pastiche, however hackneyed, can render them entirely
foreign to our humanity. Likewise, the humdrum materials of Joan
Crawford's life—"her made-over dress with little washable collar and
cuffs" and so forth—conceal a vitality and resourcefulness rising tri-
umphantly from the ignominious clichés of American life ("good
looker," "tootsie," "poor girl") into actual identity. The poem's last
line: "Ladies and Gentlemen: Miss Joan Crawford." In a similar way,
the poem implies, each member of the audience can model some
evolution of self from the conditions of mass culture, the anonymity

and anomie of urban and rural places. "Movie stars have meaning for our common selves," Field remarks in an essay. "They are great compensatory beings for our crummy lives."[22]

Field's persistent attention to female stars—not only Joan Crawford but Mae West, Garbo, Dietrich, and the mythic figures of White Jungle Queen, Bride of Frankenstein, SHE, May Caspar, and the Cat Woman—does circumscribe his poetry and lock it into the category of camp. Though his other poetry is revelatory of gay experience, he does not write about male movie stars as O'Hara does in his elegies for James Dean, or Ginsberg in his use of Laurel and Hardy, to screen their feelings about male objects of desire and the indulgences of adolescence. This keeps Field's writing securely and beguilingly within the realm of playful make-believe, remote from the critical re-visioning one associates with knowledge of the world beyond the enchantments of Hollywood. Stars and scenarios provide him, as they do so many of his disciples, with the opportunity to compose in a lush and lavish style forbidden the modern poet by the grim tensions and fashionable ironics of the postwar era. When Field writes on Mae West, or Frank Polite on Carmen Miranda, or Gerald Burns on Boris Karloff, or Charles Webb on the movie *Tarantula,* the powerful rush of uninhibited and extravagant imagery represents an implied critique of the antiromantic impulses that inform the "cool style" of so much modern verse from the period of Imagism to that of Minimalism. In this way, too, movie poems mimic the status of movies in the culture at large.

The popularity of Field's takeoffs on movies of the golden age speaks to the yearning in late 1960s culture to withdraw from the bitter and divisive struggles over civil rights and the Vietnam War into some polymorphous fantasy world of the kind enjoyed in the Platonic cave of self-projected and self-delighting desire. Hollander had inverted the lesson of Plato's parable in "Movie-Going" by endorsing the superior value of the theater over the extratheatrical: "we creep into the dull / Blaze of mid-afternoon sunshine, the hollow dole / Of the real descends on everything." *Variety Photoplays,* too, reminded a reading public undergoing too much doleful reality of the centrality of artifice to their emotional life, but at the cost of putting asunder profound emotion and the will to act on the turbulent streets of the 1960s. How moviegoing could help reform public policy became an ethical question Field, like O'Hara, evaded or treated lightly.

In the work of Adrienne Rich, however, the movies are divested of all their camp qualities in order to advise moviegoing readers how to be responsible citizens rather than fans.

Chapter 7

Anna Karina as Natasha in *Alphaville* (1965) clutches the book of poems that helps to rescue her from the dystopian civilization built by computer technology. Poets of the 1960s like Adrienne Rich aspired to write that redemptive book as their countercultural act of liberation. (Courtesy British Film Institute.)

Chapter 7

"The Poet Is at the Movies": Adrienne Rich and the New Wave

IMAGES FOR GODARD

1. Language as city:: Wittgenstein:
   Driving to the limits
   of the city of words

   the superhighway streams
   like a comic strip

   to newer suburbs
   casements of shockproof glass

   where no one yet looks out
   or toward the coast where even now

   the squatters in their shacks
   await eviction

   When all conversation
   becomes an interview
   under duress

   when we come to the limits
   of the city

   my face must have a meaning

2. To know the extremes of light
   I sit in this darkness

   To see the present flashing
   in a rearview mirror

blued in a plateglass pane
reddened in the reflection

of the red Triomphe
parked at the edge of the sea

the sea glittering in the sun
the swirls of nebula

in the espresso cup
raindrops, neon spectra

on a vinyl raincoat

3. To love, to move perpetually
   as the body changes

   a dozen times a day
   the temperature of the skin

   the feeling of rise & fall
   deadweight & buoyancy

   the eye sunk inward
   the eye bleeding with speech

   for that moment at least
   I wás you—

   To be stopped, to shoot the same scene over & over

4. At the end of *Alphaville*
   she says *I love you*

   and the film begins
   that you've said you'd never make

   because it's impossible:
   things as difficult to show
   as horror & war & sickness are

   meaning *love,*
   to speak in the mouth

   to touch the breast
   for a woman

to know the sex of a man
That film begins here

yet you don't show it
we leave the theatre

suffering from that

5. Interior monologue of the poet:
   the notes for the poem are the only poem

   the mind collecting, devouring
   all these destructibles

   the unmade studio couch the air
   shifting the abalone shells

   the mind of the poet is the only poem
   the poet is at the movies
   dreaming the film-maker's dream but differently
   free in the dark as if asleep

   free in the dusty beam of the projector
   the mind of the poet is changing

   the moment of change is the only poem[1]
   —1971

In an essay of the early 1960s Stanley Kauffmann relates an anecdote about delivering a speech containing the same ideas he incorporates into the essay. After his lecture, "a distinguished poet and a critic of the graphic arts"—he has since identified them as Stanley Kunitz and Frederic Tuten[2]—approached him, and the critic remarked, "You destroyed us. You wiped out our professions. You rendered my friend and me obsolete." Kauffmann demurred, but if his essay is any indication, he must certainly have terrified anyone in the audience who pursued an artistic field other than cinema. As Kauffmann acknowledges, "His dismal reaction had been prompted by my assertion that film is the art for which there is the greatest spontaneous appetite in America at present."[3] Kauffmann's term for this appetitive audience, "The Film Generation," has had a vigorous life in film historiography since the essay was published. It refers not to total numbers of patrons, for moviegoing had declined in America since the 1940s, but to the elite public of aesthetes historically coveted by poets and painters, as well as critics of the sister arts. Young intellectuals who sought a unique membership in the present were gravitating to "art houses" for their primal media experiences, so much so that their proprietary feeling threatened the viability of verse in a visual culture.

As Kauffmann was quick to note on the first page of his essay, imports rather than Hollywood products dominated the attention of the film generation. The films of Ingmar Bergman, Federico Fellini, Michelangelo Antonioni, Akira Kurosawa, Francois Truffaut, Jean-Luc Godard, and *many* others offered avant-garde pleasures at a time when American movies seemed to have hyperinflated into lumbering spectacles, broad comedies, and sentimental musicals. Lacking the innovative editing and bolder subject matter of the European and Japanese art film, American movies had significantly less chance of captivating a sophisticated, college-educated audience. As a member of that generation, one who graduated high school in 1960 and became enthralled by the originality and profundity of foreign films, I can testify to the accuracy of Kauffmann's commentary. Even British films seemed far advanced beyond American products, with the exception of Alfred Hitchcock, himself a British import. In retrospect one acknowledges the pretension of such a snobbish posture, and yet at the time it made a perfect fit with the restless search for unconventional behaviors that characterized the 1960s generation. One could not enjoy the existentialist philosophers and the Beat poets, the warring modes of abstract expressionist and pop art painting, the manic rhythms of rock and roll and the distractions of television and still feel comfortable with sluggishly paced and routinely plotted films like *Judgement at Nuremberg* and *The Sound of Music,* no matter how many Oscars they won. Rather than what Kauffmann called "an exhausted naturalistic technique," the new audience, including poets, sought "the new life of surfaces" offered by an experimental cinema.

The first thing to notice about Adrienne Rich's poem, then, is that it is offered in tribute to Jean-Luc Godard, the most innovative of the foreign filmmakers. Not for her the O'Hara-like homage to Hollywood's golden era; she rejects American popular culture as a subject and, by her demanding stylistics, aligns her poetry with the high cultural discourse of the art film. Rich had displayed a familiarity with French film in her early poems, alluding, for example, to Raimu in "A Marriage in the 'Sixties" and to Louis Jouvet in "Necessities of Life." In *The Will to Change* (1971) she uses French film as the dominant reference point for her interpretation of the 1960s. One poem from the volume, "Pierrot Le Fou," plays with images and sentiments from that film by Godard. Another poem adapts material from Jean Cocteau's *Orphée* to develop its lyric point. No important poet before Rich focused so extensively in a single volume on foreign film. And the other part of her title, "Images for," calls attention to the nonlinear, associative, indeed often aleatory technique for which Godard was famous. Rich's volume concludes with a long poem, "Shooting Script," that mimics the montage effect of some of Godard's more adventurous scenarios. Whether or not Rich's assertion that "the poet is at the movies" is too categorical, clearly Rich herself was studying the shape of Godard's films as a way of breaking out of her former rhetoric and developing an idiosyncratic style that spoke to her rebellious generation.

Rich directs her reader's attention to Godard for self-serving reasons, then. Godard emerged in the late 1960s as the supreme type of what we would now call a deconstructive artist. He served a dutiful apprenticeship in the medium as a film critic, studying the traditional techniques and narratives with a scholar's patience, and writing about them scrupulously in *Cahiers du Cinéma* and *Arts*. Hollywood films were his speciality, as they were the favorites of all the *Cahiers* critics, and Godard mastered their formal contrivances just as Rich began her career by assimilating the manners of Robert Frost, W. B. Yeats, and Robert Lowell. But whereas Rich's apprenticeship involved the actual composition of poems in a derivative style, Godard understood from his first day behind a camera that "as soon as you can make films, you can no longer make films like the ones that made you want to make them."[4] His first important film, *A Bout de souffle* (1960), enacted in several ways his distance from the films he admired. First, he cast Jean Seberg as the nihilistic American girl Patricia Franchini, who would rather be Swedish and named "Ingrid." Seberg was famous as Otto Preminger's discovery for the role of Joan of Arc in his rendition of *Saint Joan,* a costume drama in which her glazed expression seemed less spiritual than empty-headed—as Godard cunningly perceived. Aimlessly wandering among cars and cafes and buildings in modern Paris, the antiheroine Seberg meets her match in the disaffected Michel Poiccard (Jean-Paul Belmondo), who shapes his behavior in imitation of Humphrey Bogart roles. These inauthentic types represent the contemporary that cannot sit comfortably within the conventional shape of a Hollywood film, in part because they are signs of Hollywood itself, any more than postwar society can obey the codes and dynamics of an exhausted cultural tradition. Godard's dedramatization of plot, and depersonalization of characters, opened up opportunities for a new direction in movies: a new content and a new rhetoric.

With the loosening of conventional plot structure in favor of a more episodic and arbitrary arrangement of visual elements—something Godard claimed to have learned from Hollywood B movies where the plot was so formulaic that the director paradoxically had the freedom to fill the ninety minutes with surprising and bizarre scenes, shots, and scraps of dialogue—Godard's films began to allow into themselves an astonishing amount of diverse material that asked only to be savored for its quality of being stimulating and memorable. "You can put anything and everything into a film, but you *must* put everything," Godard wryly remarked.[5] The pleasure of a Godard movie was in the abundance of contemporary imagery one was exposed to, not because everything belonged, as in the classic well-made play or film, but precisely because the spontaneous or unexpected could jar one out of the trance induced by customary and socialized expectations. It's not that Godard had a special vision that he put into competition against the inherited structures; on the contrary, his films were a running critique of any kind of autonomous and perfected ideology. (Now they seem limited by their period ambiguities.) They offered incongruous images for the purpose of frustrating filmgoers who knew what to expect from movies, even foreign movies. They were playful to an extreme, part of the erotics of art that cultural critics were calling for in the 1960s.

As in the 1920s, then, montage form appealed to a rebellious generation seeking a refreshment of epistemological habits and narrative formulas. Montage foregrounds the image not as a serviceable unit in a tightly constructed whole that is greater than the sum of its parts, but as a thing of value in itself. In Godard's films such images are often literary allusions, verbal texts that carry one back into history, so that the films achieve that paradoxical conventionality that comes from constant attention to the traditional. In a scene from *Bande à part,* Godard cites T. S. Eliot's dictum that any work that is genuinely new is automatically traditional. As in *The Waste Land,* a Godard film will collect fragments, or what Rich calls "destructibles," in order to formulate a text that possesses, in Godard's phrase, "the essence of the moment." What holds together a film of such diverse elements is the audience's alert willingnesss to take them seriously as they surface, to overhear or eavesdrop on Godard's sensibility, moment by moment. And this is what the Film Generation gladly did.

Turning to "Images for Godard," we see that Rich's first homage to the allusive Godard is to return the favor: she begins the poem with a quotation from Wittgenstein, which she will develop as a fundamental and highly cinematic image. "Language as city" derives from Wittgenstein's remark in *Philosophical Investigations* that "our language can be seen as an ancient city: a maze of little streets and squares, of old and new houses with additions from various periods; and this surrounded by a multitude of new boroughs with straight regular streets and uniform houses."[6] The remark deliberately evokes Freud's famous comparison of the unconscious to a buried city, specifically ancient Rome, with its strata and subterranean structures. Since Freud had based his view of the unconscious on its language-generating and language-transforming potential, Wittgenstein's commentary carries with it much of Freud's attribution of psychic reality to language itself, language as the carrier of the unconscious's fundamental desires and memories.

Rich is using the ideas of three European intellectuals, then, to legitimize a view of language, and by extension verse, that breaks free from the mimetic or representational character of poetry as she has received it from her modern masters. Her earlier poems, often in conventional meter and rhyme, had preserved a clear boundary between the external and internal, between dream and reality, between the work of art and what it observed and recorded. By the mid-1960s she is obviously chafing against a poetics in which "Language as city" mandated logical and linear construction:

> They're tearing down, tearing up
> this city, block by block.
> Rooms cut in half

hang like flayed carcasses,
their old roses in rags,
famous streets have forgotten
where they were going. Only
a fact could be so dreamlike.
They're tearing down the houses
we met and lived in,
soon our two bodies will be all
left standing from that era.

                              ("Like This Together")

By the time of *Necessities of Life* (1966) her eye is fixed on demolition, on radical change, on dispossession and disintegration. The old city is like the old self and its relations, and like the received language that articulated the self, a casualty of time and the will to change. Fact is becoming dreamlike at an accelerating pace, and the verse that enacts the decade's future shock is moving with greater speed, in shorter lines and more succint, even incomplete, images. Rooms are fragmented and streets forget where they're going, like the poems that increasingly jump-cut and digress, less and less likely to proceed methodically toward an emphatic closure. This is language that streams along "like a comic strip," an astonishing trope for a poet of Rich's solemnity, but, on second thought, true to the sense of language derived from the cinema, language as a sequence of stills or shots, words laid out in discrete visual order.

It's important to remember that the experience of viewing a foreign film is in large part the experience of *reading,* especially when the films are as talky as those of the French New Wave. "I grope for the titles," Rich comments in the poem "Pierrot Le Fou." Godard's dialogue is charged with contemporary idioms, but Rich confesses that "I speak the French language like a schoolgirl of the 'forties." The disjunction of word and image is an integral and vexing part of watching a foreign film. The necessity to read the translations and relate them to the visual action keeps the spectator from immersing herself in the narrative as an environment. One maintains of necessity a critical distance from the imperfectly understood story. Perhaps the distance is analogous to that of the poet's words in a visual culture, words that translate the activity of that culture to its participants. Or put another way, the foreignness of foreign film permits the poet to rediscover the contingent quality of words in relation to visual images and social praxis. The poet as title maker, as the essential but insufficient guide to the action, is an implied metaphor in Rich's writing. When she warns about "the temptations of the projector" in "Shooting Script," she is expressing her skepticism, in part, about the still- and shot-making capacity of poetry to mangle the wholeness of human activity by its pretense to be nothing more than a transparent window opening onto an intelligible reality. It is the very groping for words that protects the onlooker from being indoctrinated by the easy flow of language or imagery in the media. Alienation from "the oppressor's language," as she calls it in *The Will to Change*, is the first step toward a reconstitution of imaginative *and* social freedom.

In *The Will to Change* Rich registers her unease with received modes of language in "The Burning of Paper Instead of Children," in which the burning of texts becomes not only a thinkable but commendable activity. Texts are part of the mortmain of history that leads to the burning of children in Vietnam and elsewhere. Burning the texts is not equivalent to burning the images that inform texts; indeed the corrosive power of images liberated from texts, as her poem demonstrates, represents the artist's genuine power to change the minds and politics of her readers. She recalls the reading habits of her childhood:

> the crocodiles in Herodotus
> the Book of the Dead
> the *Trial of Jeanne d'Arc,* so blue
> I think, It is her color
>
> and they take the book away
> because I dream of her too often
>
> love and fear in a house
> knowledge of the oppressor
> I know it hurts to burn

Rich learned early the dual powers of language: to destroy, as in the legal documents that doomed Joan of Arc, and to liberate, as her reading about Joan of Arc gives her distance on the culture of the oppressors. She too is Joan of Arc punished by her parents for too much freethinking and dreaming. As in her later poem about the

"Savage Child" of Aveyron, she will associate the oppressor's language with an attempt by a logocentric culture to confine or constrict a natural creature. Dr. Itard in that poem, very likely influenced by Truffaut's film of 1970, *L'Enfant sauvage,* resembles the forces of logic she combated in her poems of homage to the surrealistic films of Cocteau and Godard. What she says of writing applies as well to her reading of subtitled films: "A radical critique of literature, feminist in its impulse, would take the work first of all as a clue to how we live, how we have been living, how we have been led to imagine ourselves, how our language has trapped as well as liberated us."[7]

In *Leaflets* (1969), Rich had experimented with deconstructing poetic language by adapting the ghazal form of Ghalib, a couplet sequence that anticipates the nonlinear discourse of "Shooting Script" in her next volume. Leaflets is a metaphor for poems, "scraps of paper" that compete for public attention with every other visual medium. By de-meaning verse she places it more securely in the inglorious landscape of "Images for Godard." The more vernacular the poetry, the more successfully it can subvert the official language of the 1960s, which has the flat inhuman quality of a civilization at war with nature. The "superhighway" rolls out to "newer suburbs," which are described as "casements of shockproof glass." Modernistic urban design has never appealed to Rich, and her resistance to it marks her as a member of the 1960s counterculture that preferred a nineteenth-century pastoralism to the so-called progressive technology overrunning the native land. (Paving paradise and making it into a parking lot, as Joni Mitchell put it in her famous song.) Here as elsewhere Rich belongs to a modernist tradition that declares a boundary break between past and present, inventing new artistic forms under the influence of technological changes, while at the same time nostalgic for at least some of the superseded values. The enemy, of the sensitive poet as well as "squatters in their shacks," becomes the forces of eviction and dispossession, driving an ethic of nature beyond the limits of the city. And so, even in the city of words, Rich concludes the poem's first part by affirming that "my face must have a meaning." On the one hand, this is a warning to the more Wittgensteinian poets who by the 1960s, and especially afterward, will take the city of words as their exclusive locus. To what extent, Rich asks, is the experimental tradition analogous to the reconstruction of the land into an unfriendly city of superhighways and suburbs? Where is the human face in such poetry? On the other hand it protests, in the manner of C. Wright Mills, Herbert Marcuse, Paul Goodman, Theodore Roszak, and other dissidents of the 1960s, the depradations of an Establishment that increasingly seemed to be annihilating the self as a matter of policy. Again, Godard provides a model of how to feature that face in the midst of some demonized alphaville of the cultural imagination.

(A flash-forward at this point might be useful. Rich will say in a later poem, "Natural Resources" [1977]:

There are words I cannot choose again:
humanism   androgyny

Most of the critical attention has gone to the word *androgyny,* since the lines seem to reject the more generous terms of poems like "Diving into the Wreck," which concluded that the dream of a common language would be reciprocally shared by males and females. But the rejection of "humanism" is the more serious one, for it contradicts the imaginative effort of all Rich's poetry to recuperate values from a varied past and distinguish them from what is life denying and sterile. To say that the word *humanism* is tainted because it was used hypocritically and cynically by men to justify their oppression is one thing; to deny that the concept has validity is not only self-defeating, it is belied by Rich's own poetic practice, which paradoxically has grown more conservative and conventional the more aggressively she has espoused behaviors such as lesbianism and radical feminism.)

The crucial thing to say about part 2 of the poem is that it does not show us a human face. When the poet says of her presence in a movie theater, "I sit in this darkness," she is preparing us for a Platonic critique of the imagery made available by film technology as a modern style. The montage of random images—the red Triomphe, the sea, the espresso cup, the vinyl raincoat—which simply stops without any discursive commentary in this section, makes the point that imagery itself, no matter how psychedelic and eye-catching, cannot satisfy the hunger of imagination for meaning of the kind that language has always articulated. Robert Hass makes the identical point in his poem "Heroic Simile," in which a scene from Kurosawa's film *Seven Samurai* causes him to glide in reverie from extracinematic image to image until he reaches the end of his competing scenario at the film's conclusion. Then: "A man and a woman walk from the movies / to the house in the silence of separate fidelities." The heroic simile the poet makes from the film scene does not create the solidarity one desires for actual relationships; the poem's last line is "There are limits to imagination."[8] No filmmaker knows this better than Godard, and the appeal of his art is the way his words so often are a critique of his images, a contrapuntal technique that Rich no less than Hass defines as the function of poetic language.

Alphaville (1965), the occasion of the poem, illustrates this point in the clearest possible way. The film sends an earthling, Lemmy Caution (played by Eddie Constantine), to a galactic empire called Alphaville ruled by Professor von Braun and his giant computer Alpha 60. The urban landscape of Alphaville is like the one described by Rich in the opening of "Images for Godard": superhighways and suburban boxy condos and many-windowed office buildings. A city of logic, designed in a circle (Godard's symbol of a closed system), it denies cultural memory as a matter of domestic policy. This is the city built by the oppressive language of the technetronic intelligentsia. The somnambulistic spirit of the place is the brainwashed Natasha von Braun (played by Anna Karina) whom Caution will rescue on his mission to destroy Alpha 60. "The present is all we can know of life," she says. "The present is the form of all life," says the computer. Caution's real mission is to redeem this robotlike woman, whose face is a model's blank gaze throughout the movie, and bring her back to an historicized world of emotional and instinctive vitality. Godard often depicts a romantic couple in which one partner represents the nineteenth century and one the twentieth century. Caution embodies the past, if not the distant past, and he does so by means of textual allusion. Eddie Constantine himself is a sign not only of many movies he had made previously for French television and film, including a series in which he portrays "Lemmy Caution," but for the world of American hard-boiled movies he summons in his performance. His tough-guy mannerisms, especially his dialogue, are derived from the film noir tradition, as are techniques like the black-and-white lighting and the melodramatic music. Though Natasha is the blank slate of the present, her name recalls Tolstoy's heroine in *War and Peace,* just as her father's code name, "Professor Nosferatu," alludes to Murnau's great vampire film. There is an allusion to Marcel

Carné's film *Le Jour se lève* on the soundtrack, and one to Céline's novel, *Voyage au bout de la nuit*. Caution is seeking another secret agent, Harry Dickson (played by Akim Tamiroff), whose name recalls a popular series of pulp novels in France, *The Adventures of Harry Dickson*. Professors Heckel and Jeckel are characters; one hears lines like "to sleep, perchance to dream" and "mon semblable, mon frère"; a seductress named Beatrice approaches Caution; and so on. The past has been repressed in Alphaville, but it returns in a myriad of words as an architecture of references, from the agents Dick Tracy and Flash Gordon inquired about at the beginning, to the Bible in several scenes. (The hotels provide daily dictionaries rather than Bibles, since the language is changed by authorities each day to defeat the claims of the past upon the present.) Natasha is saved when she can utter the most holy words of a humanistic past as Caution spirits her out of the demonic city: "Je... vous... aime."

And so in part 3 the poem's weight is thrown heavily upon the word *love*. The homophonics of "love" and "move" in the first line make the essential point that in a world where everything changes, love must change no less than the language which names or describes it. Love is a word we read in a rearview mirror; what it actually means must be tested through moment-by-moment measurements, like the temperature of the skin. Godard has the right idea, Rich is suggesting, by use of the montage format to mimic the continuous changes of custom and language alike, but her own response is determined by her different medium of expression: "the eye sunk inward / the eye bleeding with speech." The camera eye can never sink inward; it can only transcribe what appears outwardly before it. As she says in "Pierrot Le Fou," "the eye of the camera / doesn't weep tears of blood." "The eye" of the poem is the poet's eye that is turned back to the past by the cumulative accretions of language. The quoted lines insist on speech, on the flow of poetry, on language as a highway from the closed-off self to the Other. In the poem "Pierrot Le Fou," for example, Rich is driven inward by the film's images to a memory of her own travels in France in the 1940s. "France of the superhighways, I never knew you," she says. Here she is identifying with the film's aptly-named heroine Marianne Renoir, who is animal nature. (After her lover compares her to a fox, the camera cuts to a fox; two years after the film Rich will compare herself to a vixen in "Abnegation.") The poet's duty remains the Wordsworthian one of locating and cherishing those spots of time that capture a moment of pastoral pleasure or imaginative power related to language itself, to "shoot the same scene" even if the repetition compulsion threatens to retard the process of self-transformation. What is more old-fashioned, more ritualized in expression, than love between two people? And yet the poet has to declare it, and the filmmaker to show it.

Declaring the word *love* seemed to be a national obsession in the 1960s, an era when the Film Generation tried on love beads, spent Sunday afternoons at love-ins, and finally adopted the label of Love Generation. "All You Need Is Love," sang the Beatles on their album *Magical Mystery Tour,* and the utopianism of that *idée force* resonated throughout a self-selected collectivity eager to compose themselves into a romantic frame of mind. "Say the Word. . . . The Word is Love," the Beatles demanded in another song that translated the neo-Freudianism of Norman O. Brown's *Love's Body* into lyric expression even cats and dogs could understand. Robert Indiana's word image LOVE, in which the O was tilted like a heart, was the most widely distributed visual icon of the pop movement, plagiarized (in altered form) for the cover of Erich Segal's best-selling novel, *Love Story.* Love stories were everywhere, except in Alphaville, the unlovely civilization that Godard's and Rich's generation sought to redeem. But Rich complains to Godard on behalf of Natasha, "You don't show it." In a movie that shows so much and says so much, Rich cannot discern the word love becoming sufficiently embodied.

That Godard's modernity does not extend to a philosophy of liberation for women worries Rich. Just as she identified with Joan of Arc in childhood, so she cannot help but identify with Natasha in *Alphaville.* And she doesn't like the experience. In an essay she complains that whenever a woman reads about women in the masterpieces of male writing, "she finds a terror and a dream, she finds a beautiful pale face, she finds La Belle Dame Sans Merci." The represented woman is so often "the painted model and the poet's muse."[9] From the time of *A Bout de souffle* Godard had specialized in portraying such women in antiromances like the one between the Seberg and Belmondo characters. (Seberg informs on him to the police, and he is shot to death.) Brigitte Bardot is the archetypal object of desire in Godard's film about filmmaking, *Le Mépris* (1963), and later the director will feature his second wife, Anne Wiazemsky, in similar roles.

One critic calls this fascination with the model figure a "politique des ingenues."[10] In *Alphaville* the image of Natasha is of the doe-eyed (albeit mascaraed) mannequin, virtually expressionless, a passive princess figure in need of rescue by the resourceful male. The task of the somnambulistic girl is to fall in love. Rich quotes Godard as saying that some subjects are too difficult to show, and he names horrors and war and sickness. But she sees through his words to the most important absence: "meaning: love." The typographical gap emphasizes what cannot be readily spoken, the word Godard evades in his speech, and evades, she claims, in his film. "You don't show it / we leave the theatre // suffering from that." The "suffering"—a harsh term for the spectator's sense of ungratified expectation—comes from the abrupt ending of *Alphaville,* in which the new life promised by Natasha's espousal of love is curtailed almost as if it constituted a threat to society rather than a redemption of it. Seeing the movie critically in this way, Rich achieves a visionary break-through as to the limits of the will to change enacted by the cinematic method. Rich resists the identification enforced by the conventional gender roles of the movie. And that resistance is part of the will to change.

(Another flash forward. In the poem "Waking in the Dark" [1972], Rich describes the alluring image of bodies diving into a pool in Leni Riefenstahl's film of the Berlin Olympics. But the next part of the poem draws the imagery inward into the poet's consciousness where the erotics of Riefenstahl's images are verbalized and personalized:

> Over and over, starting to wake
> I dive back to discover you
> still whispering, *touch me,* we go on
> streaming through the slow
> citylight forest ocean
> stirring our body hair.

These are the ideal subtitles for Riefenstahl's abstract surfaces and indicate the poet's unique power to extend and fulfill the scarcely implied meanings of the cinematic images. Just as the viewer suffers in the Godard poem because the filmmaker won't show the breast of a woman or the sex of a man being touched, so Riefenstahl denies the viewer intimate contact with and between bodies in favor of treating the athletes as formal abstractions. Homage and critique go hand in hand in Rich's re-visioning of the fascist masterpiece.)

And so part 5 rejoices in the poet's power not only to mimic the filmmaker who can (even when he won't, as Godard won't) show human beings enacting the language of love, but to generate the kind of reality that comes from vision, from *completing* the movie's fragmentary humanistic enterprise. Here "the notes for the poem are the only poem" because the frozen architecture of a well-made poem comprises only the suburbs, only a derivative appendage barren of the vitality possessed by the entire city of words. The closed poem (of the 1950s, for example) is like the closed circle of Alphaville, which Caution calls "Zeroville." That cold war construct must be annihilated in favor of a genuine alpha-ville or new beginning. So "the poet is at the movies" in order to dream "differently" even as she dreams along with the imagery presented to her. This is the model, it is understood, of the reader-poet relation as well: to read critically, to absorb what the poet has noticed but not to seek perfection or completion that would lead one to reject the opportunities of new life, new poems. This Emersonian doctrine shifts the creative power first from the film text to "the mind of the poet" as viewer, and then from the mind of the poet to the mind of the reader as observer in his or her turn. The poem is not what is written down, for Rich has deep suspicions about language in this book, but the poem is "the moment of change" itself, seeing through texts, including, reflexively, "Images for Godard." The poem, in a kind of mental jujitsu, uses Godard's images to critique his *and* its own practice, and does so in the spirit of Godard's own self-criticism. Godard seems to invite such antagonism when he uses his own voice as the monotonous and sinister voice of the master computer, Alpha 60.

As Lemmy Caution leads Natasha out of Alphaville, the whole of the city is disintegrating, its citizen-victims writhing and dying, its Nazi-like ambitions to take over the universe in ruins. "Don't look back," Caution cautions Natasha. The scene is an allusion not only to the flight from the accursed city of Sodom but to the rescue of Eurydice from Hades by Orpheus. Since Caution is in no sense a realized individual in the movie, but always the character "Lemmy Caution," acting always in type, one might say that what happens at the end of *Alphaville* is a rescue of the deracinated girl by the movies, and more generally by art. A running joke throughout Godard's films is the way he treats his offscreen wife Anna Karina in the movies he makes with her. Here we have the director, the *metteur en scène,* rescuing his wife from the imaginary hell he has himself created and embodies as the voice of Alpha 60. The artist becomes the Orphean hero of his own scenario, using a stand-in, Lemmy Caution, imported into this high-culture film from the depths of the comic-strip and pulp-novel milieu. "Godard is suggesting that the popular arts are the only place where we can look for a force vital enough to combat the deadening, dehumanizing, automatizing effect of those tendencies Alphaville epitomizes," Robin Wood remarks.[11] As a relentless critic of the stereotypes of popular culture, Rich resents Godard's evasion, as she sees it, of the difficult solutions in favor of a comic-strip or Hollywood-style ending. She sees the opportunity to seize the standard of Orpheus from Godard, and through her more demanding art rescue his viewers, and her readers, from the sterile city exhibited in Godard's film and in the Alpha 60s of her generation.

Once again, Godard has anticipated her rhetorical movement, however. What has made Natasha susceptible to rescue in *Alphaville* is her discovery of a book of poetry passed on to her by a previous visitor from "The Lands Without." The book is Paul Eluard's *Capitale de la douleur,* and its vibrant lines initiate in Natasha the will to change:

And because I love you everything moves . . .
One need only advance to live, to go
Straightforward towards all that you love
I was going towards you
I was moving perpetually towards the light.[12]

The surrealist Eluard offers the antidote to the ossified logic that has built Alphaville, the language as city constructed by computer intelligence. Against the expressionlesss, mechanical voice of Alpha 60, Eluard's poetry makes its eloquent protest. At one point Caution is asked by the computer, "What transforms the night into the day?" His answer is "Poetry." If Alphaville is a summary image of totalitarian newspeak, Eluard's poetry is an inspirational model for language as a liberating creative force. One shot in the film superimposes Natasha's face on the cover of Eluard's book as if to identify her as the human form of his vision. (This shot may have suggested Rich's declaration that "my face must have a meaning.") Eluard serves Godard, then, as Godard serves Rich, as a model of self-conscious and critical thinking about the one-dimensional society that constrains the energies of its citizens.

Movies, and specifically foreign movies, were helping the Film Generation, Rich's generation, to fight that battle. The city of Alphaville is in one sense a European city, a memory of Berlin and an image of modern Paris, but it is also an American city. The obvious connection is the mad scientist Professor von Braun, an allusion to Wernher von Braun, the Nazi rocket engineer who came to the United States after World War II to direct the space program. Von Braun's language is not Eluard's but rather the equation $E = mc^2$, which flashes intermittently on the screen in Godard's film. The use of the American actor Eddie Constantine as von Braun's nemesis dramatizes a war within America between the forces of repression and the forces of subversion, the culture of a militarized Washington and the counterculture of vivacious presences like Elvis Presley, James Dean, Lenny Bruce, Humphrey Bogart, Marilyn Monroe . . . and any other figures who speak to the younger generation. Though Rich shunned the use of such pop icons, she pursued her quest to slay the dragon by recourse to the nourishing myths of salvation refracted through films like Godard's that took popular culture seriously.

A likely source for Rich's poem is Robert Duncan's "Ingmar Bergman's *SEVENTH SEAL*" (1960), another verse meditation on a European art film. If *Alphaville* is a futuristic fable that is also a documentary account of modern Paris, Bergman's film is a depiction of medieval life recognizable as the spiritual condition of the late 1950s. "It's our age!" Duncan exclaims as he watches the film. "The malignant stupidity of statesmen rules. . . . Now the black horror cometh again."[13] Just as Godard and Rich focus on Karina as the humanistic soul that must be rescued from the cold war malaise, so Bergman and Duncan focus on the holy family that escapes the figure of Death as he stalks and finally takes the knight in their contest of values. Duncan identifies with the clown's strategy: to evade Death by choosing an existential "happiness" as his condition.

Duncan does not involve poetry in his decision to choose happiness, perhaps because a poetry of personal satisfaction might sound like a sellout in the plague years of the 1950s. Rich achieves a greater depth than Duncan by uniting poetry and happiness in the poem that precedes "Images for Godard." In "I Dream I'm the Death of Orpheus," she becomes the feminist heroine of Jean Cocteau's film, *Orphée*. In this occult poem Rich seizes the initiative implied by the archetype of the rescue from hell basic to Cocteau's and Godard's films. In Cocteau's film Death, played by Maria Casarès, loves Orpheus (Jean Marais) and kills his wife in a fit of jealousy. Orpheus journeys to hell to reclaim Eurydice, and shortly after he has again lost her he is killed in a brawl by the modern-day Bacchantes. Death, called the Princess, allows Orpheus to return to earth and then turns to face her punishment from the authorities.

Why should Rich fantasize about enacting the figure of Death? In part because Death is portrayed as "feeling the fulness of her powers," becoming a *subject* in the texts produced by her enthralled poet. Rich seems to be captivated by this fantasy of a powerful woman who commands her motorcyclists and her chauffeur with the same iron will as she does her lover:

> *Princess:* Hold me tight Orpheus. Hold me tight.
> *Orpheus:* You are burning me like ice.
> *Princess:* I can still feel your human warmth; it's good.
> *Orpheus:* I love you.
> *Princess:* I love you. Will you obey me?
> *Orpheus:* I will obey you.
> *Princess:* Whatever I may ask?
> *Orpheus:* Whatever you may ask.
> *Princess:* Even if I condemn you, if I torture you?
> *Orpheus:* I belong to you and I'll never leave you.[14]

Their love will continue to prevail, thanks to the power she has granted him. This is, on a mythic level, the enactment of love denied the viewer in Godard's film, where the zero of Natasha is destined to be completely reconstructed by the abrasive macho ethics of her savior, Lemmy Caution. As "a woman sworn to lucidity" who "sees through the mayhem," the speaker of Rich's poem is also the implied poet walking backward on the other side of the mirror, contesting, on the basis of her experience in the psychosexual hell of the 1960s, the distorted world of reason and logic responsible for the Alphavilles of her era. In a crude reduction, the feminist poet is death to the poetry and the civilization constructed by men out of touch with the subversive aims of a feminist ideology. Just as Cocteau suggests that Orpheus wills the death of Eurydice through his aspiration for the more intense relationship with the Princess, so Rich figuratively slays the Eurydice part of herself in favor of the more self-defining and poetry-producing feminist self. Rich entirely ignores the sentimental ending of Cocteau's film, in which Orpheus and a pregnant Eurydice are joyfully reunited. Rich's poem shuts out Eurydice and the domestic sphere entirely. For the homosexual poet Jean Cocteau, who had carried on a love affair with Jean Marais offscreen, identification with the Princess came as naturally as his identification with Orpheus. He speaks this line as a voiceover: "The Death of the Poet must sacrifice herself to make him immortal." His film, though idyllic in tone, submits Death to a tragic fate in order to affirm the very art we are witnessing. Rich rediscovers *her* powers of composition, her purpose as an artist and her destiny as a woman, by means of Cocteau's dream-film, "dreaming the film-maker's dream but differently," as she says in "Images for Godard."

The submergence into Hades in this poem, and the ascent back to our everyday world, anticipates the title poem of Rich's next volume, *Diving into the Wreck*. One can read this poem on several levels, but coming to it directly from our discussion of *The Will to Change,* one is likely to identify the wreck on the ocean floor as a thematic equivalent of the city of words built by the patriarchs which the lone hero sets out to raze and redeem. The "I" of the poem is presumably a woman, but she is dressed in "body-armor" that recalls the figure of Orion from an earlier poem, a fantasy figure for her male animus. The speaker of Rich's poem has "read the book of myths" that guides her into the underworld. "The words are purposes. / The words are maps." The wreck is the negative example of a self-destroying civilization that must be confronted and overcome by the power of action, including linguistic action. When the speaker surfaces she/he will be "carrying a knife, a camera / a book of myths / in which / our names do not appear." The writhing bodies of the damned in Alphaville and *Orphée* are left behind for a new order founded on the words "I love you." In this poem, the new order takes the form of an androgynous ideal in which the speaker and her animus, like Death and Orpheus, fuse into one: "We are, I am, you are / . . . the one who find our way / back to this scene" (that is, to earth). The pronouns tell the story of an inward eye that recognizes the soul of love, the harmony of feeling between others. Rich's most important poems from now on—"Twenty-One Love Poems," "Transcendental Etude," "Paula Becker to Clara Westhoff"—will represent the Eluard-like force of love poetry to assault and destroy the entrenched capitals of dolor. And, significantly, Rich leaves behind the cinematic structure as a time-specific form that has performed its subversive duty and now must be replaced by the more coherent poetics arising from a feminist ideology. Thus, acting as the feminist subject, not the ghostly object of male narrative, Rich offers her act of consciousness as a model for her generation. It may be a Film Generation, but finally what it seeks is a book of myths as powerful in effect as Eluard's book of poems. *The Will to Change* is one such book, carried back from the movies it in part critiques.

(A final flash forward. In the poem "Frame" [1981], Rich watches from a distance, "just outside the frame" or "just beyond the frame" or "at the edge of the frame," as a black female student is harassed, arrested, and finally beaten by a white male police officer who suspects her of... something. The humiliation and abuse is feelingly described, but always as a spectator of this moving picture of contemporary life who cannot "break frame," in movie parlance. Rich's movie of a poem is offered as a documentary:

> *What I am telling you*
> *is told by a white woman who they will say*
> *was never there. I say I am there.*

The italics are like the use of photographic negatives in both *Alphaville* and *Orphée,* revelations of the shadowy world of repressed reality that film and poetry have perpetually borne witness to. Rich's movie is like Godard's book of poetry, an aesthetic strike against injustice. "Frame" is a poem designed to breed new poems of the same kind, but clearly what interests Rich, still, is this polemical question: once the spectators of this treatment have shut the book, left the theater of her imagination, what will they do to make such abuses part of the wreckage of time past?)

When the octoroon Jules Gaspard d'Estaing signs on as a hired gun for a fearful town in the film *Invitation to a Gunfighter* (1964), he signs his death warrant. This allegory of the black man in America made perfect sense to poets who knew how to read the fate of Black Power in the 1960s and afterward.

Chapter 8

"Mama How Come Black Men Don't Get to Be Heroes?": Colorizing American Experience

INVITATION TO A GUNFIGHTER

you rode into town on a mighty tall horse, Durango
and now it's time for that last showdown

and the townspeople who sired you
have all turned against you
in their arrogance ignorance and fear
and the subject of your love
is as fickle as the wind

and you're punch-drunk as a skunk in a trunk
looting and shooting for pleasure—tearing up
their peace of mind

and they're all too scared to take you on—
the gutless lot of 'em

and you're too bitter and fed up with the bad hand
fate has dealt you in the form of black skin
and deadly aim

it's time to get out of town, Durango
time to get the first thang smokin'
go on and get on
to whatevah is waitin' in that wild way out yonder

time to take that long slow technicolor ride

before they ambush you in the saddle
and leave you face up in the sun[1]

—1990

Born in 1943, I am probably typical of most white males of my generation in my addiction as a child to western movies. A small number of these I saw in theaters, especially at matinees where serials like *The Durango Kid* and a B feature starring Hopalong Cassidy or John Wayne were Saturday afternoon staples. But I viewed the majority of westerns on television, developing a special fondness for Ray ("Crash") Corrigan, Bob Steele, and Hoot Gibson. Armed with my white Hoppy holster and gun, I would join friends after school and on summer days for mimed shoot-outs with the bad guys, picking them off where they hid in trees—these were usually Indians—or in *High Noon*–style duels where the man in black leaped out from behind hedges or advanced toward me from the other end of the street.

Stories about the wild west appealed to me for the same reasons they attracted city kids in the nineteenth century: they provided a heroic model of masculine risk taking and character building in a native landscape. There were plenty of cowboys, cattle, and cattle rustlers in California and stations east during the late 1940s and 1950s, so that the fantasy of actually running off to join the Three Mesquiteers had an invigorating touch of possibility. I practiced the terse, tough-guy linguistic style of cowboys just in case I ever got the opportunity to mount some spotless white horse and ride out against the "hostiles" in what was even then called the "inland empire" of California. And unquestionably the scenarios of physical struggle appealed to me and my friends, all of us athletic but never the kind to engage in brawling. "The staging and viewing of violent spectacles are among the genre's prime attractions," writes Philip French, who sees "the murderous algebra of the Western" as its defining artistic form.[2]

For this reason, many film critics have argued that the western thrived in the 1940s and 1950s because its narrative situations recalled and simulated the world war of recent memory, as well as the cold war that pitted good against evil with the same simplistic archetypes. Probably I knew this intuitively as a child, if only because some actors, like John Wayne, Alan Ladd, Robert Taylor, and Ronald Reagan moved between westerns and war movies as virtually the same character; and because the Russians and Red Chinese I was taught to hate and fear were so abstract to my imagination that any villain on the screen could be accommodated to the threatening alien figure constructed by years of radio, newspaper, and magazine copy. It seems likely that my fantasies of holding off hordes of Indians from fort or village had something to do with the drills in grammar school where I was trained to hide under the seat in case of nuclear attack, or the trauma of seeing movies like *Invasion U.S.A.*, in which marauding hordes of Communists raped and murdered innocent Americans on the west coast. Having assumed the habit of decoding and fantasy substitution, I was well on my way to Indian hating as a rite of citizenship. But one day I asked my parents about the occasional cross-burning in the Baldwin Hills above my home in Culver City, and when I learned that I, as a Jew, was a despised alien in so many other people's fantasies, my devotion to the western genre began to wane.

It never occurred to me then to wonder how present-day Native Americans might feel about films in which General Sheridan's famous remark that "the only good Indian is a dead Indian" informs the scenario. There *were* good Indians in the movies: loyal scouts and sidekicks, peace-loving tribes that let the settlers share, or take over, their land. And after the groundbreaking *Broken Arrow* (1950), an occasional film of overt sympathy with the Indians' situation appeared, culminating in the Academy Award–winning *Dances with Wolves* in 1990. But the majority of westerns before the 1960s made the red man into a menacing figure, the scourge of innocent settlers, whose savagery justified the white man's vindictive violence inflicted upon the tribes. Such a morality play must have forged an oppositional stance among Native American spectators at an early age, as they watched all the horrors enacted upon them in their history endorsed by the melodramatic rhetoric of the western movie.

Louise Erdrich, a poet of Chippewa descent, recalls in her poem "Dear John Wayne" how in North Dakota she and her teenage friends would watch westerns at a drive-in, where the domineering technology that brings John Wayne's face into focus above them symbolizes the immense power of the civilization the white settlers brought into the prairies:

> The sky fills, acres of blue squint and eye
> that the crowd cheers. His face moves over us,
> a thick cloud of vengeance, pitted
> like the land that was once flesh. Each rut,
> each scar makes a promise: *It is*
> *not over, this fight, not as long as you resist.*
>
> *Everything we see belongs to us.*[3]

The actor's smile shows them "a horizon of teeth." His colossal presence confines them to a small reservation, a low ceiling of opportunity, a sense of the futility of resistance. The phrase "His face moves over us," adapted from the opening of Genesis, suggests a godlike figure of vengeance and wrath, punishing the infidels by firepower and by denial of the blessings needed for redemption in his new Zion. He has taken from them not only their land but their self-respect, their humanity. When the group of kids drives away, drunk and noisy, she can hear his monitory voice in her head, recording their feckless behavior as a rationale for further punishment. Referring to Wayne's death by cancer in the final lines, she remarks mordantly, "Even his disease was the idea of taking everything. / Those cells, burning, doubling, splitting out of their skins." Erdrich's Dear John letter is not an elegy in the manner of Frank O'Hara on James Dean or so many poets on Marilyn Monroe, an expression of homage and affection, but an antielegy, a bitter commentary from the victim's-eye view of the movie mythology that continued to oppress Native Americans long after the white settlers had dispossesed them of their heritage.

In her prose poem "Angel Baby Blues," Wanda Coleman recalls a childhood spent "hating John Wayne rooting for the chinks Japs Apaches cannibals." Hating John Wayne became something of a national pastime during the 1960s, when the Vietnam War and the civil rights movement initiated a revision of national mythology among the generation raised on westerns. Indeed, westerns virtually disappeared after the mid-1970s, and one reason is that they could not respond to the child's question posed in Coleman's blues lament: "mama how come black men don't get to be heroes . . . and where are the heroines who look like me?"[4] In actual fact, some 25 percent of working cowboys on the frontier were black, as William Loren Katz has documented in *The Black West*. And after the 1960s there were a few "soul westerns" featuring black gunfighters, such as *Soul Soldiers* (1970), *Buck and the Preacher* (1972), *Charley One-Eye* (1972), and *The Legend of Nigger Charley* (1972). But something about the genre militated against switching the categories of black and white. Reform-minded filmmakers found it easier to move the formulas of westerns into the urban space, where macho black heroes could achieve more credible triumphs, or into outer space, where the good alien had always been a consolatory sci-fi convention.

Coleman's poem "Invitation to a Gunfighter," written in the 1980s, captures a complex period in American culture because it is informed by the assumptions of the classic western *and* by the countercultural response of the 1960s when African-Americans picked up the gun in an effort to write themselves into the A budget scenario of modern American history, *and* by the aftermath, when Black Power subsided under the dual pressures of liberal reform and conservative backlash. The sarcastic wit of Coleman's poem, supposedly directed at the hapless gunfighter, assaults the reader as well, especially the white reader, who recognizes that he or she is one of the "gutless" townspeople in need of a white knight, or the Duke, to drive this historical menace out of sight and out of mind.

Who is this gunfighter? The first thing to say is that he is someone with black skin who is uppity enough to take the mythology of the western movies seriously. This native son has the name Durango, derived from westerns where heroes and villains alike are commonly named for western places. Usually the name "Kid" is preceded by the place name, as for example, Idaho, Oklahoma, Mojave, Pecos, San Antonio, Silver City, El Paso, Michigan, and dozens more in the pantheon. Here the western genre gives Coleman the opening she needs for her social fable. The gunfighter in most western movies is a nomad known only by his name, an outcast, a loner who can't settle down and become part of the domestic tranquility of the community. The sign of his ambiguous relationship with the townspeople is his gun, which he uses either to defend the town from its enemies of whatever color, or to threaten the town with depredations until a rival gunfighter challenges and defeats him. Antisocial impulses link the hero and the villain. The sheriff is sometimes an ex-outlaw, the outlaw is sometimes an ex-lawman. The rhetorical action of the film is often a wooing of one side by the other, as the costs and benefits of defending or preying upon the community are calculated. In the precise synecdoche of common idiom, the person becomes "a hired gun," whether deputy or outlaw. His identity is fixed by whom he kills, but also by the authority that conscripts him.

One such gunfighter is Jules Gaspard d'Estaing, the antihero of the film *Invitation to a Gunfighter* (1964). As played by Yul Brynner, d'Estaing is a gentlemanly Creole in a black suit whose mother was a quadroon slave sold by his father. "I'm a man with a gun" is all the identity beyond his name that d'Estaing acknowledges to the townspeople who hire him to kill a Confederate soldier returning from the Civil War to claim a homestead seized by the town's leading citizen, a ruthless businessman. D'Estaing scares the authorities by getting drunk and shooting off both his gun and his mouth in a rage of protest against his morally pernicious situation. He refuses to leave town to save his skin. Finally, he is shot to death by the corrupt businessman who is killed in turn by the Confederate soldier. D'Estaing's body is carried off in the final scene by Mexicans and whites acting in solidarity, a tragic figure sacrificed to redeem the sins of the townspeople.

In their standard history of the genre, George N. Fenin and William K. Everson remark that "in 1940 the tendency to glamorize outlaws began in earnest, most notably in Henry King's *Jesse James*."[5] As with gangster movies, whenever an outlaw is humanized or glamorized, the audience is invited to recognize the excluded or alienated figure as legitimately American. That is, the outlaw is conceived as a sign of the essential national character. In this reading, the American as historical type was self-created by the subversive act of revolution against the parent authority of England during the late eighteenth century, and grew to adulthood by pushing across boundaries in the westward movement that settled the continent. At each stage of development violence initiated and resolved the new definition of the individual in a society whose laws could only be provisional stays against the self-interested claims of an imperial consciousness. The Civil War is often used in westerns like *Invitation to a Gunfighter* as a trope of the political and moral chaos that empowers its embittered veterans for a life of semi-justified aggression against corrupt communities, banks, railroads, and the law itself. Emerson's and Thoreau's essays became the canonical authority for the continuing assault of Americans upon the idea of authority. "Whoso would be a man must be a nonconformist," Emerson wrote in "Self-Reliance."

"He who would gather immortal palms must not be hindered by the name of goodness, but must explore if it be goodness. Nothing is at last sacred but the integrity of our own mind. Absolve you to yourself, and you shall have the suffrage of the world." Much of the American literary tradition, as critics have repeatedly demonstrated, proceeds from this endowment of legitimacy upon the individual's stance of resistance to the ideal of social solidarity.

If the outlaw can be considered the essence of the American type, then African-Americans have a good claim to be the essential Americans. Jim Crow laws, lynchings, and a pervasive stereotyping in every medium of social discourse made the point a million times over that the Negro was an embarrassment and a danger to the social elements conformed against whoever was "diff'rent." Richard Wright had argued that the black man is America's metaphor long before the idea became popularized in the postwar period, when Ralph Ellison, for example, could claim that "in a sense, the Negro was the gauge of the human condition as it waxed and waned in our democracy."[6] Radical writers of the 1960s and 1970s asserted that Establishment white society in the United States had become as foreign to the American spirit as the English colonial governors, and that a second revolution in the name of Black Power was necessary to reclaim the native character and redeem the American Zion.

Black poets often had reference to white popular culture in order to illustrate how such a reclamation could take place. These authors did not have to read Gramsci or the Frankfurt School to recognize that radio, films, journalism, and television constituted an ideological hegemony that had shaped or colonized the political consciousness of the American public, including blacks. Hating John Wayne became the paradigm for such resistance to role modeling for citizenship. Don L. Lee wrote to his black readers, "If all you are exposed to is Charlie Chan, you'll have a Charlie Chan mentality. A better example is Tarzan. Remember Tarzan grew out of one man's imagination, but because of pervading anti-black conditions, he immediately became a nation's consciousness. What Tarzan did was not only to turn us away from Africa, but from ourselves."[7] Lee's poetry demands that readers stop thinking of "Tony Curtis, Twiggy" as "cool," stop getting their ideas of themselves from the black characters in TV shows like *Julia* and *The Mod Squad,* and especially, as in his poem "Wake Up Niggers (you ain't part Indian)," to stop emulating Tonto, the white hero's loyal sidekick. Similarly, Amiri Baraka/ LeRoi Jones in his playlet *Jello* shows a subversive Rochester murdering Jack Benny, and usurping his custodial power. Gwendolyn Brooks addresses a poem "To Those of My Sisters Who Kept Their Naturals" and praises them in this way:

> You never worshipped Marilyn Monroe.
> You say: Farrah's hair is hers.
> You have not wanted to be white.[8]

Wanting to be a white woman is the charge Welton Smith lodged in a poem of the 1960s against black women *and* black men too brainwashed to join the war of liberation: "you want to be lois lane, audrey hepburn, ma perkins, lana turner, jean harlow, kim stanley, may [*sic*] west, marilyn monroe, sophie tucker, betty crocker, tallulah bankhead, judy canova, shirley temple, and trigger."[9] Such accusations could be cited indefinitely, and testify to the conviction among those who felt colonized that if an African-American nation were ever to be created from the ruins of white civilization—and some advocates conceived of a separate and sovereign territory carved out of the western states—black people needed to reject white media icons in favor of black ones.

Withdrawal from white paradigms means that blacks should construct for themselves alternative narrative structures germane to their own ethnic identity. When Ishmael Reed proclaims in a widely-anthologized poem, "I am a cowboy in the boat of Ra," he is imagining an Afrocentric character for himself that both exploits and ironizes the conventional myths of the West and the western:

> I am a cowboy in the boat of Ra,
> sidewinders in the saloons of fools
> bit my forehead like O
> the untrustworthiness of Egyptologists
> who do not know their trips. Who was that
> dog-faced man? they asked, the day I rode
> from town.[10]

The last sentence refers to the closing speech of every Lone Ranger episode ("Who was that masked man?"), as the savior of the community rides into the countryside with his trusty sidekick. During the 1960s black poets conspired to reverse the roles of The Lone Ranger and Tonto, giving supreme power to the man of color so long subordinated by a white master. Reed plots an insurrection in which he rides into town, a mysterious stranger, with an Afrocentric cultural identity powerful enough to hijack the stage of Western civilization, and dispossess it of its confident mythology. The western movie gives this desperado poet the opening he needs to insert himself into white fantasy worlds in the subversive role prepared for him by so many narratives of young guns breaking the peace.

Wanda Coleman's persona non grata of the black gunfighter is a means of measuring her own distance from a society seemingly immune to the rhetoric of civil rights. For her, too, the wild west is the West, including the segregated domains of socioeconomic power in the author's own personal experience. Horse operas enable her to make signifyin' fun of her situation using the genre's own terms and tropes. In "Job Hunter," the western movie imagery is displaced to the westernmost American city. The speaker as "outlaw" has been prowling Los Angeles, willing to test her hard-won business skills against the white Establishment. The poem marches toward its serio-comic denouement:

> it's high noon
> the sheriff is an IBM executive
> it shoots 120 words per secretary
> i reach for the white-out
> it's too fast for me
> i'm blown to blazes
>
> it's the new west, Durango
> the sun never sets
> and death is an elevator on its way
> down to the lobby[11]

As in "Invitation to a Gunfighter," this poem uses western movies to situate the speaker credibly within the dreary social dynamics familiar to a black person. Coleman imagines herself as the only kind of gunfighter she can be in the "badlands" of the corporate society: a job hunter, not a bounty hunter, a supplicant whose mere presence at an interview triggers a nervous shoot-out in which her ambition to integrate causes her to be "whited-out," that is, her name removed from the job application files. Presumably the white audience cheers, and the black audience grudgingly acknowledges the inevitable victory of the "dough-flesh /desk-riders" who have the power to fire whomever and whenever they wish.

Coleman is a free-spirited resident of Watts, a fiction writer as well as a poet, and the winner of an Emmy award in 1976 for her scripts for *Days of Our Lives*. When she wishes to characterize the "new west," she often uses Hollywood as a metaphor for the white power structure she knows at firsthand. Hollywood is sometimes the moviemaking capital, as in the poem "Casting Call," in which Coleman as aspiring actress is looked over by the camera crew and the unemployment office and pronounced ill equipped for success. *"We don't do black on black"* she is told emphatically. In her poem, "Trying to Get In," Coleman writes, "i stand at the door of hollywood. beat at it."[12] In other poems Hollywood is the site of elite privilege of any kind—the academy, the social circles of Beverly Hills and Bel-Air, and the literary citadel that she can never storm. Instead, she nurses her forty-five hundred rejection slips, wondering when she will be admitted to the tonier parts of the city. In poems like "On Heaven Street at One A.M.," "Hollywood Zen," "The Co-Star," and "Sessions" Coleman depicts one-on-one showdowns in the movie capital that show just how much self-reliance is necessary to land a role in movie-made America. The "death" she suffers at the end of "Job Hunter" may be a somewhat exaggerated way of figuring each rejection, but as the closure of every western movie, the experience of being shot down figures accurately the emotional feel of her encounters with the sheriffs of the new west.

The "Durango" of "Invitation to a Gunfighter" is more threatening than the "Durango" of "Job Hunter," however, even though they are clearly related as outlaws in their respective frontiers. This "Durango" comes from the Black Power struggles of the 1960s and early 1970s; he's an amalgam of the names collected by Gwendolyn Brooks in her poem on the Blackstone Rangers: "King, / Black Jesus, Stokely, Malcolm X, or Rap."[13] One might add other names: the Eldridge Cleaver of *Soul on Ice*, Huey Newton, Bobby Seale, Bobby Hutton, George Jackson. It's crucial to remember that the black poets of the 1960s and early 1970s deliberately and persistently honored the gunfighter, or more generally, the rebel, with poems of homage. As the 1960s progressed, the violent deaths of Medgar Evers, Malcolm X, and Martin Luther King, not to mention many blacks in the South, including children, made the nation look like a moral wilderness surpassing even the imagination of the western. As the uprisings in Watts, Detroit, Newark, Attica, and elsewhere intensified the sense of slave rebellion among the disaffected and desperate of the black community, poets turned to the tradition of regeneration through violence in American culture. Nikki Giovanni's mantra is the most famous of the decade:

Nigger
Can you kill
Can you kill
Can a nigger kill a honkie
Can a nigger kill the Man
Can you kill nigger
Huh? nigger can you
kill
*
We ain't got to prove we can die
We got to prove we can kill[14]

Sonia Sanchez expresses the same sentiment:

we got some BAADD
thots and actions
                    like off those white mothafuckers
                    and rip it off if it ain't nailed
                    down and surround those wite/
                    knee / grow pigs & don't let them
                    live to come back again into
                    our neighborhoods . . .[15]

By performance poems such as these, with their percussive sound effects and street epithets, black poets constructed the figure of Durango, "too bitter and fed up with the bad hand / fate has dealt you in the form of black skin / and deadly aim." By "looting and shooting for pleasure" Durango revenged himself in the manner the black poets advised, making himself into the Terror represented in western movies as marauding Indians or outlaw gangs.

Indeed, in his poem "Black Art" Amiri Baraka called for a poetry as violent as the fists and guns used on blacks by whites: "We want 'poems that kill.' / Assassin poems, Poems that shoot / guns." Any other kind of poem is "bullshit," he says, fit only for "mulatto bitches / whose brains are red jelly stuck / between 'lizabeth taylor's toes."[16] Elizabeth Taylor may seem an unlikely antagonist to place among the cops, landlords, and politicians who populate the poem's urban land-scape, but Baraka recognizes that white models of glamour constitute the ultimate oppressors in a media culture. His claim to carry forward the work of emancipation depends on his ability to shape a poetry of violence that will extirpate from the brains of black people the seduc-tive images of white movie stars. Directing attention away from the blandishments of Hollywood and toward black artists—preeminently jazz artists—is not just a matter of taste but a primary act of slave rebellion for his generation.

The genealogy of the rebel figure in black literature is very com-plex. Scholars have usefully traced it back to the escaped renegade of nineteenth-century slave narratives, of which Frederick Douglass's autobiographies provide the most comprehensive model, as well as historical agents of violence like Nat Turner and Cinquez of the slave ship *Amistad*. But just as narratives about slave rebellion justify their claims to be essentially American by their kinship with Emersonian ideas of extralegality and self-reliance, so the "Heroism in the New Black Poetry," to use D. H. Melhem's phrase, derives inevitably from spectacles of heroism in the dominant culture, including the movies. Amiri Baraka remarks in an interview in Melhem's book, "I've been influenced by all the moviemakers that I've seen. I'm a moviegoer. I've always been a moviegoer. It always insults me when people try to say that movies are some kind of inferior art form. I can never understand that. That always seems to me the most bizarre thing in the world to say."[17] As moviegoers, the poets who construed the Black Panthers or figures like Malcolm X as heroes naturally made use of movie formulas, and especially the violence and melo-drama of the western, to glamorize their outlaws. Larry Neal's poem on Malcolm X, for example, describes his Michigan Kid traveling east rather than west in order to fulfill his destiny.

Out of the Midwestern bleakness, I sprang, pushed eastward,
past shack on country nigger shack, across the wilderness
of North America.
I hustler. I pimp. I unfulfilled black man
bursting with destiny.
New York City Slim called me Big Red,
and there was no escape, close nights of the smell of death.
Pimp. Hustler. The day fills these rooms.
I'm talking about New York. Harlem.[18]

Robert Hayden describes the same existential, self-created figure in
"El-Hajj Malik El-Shabazz." Hayden's Malcolm X takes to the
road—"he fled his name, became the quarry of / his own obsessed
pursuit"—and finally adopts the Muslim name that titles the poem,
only to be shot down by assassins who have been the implied shad-
ows of violence from the leader's own origins.[19] Leaders like Mal-
colm X are more than political agents; they are self-willed seekers of
a name and an archetypal identity that transcends temporal issues.
Hayden compares Malcolm X to Captain Ahab, whose quest is to
"strike through the mask" and lay bare the fundamental reality of
human experience. Like the films that create characters bigger than
life, as indicated by their capitalized code names—The Virginian, The
Gunfighter, The Plainsman, The Westerner—such Black Power
figures emerge from the poetry of their admiring bards as archetypes
of resistance, revolutionary leaders available to every generation.

Hollywood was unwilling to glamorize anything more than the
"pimp . . . hustler" part of the exemplary history of up-from-the-
depths figures like Malcolm X. A version of the black experience
became available in films like *Sweet Sweetback's Baadasssss Song*—with
its final message printed on the screen, "A BAADASSSSS NIGGER
IS COMING BACK TO COLLECT SOME DUES"—or *Shaft* or
Superfly or *Slaughter* or *The Mack* or *Hammer*. The title figures of these
blaxploitation pics are examples of the racial type identified by
Donald Bogle as the stereotypical "buck" or "hardman" going all the
way back to the rapacious Gus in *Birth of a Nation,* "looting and
shooting for pleasure." Bogle calls such films of macho black aggres-
siveness "daydreams of triumph" that mirror the conventions of
white melodramas like the western in which the hostiles are beaten

down by white authority. But just as the daydreams of triumph inscribed in the poems of Gwendolyn Brooks, Larry Neal, Sonia Sanchez, Don L. Lee, Nikki Giovanni, Ishmael Reed, Amiri Baraka, and others yielded to more moderate statements, or were pushed in the late 1970s and 1980s to the margin of public attention, so these films metamorphosed into the feel-good ironics of Eddie Murphy and Richard Pryor vehicles. Bogle remarks that "the great subconscious goal of the 1980s may often have been to rid American films of the late 1960s/early 1970s rebellious figures. In actuality, the movies wanted audiences to believe that such figures no longer existed, or, if they did, they could really be tamed, disposed of, or absorbed into the system."[20]

Thus, the advice given to the gunslinger in Coleman's poem and in the film with the same title is unequivocal: get lost. "It's time to get out of town," she says, and the repetition of "time" sounds the knell twice afterward for this enemy of the people. Coleman's admonition is after-the-fact advice, for by the time she writes the poem the doomed gunfighter had already become a subject for belated elegy. Malcolm X and Huey Newton were actually slain, not by Mister Charlie but by "the townspeople who sired you," and other Black Power figures did "take that long slow technicolor ride" out of public consciousness into the anonymity of the "wild way out yonder" beyond the media's selective gaze. The poem bids farewell at once to the weapon-wielding activist and to the poets who believed art should be a weapon trained upon a culpable white community. "Durango" is now a spectacle to be recalled, by the townspeople who read the poem, with a shudder, a whisper of "good riddance," and the kind of nostalgia that allows desperadoes a certain glamour in retrospect. As irony and nostalgia usurp the bardic tributes of former days, history becomes legend; Spike Lee produces a life of the fallen Malcolm, who safely terrorizes the Establishment in some Dodge City of the historical imagination preserved by set decorators and costume designers. Meanwhile, the surviving Black Power spokesmen wander the hinterlands of the public imagination, like aged gunfighters in the movies, where journalists, and even poets, can gain some repute by taking a remorseful shot at them.

Robert Hayden (born 1913) told me that one of his earliest memories was of the turmoil caused in his mixed-race Detroit neighborhood by showings of *Birth of a Nation*. He recalled the fear in the household as whites stirred up by the heroics of the Ku Klux Klan in Griffith's film ran shouting through the streets, breaking windows and setting fires. One film he spoke lovingly about, however, was Lon Chaney's silent version of *The Phantom of the Opera* (1925). Hayden savored the disguise and unmasking of the hideous Erik, the scenes under the Opera, the final pursuit of the phantom by an enraged mob that flings him into the Seine—and most of all Hayden thrilled at fifty years distance to the Technicolor scene of Erik costumed as Red Death. Hayden would rise and imitate the daunting looks and dashing gestures of the Opera's specter as he descended the staircase, appalling the Paris beau monde. It does not take Sigmund Freud to see that Hayden read the film as a parable of his own status, a talented outcast in a civilization that feared his colored presence. Erik could have no public role except as a spook, a haunt, a disturbing shadow that must be extirpated by violence when and if it rose from the depths to threaten the higher culture.

Characteristically, Hayden did not approach these or other movies in a polemical way in his poetry. Rather, "Double Feature" is one of many nostalgic genre pieces devoted to the Paradise Valley neighborhood of Detroit where he spent his childhood.

At Dunbar, Castle or Arcade
we rode with the exotic sheik
through deserts of erotic flowers;
held in the siren madonna's arms
were safe from the bill-collector's power.

Forgave the rats and roaches we
could not defeat, beguiled by jazzbo
strutting of a mouse. And when
the Swell Guy, roused to noblest wrath
shot down all those weakéd men,

Oh how we cheered to see the good we were
destroy the bad we'd never be.
What mattered then the false, the true
at Dunbar, Castle or Arcade,
where we were other for an hour or two?[21]

There is no way of telling from this full-throated poem that the author is black, though when one knows his color the last line is especially poignant. Movies allowed Hayden to cross the color line, inhabiting the blessed position of the "other" for a short period, the "Swell Guy" like William S. Hart or Tom Mix who defended a fragile civilization from its discontents, before returning not only to the bill collector but to the cultural situation that stigmatized people of color as "bad" not "good." (For example, the "exotic sheik" portrayed by Rudolph Valentino is treated as a fearsome seducer, and his passion for Agnes Ayres as just short of bestial, until it is revealed in the last scene that he is not an Arab but the son of an English nobleman and a Spanish lady.) Hayden uses the movies here as a means of registering his willingness to forgive. His gratitude for the pleasure of the movies has the effect of repressing rebellious feelings of the kind he will attribute in other poems to Nat Turner, Cinquez, Harriet Tubman, and the martyrs of the 1960s' "mourning time." The poem implies that the movies had helped to make him into a "good" man by providing him with a bracing, if often "false" morality play.

"Double Feature," a late poem in Hayden's oeuvre, postdates his meditations on the 1960s; like other works from his last book, *American Journal,* it seeks to evoke a means of healing the wounds opened in the national psyche by a decade of racial violence. Hayden's palliative—one could not call it a solution—is the Romantic-nostalgic strategy of the New York poets, who summoned the uncritical eye of childhood as a model for pluralist tolerance and personal well-being in a society undergoing radical change. The faith in high art as a redemptive force exhibited in Hayden's poems extends to popular culture in "Double Feature." Movies are not "poison light," as Ishmael Reed calls them, but a vital restorative in effecting a joyful and justice-seeking body politic. Hayden's commitment to a color-blind or universalist aesthetic made him vulnerable to criticism by many contemporaries less forgiving of Hollywood. James Baldwin, for example, incorporates the sentiments of "Double Feature" into his early fiction and then derides them in his later polemic *The Devil Finds Work* (1976) as the apologetics of an Uncle Tom.

Baldwin's autobiographical novel, *Go Tell It on the Mountain* (1953), established the terms by which his later revisionist essay can be understood. For the boy John Grimes, raised in a pious if contentious Harlem family, the movies are an escape from the restricted life to which his color and his poverty condemn him. And yet, to the extent that movies represent escape from church and family, his destined salvation, they also represent damnation. Moviegoing is an intensified experience of sin for the boy, not just in his rebellious act of attending these forbidden pleasures but in the charismatic sinners he gazes at while seated comfortably in "the gloom of Hell." In one scene he watches a movie that sounds like *Of Human Bondage* and feels a powerful attraction to the sadistic woman who again and again betrays the innocent student who loves her. John is seized, surprisingly, with sympathy: "He wanted to be like her, only more powerful, more thorough, and more cruel; to make those around him, all who hurt him, suffer as she made the student suffer, and laugh in their faces when they asked pity for their pain. . . . One day he would talk like that, he would face them and tell them how much he hated them, how they had made him suffer, how he would pay them back!"22

When the woman dies, John, Hollywood's ideal moviegoer, is struck with remorse for the vicarious empowerment he had experienced in watching her cruel treatment of the student. He has learned to abhor the temptation of revenge, and that "it was the Lord who had led him into this theater to show him an example of the wages of sin." By revealing to him, in his moment of sympathy with the scarlet woman, his own iniquity, the Lord has put John on the narrow path, which he pursues until the end of the novel when he becomes a preacher like his father. The child is redeemed by his capacity for self-knowledge and his will to act upon the moralistic messages delivered to him by Hollywood—virtually a second church if rightly understood. Race is simply not an issue in this case study of the impact of film. Having performed their miracle, movies play no part in the novel after this scene.

The Devil Finds Work is a much angrier look at the subject. Now that the civil rights struggles and the passions of the 1960s and early 1970s have intervened, Baldwin remembers his childhood fascination with movies in a different way than when trying in *Go Tell It on the Mountain* to account for his own career as a boy preacher. In this essay Baldwin offers John Grimes's desire for revenge as a positive guide to revolutionary action. Baldwin's polemical purpose leads him not to melodramas like *Of Human Bondage* but to social protest films that construed reality as a struggle of the privileged and the oppressed—a recognizable scenario of young James's Harlem experiences. Because "we were all niggers in the thirties," the anger of screen whites and black audiences converged in at least an illusion of solidarity. In the 1930s blacks were given no image of black rebellion, neither in westerns where a film celebrating Cochise or Sitting Bull would have served the purpose, nor, of course, any film chronicling black insurrection analogous to the novel *Native Son*. But Baldwin recognizes that films like *A Tale of Two Cities, Fury,* and *You Only Live Once,* and any picture that featured prisoners, were relevant to his experience and his destiny. *Prisoner of Shark Island,* he tells us, exerted an attraction solely on the basis of its title. But these stories could never be *his* stories because the historical settings were always foreign, even, as in *Dead End,* when the location was proximate to his ghetto home. And the actors, or "escape personalities," as he calls them, could never offer him genuine escape because of their skin color.

After the 1930s, according to Baldwin, filmgoers were denied realistic social commentary, at least of the revolutionary kind practiced in the Depression era when anger against the system was a more saleable commodity. Now the movies began to close out the black audience, not only by continuing to deny blacks entrance to any but singing-and-dancing roles, but by reducing the scope and seriousness of proletarian films that depicted a reality blacks shared with whites and thus could have used as tutorial instruments for initiating radical social change. Films became escapist, practicing "the American self-evasion, which is all this country has as history."[23] Especially evasive, in Baldwin's view, are films like *The Defiant Ones* and *In the Heat of the Night* that create black characters who are admirable to the extent they forgive and befriend and even love their white coactors. (This is the formula Donald Bogle calls "the huckfinn fixation.") By underestimating black rage such films constitute an erasure of the racial problem from the screen; they offer pat resolutions relieving whites of responsibility at the same time they evade the spectacle of historical depredations. Writing this book in the mid-1970s, then, Baldwin sees all the movies in which Sidney Poitier portrays some virtuous or even saintly figure as attempts to exorcise the black gunfighter from the conceptual field of white and black audiences alike.

That Baldwin prefers to approach the movies as an adversarial critic can be seen most clearly in the longest of his poems, "Staggerlee wonders," a meditation on the America of the 1980s that uses the persona of the murderous Staggerlee to score points against the culture of violence in white America. In folk balladry Staggerlee is the unredeemable black gunfighter who shoots his friend Billy Lyons in a quarrel over a Stetson hat. That Baldwin adopts this persona to rage against the racism of America, as institutionalized in the ascension to power of Ronald Reagan, suggests something of the poet's vindictive feelings toward a culture that has given him such dead-end folk heroes while blazoning the likes of John Wayne and Ronald Reagan as champions:

> Oh, noble Duke Wayne,
> be careful in them happy hunting grounds.
> They say the only good Indian
> is a dead Indian,
> but what I say is,
> you can't be too careful, you hear?
> Oh, towering Ronald Reagan,
> wise and resigned lover of the redwoods,
> deeply beloved, winning man-child of the yearning Republic,
> from diaper to football field to Warner Brothers sound-stages,
> be thou our grinning, gently phallic, Big Boy of all the ages![24]

Baldwin's sarcastic tribute to Ronald Reagan calls attention to a source of despair for blacks during the 1980s. Bad enough, they might say, that movies reflected the racism of American whites, intensified into myth by the experience of the frontier. As in Louise Erdrich's poem, John Wayne's war against people of color, from *Stagecoach* to *The Green Berets,* signifies the cancer that threatens long-time historical victims "on the auction block / of Manifest Destiny." The rise of Ronald Reagan to power ensured that the racism of the movies would be reduplicated with double power by a national government whose values came entirely from the simplifications of the movies. What chance was there for Americans to outgrow their juvenile myths when the "Big Boy of all the ages" continued to set national policy according to the melodramatic formulas of B movies?

(Baldwin would no doubt attribute the homophobia he associates with "gently phallic" figures like Wayne and Reagan to the same persistence of nineteenth-century cultural vision. As a homosexual,

Baldwin has another reason to protest the movies' construction of an exclusive politics of gender.)

The Devil Finds Work can be seen, among other things, as a denial of credibility and authenticity to the medium. Baldwin's own disenchanting experiences in Hollywood no doubt nourished his unfavorable attitude. In 1968 he was working on a screenplay for Columbia Pictures about Malcolm X when reports of the assassination of Martin Luther King reached him. Traumatized by the news, he returned to the script with renewed fervor, and soon got into an argument with Columbia over their interference in his project. Malcolm X had once said to Baldwin, "I'm the warrior of this revolution and you're the poet."[25] Baldwin's inability to act as the Homer for Malcolm X's exploits, or to realize his desire to film the life of George Jackson, no doubt contributed to his indictment of the movies as terminally evasive of historical reality. In his poems Baldwin alluded to *Superman* and *The Godfather,* and praised Simone Signoret and Lena Horne, but *The Devil Finds Work* shows that his pleasure in the movies was persistently clouded by their treatment of the racial situation. He loathed "coon" actors like Stepin Fetchit, Willie Best, and Mantan Moreland, and he lamented the good-intentioned films of the 1950s and 1960s, from *Intruder in the Dust* through *Guess Who's Coming to Dinner,* as insufficient for the monumental changes in attitude required by centuries of racial oppression and prejudice. Baldwin does not advise any reader to withdraw from the movies; but his book is a cautionary one, warning black readers that the medium is part of the problem, not part of the solution.

Baldwin's suspicion of the movies, with that of other black writers, helped to make an oppositional stance normative for black poets of the 1980s and 1990s. It has strengthened their ability to expose and condemn movies on racial themes, but it has also diminished their opportunities for creative play by imposing upon them a political agenda forged and sanctified in the civil rights era. Younger authors who inevitably see themselves as the beneficiaries of the revolutionary re-visioning of popular culture undertaken by the older generation are susceptible to charges of ingratitude if they seem to compliment their image in Hollywood's mirror. But just as Baldwin had freed himself from the influence of his predecessor Richard Wright by means of his critical essay "Everyone's Protest Novel," so some black poets have tried to free themselves from the thematic constraints of movie discourse imposed by Baldwin and the poets discussed above. Thylias Moss's poem "Birmingham Brown's Turn" (1991), for example, selects as an object of praise not some weapon-wielding black man dangerous to whites, but a seemingly degraded role, that of the chauffeur for Charlie Chan in the parodic *Charlie Chan and the Curse of the Dragon Queen* (1981). Peter Ustinov is only the most recent white man to portray the Chinese detective, suggesting an anxiety about racial identity on the part of filmmakers and audiences alike. But the driving agent in the film is no white in yellowface, or blackface, no "caricature" or "effigy." Birmingham Brown knows who he is and where he is going, Moss asserts, and his cool "entitlement" reassures her about the place and fate of black people in a friendlier decade than the 1950s or 1960s. Brown is an authentic and vibrant example of an American whose profession makes him one with the natural world prolifically summoned in the poem as part of the chauffeur's continual presence on the open road. The poem cannot be called complacent about the "bottom-hugging black // race," but in the manner of Robert Hayden it rejects the temptation to bitterness in favor of an upbeat endorsement of the survival skills black writers admire in their people. As Moss says of Hattie McDaniel in another poem, "This one is about dignity. . . . she / is what outlived Tara in significance."[26]

Moss's poems seem to critique Wanda Coleman's lament that movies have never presented her with a recognizable image of a black hero or of herself. As an elegist for the Black Arts generation, Coleman has reason to be bitter that black aspirations reached the screen in such distorted ways, even in the 1970s. More recently, however, the achievements of the New Black Wave in the 1990s (Bill Duke, Spike Lee, Matty Rich, John Singleton, Mario Van Peebles) have begun to circulate the sound and imagery of ghetto streets to all Americans. Rap lyrics on the soundtrack are bringing news of black attitudes to many spectators who don't read poetry or watch MTV. And these attitudes are not always those of formulaic resentment against white power. In John Singleton's film *Poetic Justice* (1993), the young black woman named Justice uses Maya Angelou's poems to explain to herself and her black cocharacters how personal needs, not political agendas, deserve attention if meaningful reform is ever to occur in the lives of people of color. Such films open a moral space for the redefinition of black society as a congregation of individuals, not types, even in the devastated locale of South-Central Los Angeles. The theoreticians of the Black Arts movement hoped that some new mythology based on black history could be constructed to compete with an oppressive and evasive white mythology signified by the western. Black film and black poetry could then cooperate at last in articulating the recognizable consciousness of the race. Whether or not this convergence comes to pass, the New Black Cinema presents new challenges to black poets, who will keep us posted on whether Hollywood does or does not continue to play the Devil when it represents the most recent history of different races in America.

Humbert Humbert reads Poe's poem "Ulalume" to a skeptical Lolita who would be right to suspect him of wanting to make her another doomed nymphet of the romantic imagination. Whether it is possible to escape from imposed roles in a post-modernist culture is the fundamental question of poetry on the movies in the 1980s and 1990s.

Fin de Siècle: Jorie Graham and the Rites of Self-Renewal in a Culture of Film

Now the theater's skylight is opened and noon slides in.
I watch as it overpowers the electric lights,
    whiting the story out one layer further

till it's just a smoldering of whites
    where she sits up, and her stretch of flesh
is just a roiling up of graynesses,
    vague stutterings of
light with motion in them, bits of moving zeros

in the infinite virtuality of light,
    some *likeness* in it but not particulate,
a grave of possible shapes called *likeness*—see it?—something
    scrawling up there that could be skin or daylight or even

the expressway now that he's gotten her to leave with him—
    (it happened rather fast) (do you recall)—

the man up front screaming the President's been shot, waving
    his hat, slamming one hand flat
over the open
    to somehow get
our attention,
in Dallas, behind him the scorcher—whites, grays,
    laying themselves across his face—
him like a beggar in front of us, holding his hat—

> I don't recall what I did,
> I don't recall what the right thing to do would be,
> I wanted someone to love. . . .[1]

—1991

The 1980s was the decade in which theories of popular culture fostered by the triumph of the visual media finally caught up with not only academia but the entire intellectual community. Perhaps it was Ronald Reagan's presidency that irresistibly enforced on every thinking person the association of movies and television with hegemonic power, or perhaps the maturing into middle age of the first generation to grow up with television in the house made the fact unavoidable at last. For whatever reason, postmodernism as an explanatory term for the new cultural environment became a household word. Postmodernism has been described as an era, or more precisely a condition of being, in which simulation and hyperreality usurp the traditional modes of belief and activity. "All the great humanistic criteria of value," writes Jean Baudrillard, "all the values of a civilization of moral, aesthetic, and practical judgement, vanish in our system of images and signs."[2] The characteristic drama of postmodernism is the struggle to achieve authenticity in an environment so filled with mediated phenomena that one feels constantly like a character in a movie . . . or worse. In a decade when theorists were cheerfully asserting that the self was a cultural construct, and reality a discourse of the dominant ideologies, poets could be expected to investigate with increasing sophistication, and desperation, the intertangled links between their imagination and the prolific representations that nourished it as they grew into maturity.

Poets have always sought to identify the origins of their inner life, especially after Romanticism made such self-interpetation a rite of passage into authorship. In *The Prelude* Wordsworth traced his song back to the voice of the Derwent river flowing into his childhood dreams. For Shelley, a vision of the "Spirit of Beauty" vouchsafed to him as a boy in a "starlight wood" caused him to dedicate his powers to reforming the world through poetry. In "Out of the Cradle Endlessly Rocking," Whitman attributes his awakening as the author of "myriad thence-arous'd words" to hearing a mockingbird sing by the Paumanok shore. A century later, the story of origins is less likely to consult transcendent nature when situating the poet as an intermediary between a source of power and an audience in need of empowerment. It is more likely to involve the epiphanic visit to a movie theater, and the discovery of how the poet has insinuated herself into the mediated body of historical reality.

Jorie Graham's "Fission," the longest and most complex of all the poems we have thus far examined, performs this hermeneutical task. It seeks to interpret an originary moment as a text full of convoluted meanings. The text is an event of more than personal significance. It is a Friday afternoon in November of 1963, when a showing of the movie *Lolita* at which the poet is present, a girl of twelve years, is interrupted by the announcement of President Kennedy's assassination. This public calamity that split the consciousness of every American provoked a fission of identity in the poet as well, and by means of the imagery of light splitting off from light—the light of the movie projector, the houselights, the light of the actual world let in through the skylight—Graham reads the event as a moment of rupture and reproduction, of mortification and achieved freedom, as her new self splits off from the innocent she had been when she entered the theater. The parable of Plato's cave serves her narrative purpose throughout the poem by indicating how decisively a new vision effects the decease of a former state of being. In Graham's apocalyptic poem, the death of Lolita's mother that fissions off the orphaned virgin into the predatory care of Humbert Humbert, and the wrenching revelation of John F. Kennedy's assassination, occur simultaneously as dual forces acting upon the poet's suddenly disintegrated consciousness.

Graham's poem has a fin de siècle quality because of its retro fascination with the 1960s as a fountainhead of contemporary culture. The movies of the prepostmodern period compel attention not only for obvious reasons of nostalgia among middle-aged poets but because they seem to occupy a historical period of more authenticity, more *credibility*—a period before theorizing about spectacle became a self-conscious tic that made everyone, including poets, skeptical analysts of their own spectatorial practice. It is no accident that Kennedy has been appropriated for the same retrospective uses. As 1963 fades into ancient history, far far distant from the infinitely renewable present of the media carnival, Kennedy has become a fictive personality

whose life and death are recycled into every imaginable kind of enter-
tainment, including poems like "Fission." It may be easiest to enter
Graham's poem by a consideration of Kennedy's ghostly role in it.

When Kennedy was inaugurated in 1961 Robert Frost wrote a
panegyrical poem in which he constructed Kennedy as a kind of sun
king:

> It makes the prophet in us all presage
> The glory of a next Augustan age
> Of a power leading from its strength and pride,
> Of young ambition eager to be tried,
> Firm in our free beliefs without dismay,
> In any game the nations want to play.
> A golden age of poetry and power
> Of which this noonday's the beginning hour.[3]

Norman Mailer had sounded this same note in an influential article
for *Esquire* magazine the year before, titled "Superman Comes to the
Supermarket." Mailer had scorned Adlai Stevenson as a debilitated
figure of the Democratic party's past and hailed Kennedy as a new
kind of hero, a Blakean spirit of virility and creative energy who
would extinguish the Urizenic influence of Eisenhower and his ser-
pentine shadow Nixon. Thanks in part to Mailer and Frost, the my-
thology of Kennedy as a conquering King Arthur presiding over a
Camelot of the best and brightest men in the realm passed into the
folklore of American culture, there to be gradually deconstructed in
the light of posthumous revelations about his sexual infidelities. (The
Camelot legend called for Jackie to play the unfaithful Guinevere, but
history did not fall for this patriarchal ruse.) Kennedy accomplished
a fair amount of legislation, but he will always be most famous for
his assassination. The abrupt closing of his "new order of the ages,"
as Frost called it, put him in the same category with Marilyn Monroe,
another glamorous fatality of the early 1960s, whose name has been
linked with Kennedy's for more reasons than one ever since.

Because the Democratic convention of 1960 was held in Los
Angeles, at the Sports Arena, Mailer's connection of Kennedy to
Hollywood archetypes appears at first a clever trope; but Mailer
makes it clear that he means to be more than clever. The convention,
he asserts, represents a boundary break with the past of epoch-mak-

ing significance: "it was . . . one of the most important conventions in America's history, it could prove conceivably to be the most important."[4] The first part of Mailer's essay traces the decline of America from an Emersonian realm of independence and assured selfhood to a nearly totalitarian state presided over by the FBI and CIA, the mirror image of a soulless Soviet regime it devotes all its wealth and energy to combat. The hope of America has been preserved, however, in the movie archetypes of nineteenth-century heroism, for the first movie theaters, serendipitously, were erected just at the time the frontier closed. The necessity, then—and Mailer gleefully acknowledges the risk in this prospect—is to elect someone who embodies in actuality the rugged good looks and adventurous temperament that Americans have come to expect only in the movies: "The Democrats were going to nominate a man, who, no matter how serious his political dedication might be, was indisputably and willy-nilly going to be seen as a great box-office actor, and the consequences of that were staggering and not at all easy to calculate."[5] Kennedy is a superman, then, because he embodies the myth of America as a place of unlimited power and freedom. He alone would have the courage and resourcefulness to face down the Washington bogeymen in some fateful encounter of the type so familiar to Americans from their popular culture.

By the time Mailer collected this essay into his volume of 1963, *The Presidential Papers,* prophetic claims like these already seemed hollow to him, and he used his introduction to deplore the shortcomings of a president who inflicted the Bay of Pigs on the world, refused to rein in J. Edgar Hoover and other dictatorial bureaucrats, endangered the world by his frantic *High Noon* showdown with the Soviet Union over missiles in Cuba, and showed too much caution when faced with the civil rights struggles in the South. But no sooner did Mailer's book appear than Kennedy's assassination and canonization fulfilled the original prophecies; Kennedy passed into legend as precisely the kind of movie figure Mailer had apotheosized. The squalid careers of Lyndon Johnson and Richard Nixon drove many public intellectuals back upon the sanctimonious image of Kennedy's bright and shining presidency—as it seemed in retrospect. In the shorthand of America's dreamwork, the tragically short tenure of the young president irresistibly made him a symbol of America's truncated hopes and dreams.

In Don DeLillo's novel *Libra* (1988), Lee Harvey Oswald is at-
tracted to John Wayne, who makes an appearance in Corregidora
while shooting a movie in the Pacific.

> He wants to get close to John Wayne, say something authen-
> tic. He watches John Wayne talk and laugh. It's remarkable and
> startling to see the screen laugh repeated in life. It makes him
> feel good. The man is doubly real. He does not cheat or disap-
> point.[6]

In the structure of the novel, John Wayne is clearly a foretype of John
Kennedy, whom Oswald idealizes in the manner of Mailer. (Mailer's
essay is certainly an influence on DeLillo's novel.) According to these
writers, then, the election and tragic death of Kennedy is a movie
fantasy played out in public life as a ceremony of masculinity. Both
writers represent the period of American history since 1963 as a
thwarted renaissance, a benign patriarchal order subverted by the
oedipal violence of the assassin who stands for all envious spectators.
When the repressed Kennedy returns in the 1980s, carried into office
on the promise that once again it is morning in America, the stan-
dard-bearer is an actor who is "doubly real," Ronald Reagan, who
strains to mimic John Wayne and admires the cold war macho of
John Kennedy.

Why did Kennedy have to die? This is the question of a nostalgic
polity, dramatized most recently in hagiographical films such as *JFK*
and *In the Line of Fire,* and in Mailer's epic novel, *Harlot's Ghost.*
Kennedy's death remains "the beginning hour," the alpha point of
postmodern history, and the only way of defeating its spell is by
confronting it with an iconography of equal and opposite force. Jorie
Graham's poem attempts such a task: not to demythologize, which
would secure the power of Kennedy's martyrdom, but to remytholo-
gize by crossing the death in Dallas with some moment of a female
self's nascent awakening to life. Graham's daring choice for such a
crossing is Stanley Kubrick's film of Vladimir Nabokov's novel,
Lolita. Graham constructs a dramatic encounter of film and historical
reality in order to liberate herself from the forces that threaten to
constrict her freedom within the bounds of a powerful national my-
thology. From the conflict ultimately inscribed on her own body in
the form of competing sources of light, she emerges as a shining

starlike presence, and also as the contested site of her self-divided culture.

In a poem on Eurydice in *The End of Beauty* Graham remarks of her subject, "what she dreamed / was of disappearing into the seen / not of disappearing, lord, into the real."[7] The opposition of the seen and the real is central to "Fission" as well. The seen is an aesthetic space that Graham locates, in many of her poems about paintings, as outside of historical circumstance, at a still point which is the place of light's absolute presence. As she is careful to point out, however, for the human spectator the experience of transcendent light inevitably marks a turning point in personal history, separating a before-experience of the artwork from the aftermath of seeing. In "Pollock and Canvas," for example, the artwork is a "garment of light . . . parting the past from the future." This effect derives from the dramatic, often narrative *forms* assumed by light in an artwork. "Fission" is the first time in her work that a movie (rather than a painting) will be used as a medium of the apocalyptic. *Lolita* is nothing but light, "a corridor of light . . . the tunnel / of image-making dots licking the white sheet awake . . . the arm of screen-building light," that holds the young spectator spellbound as she surrenders herself (presumably) to identification with the "seen" figure of the nymph on the screen. ("Nymphet" hardly seems the right word for the fourteen-year-old actress, Sue Lyon, mature for her age, who plays Nabokov's demoniac child.) Light encloses actress and spectator into a unity, an imaginative "shape all light," to borrow a phrase from Shelley. The seen is an immortal moment of apprehension, duplicated later in the poem when the light of the dislocated projector covers the speaker with Lolita's narrative:

> Where the three lights merged:
>   where the image licked my small body from the front, the
>   story playing
>
> all over my face, my
>   forwardness

The conclusion of the poem catches the young poet at a moment of potential growth, when she is expelled from Plato's cave still trailing shroudlike clouds of artificial light on her body. Now she, rather than the screen images, is the "likeness" of a forward-moving narrative subject: a chief executive of her fate. This opening poem in *Region of Unlikeness,* then, resembles the opening poem of *The End of Beauty* in which Eve is sited at the moment of "freedom" from the blissful enclosure in the ruptured patriarchal space called Eden, "the rip in the fabric where the action [of history] begins."

In popular myth it is Eve who brings death into the world by exercising a forbidden choice. She severs a glorious past from a future full of suffering and mortality. Lolita is another female both fatal and fated, for in Nabokov's novel, as in his original screenplay, she dies in childbirth of a stillborn child not long after Humbert, having killed his shadow-self Quilty, dies of a heart attack. Stanley Kubrick changed this ending to preserve Lolita, give her a future in Alaska, the new frontier, rather than render her the victim of Humbert's Poe-haunted imagination, another Ulalume or Annabel Lee. In the film (as in the novel), Humbert reads "Ulalume" to Lolita as a means of revealing to her that he adores and covets the fantasy nymph he shares with his favorite author. Lolita resists with characteristic insouciance by making fun of the poem's "corny" language. And yet, Nabokov's joke within a joke is that he is replacing the life of the doomed maiden Lolita by his powers of language, terminating her freedom and closing it into a book. Lolita is a symbol of virgin America as it looks, seductively, to Old World intellectuals like Humbert and Nabokov himself. The question posed by the end of "Fission" is whether a young woman endangered by two patriarchal and possessive myths—that of *Lolita* and that of the superhero Kennedy—can break free and continue to thrive. It is recognizably a feminist question, an act of cultural mimesis in the 1990s which rightly locates the early 1960s as the origin of women's organized resistance to the constraints of male domination.

The person of Lolita in novel and film is not an authentic being. Like Natasha in Godard's *Alphaville* she is a linguistic or poetic cipher available for capture by the male interpreters or governors of her fate. Lolita is "really" Dolores Haze, a girl on the verge of identity, first sighted by Humbert and ourselves, and by Graham in this poem, in her garden, "the dream called / *new world.*" Humbert sees her as one of Poe's nymphs; Quilty at the high school dance utters her name "Dolores" and, audibly under his breath, "the tears and the roses" from Swinburne's poem "Dolores." Lolita's mother refers to her as a "starlet," and later Humbert too will reprimand her as "our little starlet" after her debut as an enchantress in the high school play. She is cast in whatever scenario others require of her, including "the TV writer" Quilty's promise of "an engagement in Hollywood" if she will make an "art movie" with his degenerate companions in their hideaway. Lost among assigned roles and constructed signs, Lolita, who so desperately wants someone to love, nevertheless exclaims at Humbert, a figure for all her pursuers and manipulators, "Why don't you leave me alone!"

This American Eve enters Graham's poem as an erotic symbol whose postlapsarian fate, crossed with Kennedy's, foreshadows the 1960s and their aftermath. "Fission" is a monument that speaks in two voices. First, it says that the poet seeking to articulate the trauma of recent American history through her own is fixated in that stop-time moment of overpowering historical reality. (That is, the events in "Fission" are offered in part as an explanation for the obsession with what is illuminated, enlightened, or "seen" in Graham's oeuvre.) But the poem also measures how effectively the poet can take up where Lolita leaves off, released by the experience of death to "love" and to "marry marry marry" in an act of "forwardness." In order to secure this identification of the two adolescent girls, Graham has to telescope events from the film. In the poem we jump swiftly from Humbert's first view of the sunbathing girl to the mother's death to the road scenes featuring the couple's drive to Beardsley College in Ohio. In retrospect these scenes that cover an hour or so of film time are presented as occurring during the few minutes of panic in the movie theater. The shrinkage of film time is necessary to simulate the accelerated apprehension of the spectator that like the movie heroine she is now abandoned to a fate rushing toward her with the single-mindedness of Humbert himself.

"Forwardness" is part of Lolita's film experience, and the life history of the poet as well, but the poem articulates too the "immobilism," "the being-in-place more alive than the being" that characterizes the experience of spectatorship. The ending of the poem outlines the terms of escape from the constricting influence of movies and of a reality derived, as in the case of John Kennedy's adventurous life and tragic death, from fictive formulas popularized by the movies. "Choice" is presented as an act of will that "rips the wrappings of light" playing upon her Lolita-like flesh. Her resistance to the

234   The American Poet at the Movies

seductive enfoldings of light repeats the efforts of many poets we
have studied. And Graham resists as well "the / ever-tighter wrap-
pings / of the layers of the / real." Inscribed with the transcontinental
motion of Lolita, and aural messages about the dead president, she
answers back to the seminal moment by conceiving a poem that
incorporates it as a form of new life for the former moviegoers of the
Film Generation. The poem is an autobiography of its own concep-
tion, like the Romantic poems of Wordsworth, Shelley, and
Whitman already cited, holding the reader no less than the author by
the desperate urgency of its dramatic event. The last voice we hear is
a histrionic appeal that blocks our exit from the poem, trying to hold
us immobile ("Don't move, don't / wreck the shroud, don't move—").
Our act of choice that wrecks the completed beauty of the text by
escaping from its spell simulates the movement of the poet out of
her predicament of 1963 toward the achieved mastery of the poem
"Fission."

Graham's strategy, in other words, is the same as Adrienne
Rich's in her encounter with *Alphaville:* "dreaming the film-maker's
dream but differently." The difference refers not so much to the
historical context, in which Reagan or Bush replaces Kennedy as
Captain America, but to the medium by which the adult poet
achieves a selfhood that all cultural forces *except* poetry conspire to
deny her. Poetry is the Lacanian "Symbolic" that gives its creator a
language for identity formation, a vehicle for desire. In the psycho-
analytic terms favored by Lacan's followers, poetry is a surrogate for
the "fundamental lack" or absence of reality that makes every filmgo-
ing experience a psychic castration. Self-generated language fills the
gap between projector and screen, screen and spectator, spectator and
source of film imagery. Language, especially in the form of a rival
narrative, asserts the free self against whatever conspires to keep the
self wounded, mutilated, incomplete.

In the 1980s and 1990s the social function of poetry remains one
of liberation, breaking open the frames that limit consciousness, in-
cluding (in Rich's and Graham's view) a too-tidy verse form, by
innovative free-verse technique. To the extent that poetry by women
has emerged as the most powerful new force in the last two decades,
Graham's poem is paradigmatic of its era. In poems like "Fission"
Graham realizes Frost's "new order of the ages" as a textual rebuke
to older aesthetic, social, and political behaviors. Rich's experiments

in *The Will to Change* have certainly exerted influence on Graham's practice, not least by leading her to primal cinematic texts as the occasion for countercultural self-definition.

The light of cinema never loses its association with the solar myth of the Enlightenment, in which knowledge is derived from the seen, and ignorance and superstition are banished. Light brings all things into visible existence and thus into conscious apprehension. Because light is indiscriminate, it remains a metaphor for anything, for the totality of existence. But the vexed relations of the light of artifice and the light of actuality outside the theater trouble the poet in the 1990s. In Graham's poem the overlappings of light upon light are captured in the superposition or layering of image upon image, the repetitions of word and phrase, and the startling shifts in visual syntax as short and long lines are mixed together to involve the reader in the speaker's mental confusions. The multiple sources of light bearing down upon the juvenile protagonist impress upon her imagination the associations of light with sexuality and death that recall humankind's primal scene in the Garden when a God of light expelled Eve and Adam into the endless shooting script of mortal experience. In the poem the light let in from the skylight whites out the film, and its actors become "moving zeros . . . a grave of possible shapes." Light is the reality of selfhood and death, in other words, the death inflicted by a Creator upon his freed subjects.

The poet's revenge, having been made one with these zeros when the projector inscribes her flesh with Lolita's story, is to create a secondary world of enduring power, a world in which "the infinite virtuality of light" glows in a unique frame of her devising. Humbert himself is not a poet. When Charlotte asks him what he is doing while he writes in his diary, he responds falsely: "I was writing a poem." Lolita is his poem and his life terminates when she moves forward from his possessive imagination of her into an authentic life as a mother-to-be on the American frontier. By doing what Humbert cannot do, Graham, in Baudrillard's terms, does *not* vanish but becomes visible as a woman poet amidst the signs and images of her culture. But her triumph, as a creator and also as a celebrity who seeks to embody the idea of America as powerfully as Kennedy or Nabokov, has the same ethical ambiguity as the fictive forces she outmaneuvers. By writing the poem, Graham has turned her self into a property for exhibition, a high-culture version of the pop icon

(Lolita) she has appropriated in order to acquire more prestige in a media culture. Now she too has become a type of Poe, offering to readers this seductively crafted and brightly lit narrative of a teen's desperate entrapment in the machinations of mortal circumstance.

The success of Graham's poem depends on its tone of sincerity; we believe she is narrating an actual event from her life, and perhaps we would think less of the poem if we discovered that it was entirely fictitious. The poem would fit well in a collection of memoirs by twenty-three different authors published in 1991, *The Movie That Changed My Life,* edited by poet David Rosenberg. The brunt of many essays is the way a particular film severed past from future by redefining the spectator's sense of self, especially in terms of gender and sexuality. "It split my childhood in two," says Clark Blaise of *The Thing* in a typical expression of such fission. Russell Banks writes of seeing *Bambi* as a child: "One person . . . seems to have died that afternoon; and another—a child defined by his gender—got born."[8] *Bambi* and *The Thing,* then, like *Lolita,* come as exterminating angels of revelation. It would be naive to treat them as fictive, any more than the new self they create of the spectator is fictive. Or say that all selves are movie made in the sense Banks and Blaise and Graham intend. In a postmodern culture that increasingly defines as reality what is seen through the cinematic aperture, what remains indisputably real are the roles, the characters, even the actors who live among us with an authenticity loaned to them by our own sense of contingency or fictiveness.

Walker Percy has caught this sentiment in an early scene of his novel, *The Moviegoer* (1960). The narrator Binx Bolling notices William Holden on a New Orleans street, on his way to Galatoire's restaurant. A couple nearby notices the star as well:

> Now they spot Holden. The girl nudges her companion. The boy perks up for a second, but seeing Holden doesn't really help him. On the contrary. He can only contrast Holden's resplendent reality with his own shadowy and precarious existence. Obviously he is more miserable than ever.

The boy is saved from his sense of insufficient being when he casually offers Holden a light, as if the star were just any stranger. "The boy has done it! He has won title to his own existence, as plenary an existence now as Holden's, by refusing to be stampeded. . . . He is a citizen like Holden; two men of the world they are."[9] That is, the boy does not acknowledge his inferior status as a noncelebrity by fawning over Holden; rather, he shares the scene with Holden as a costar before the admiring eyes of his partner. Binx Bolling's task will be to achieve a similar reality by treating the movies as less important than they have been in his life. After the trauma of his service in the Korean War, he has turned to the movies as an alternative to the "everydayness" that is suffocating him, but the habit makes matters worse, for he can never escape the sense of diminished being that comes with measuring himself by the movies. He suffers from the "unbearable lightness of being," in Milan Kundera's fine phrase, and needs the gravity of personal crisis to bring him down to earth. His beloved cousin's suicide attempt effects his change of heart, and he marries her in order to anchor his dream life with responsibilities. Finally, he has a chance of attaining some self-image as resonant as his heroic father, though we sense in the bittersweet conclusion of the book that the presence of stars like Holden—and Binx's favorite, Rory Calhoun—will always make him feel a part of the "malaise."

Contemporary poems are often forums in which the poet arranges an encounter between some ordinary persona and the star. The author features the confrontation as revelatory, a moment that will change his or her life. As we have seen, this has been a regular feature of movie poems since Vachel Lindsay's on Mae Marsh, rising to a crescendo in the 1950s and 1960s, when the crisis of the film industry engendered a large number of elegies and homages. The losses of that later period remain the informing subject matter of recent poems; the closing first of Hollywood's golden age, and then its silver age, persists as a convenient trope for the annihilation of the poet's childhood innocence as well as his or her self-renewal as creator, if only as a re-creator of originary myths. In this sense postmodern poets remain spellbound to the discursive formulas of their predecessors, in the manner of moviemakers. But even to think of Lindsay or Hart Crane is to recognize that something more complex and interesting is happening at century's end, as poets seek to construct a more intimate relationship with the icons of commercial culture. In a poem called "Plato's Retreat" David Lehman notes how "The voyeur and the exhibitionist meet / On the sunny side of the street," and make common cause as "their bodies merge / At the vanishing point of resemblance."[10] As both voyants and voyeurs, poets of the 1980s and 1990s insist on being greedy consumers of the popular culture that entertains the masses, no longer aloof from it, as the modernists at least pretended to be. By this means they have the chance to gain back the audience they have lost to more attractive media. Voyeurs and then exhibitionists in turn, these poets gladly allow mass culture to percolate upward into elite forms of lyric and narrative, there to shine in all their glamorous vitality for a postmodernist audience infatuated with moving pictures.

An especially interesting example is Paul Monette's long poem, "Musical Comedy" (1981). The poem is composed of five letters written by Noel Coward to Marlene Dietrich as Coward makes his way across the American West by rail on the Twentieth Century. Coward meets Greta Garbo on board, and they begin to write a play together. When she shocks him by suggesting they make love—he begs off for reasons of homosexuality—the relationship ends, and she leaves the train. Coward ends the poem with a newly written song, an envoi for the romance that never was.

The meeting with Garbo is, in a fashion, comparable to the final scene of Graham's poem, but instead of the erotic image rendered as light, here it is presented as flesh. For straight readers who are movie-goers the moment of proposition sounds like a dream come true:

> "Let's go to bed."
>   "But we won't sleep," I said,
> dead at the piano. We had written
> two acts in fourteen hours, right on schedule,
> and said let's break to catch our breaths. Outside,
> a desert warred with a stack of mountains.
>   "No,
> I mean let's fuck."[11]

Garbo is acting in character as a temptress, a screen image come down into the realm of men. If Coward were heterosexual, would he casually take on the required task, as Walker Percy's young man accommodates William Holden in the streets of New Orleans? That would be a way of playing the role so that the boundary of reality and cinema is transgressed. But Coward resists; his difference stands here for the fictiveness of the reader/spectator who can in no way mate with the screen goddess. Instead Coward retreats to his cabin and there has sex with a Native American man on board who has earlier claimed to have had sex with Garbo just after she boarded the train. In their nocturnal play, each man treats the other as Garbo, while the "real" woman burns in her stateroom, at the proper aesthetic distance from the everyday copulation.

Monette is writing a social comedy that is also a parable of our confrontation with the imaginary world of the movies. Is he also writing a "sincere" personal poem? Garbo is a favorite of homosexuals, who find her androgynous demeanor and her mannerist acting an inspiration. Monette, a gay poet, performs as Noel Coward in a fantasy of encountering celebrity. Certainly his ebullient wit persuades us that he fits the role. The poem is likely to have a special meaning for gay readers who are brought into contact with their adored idol, only to be scorned by her disapproval because of their sexual orientation. "I thought / we were after loftier things than us," Coward says plaintively, and she snaps, "I want to be alone for a while." The scene is a paradigm of the straight world responding to gay identity. Garbo leaves the train to return to "Eric," whom she claims owns the railroad company, a man secure in his masculinity and a powerful presence in the actual world. Coward survives this humiliation, indeed makes a charming story of it for Marlene Dietrich, the ideal reader of his misadventures. His self is unfissioned; he continues to write his jolly songs. Monette's parable for the gay community—advising them not to be changed by the relentless and urgent heterosexual demands of Hollywood—affirms that the movies make nothing happen. No need to change your spots, because there's always an Indian—*some* other marginalized victim of the Erics of the world—who'll share your bed.

One could profitably compare this last poem in *No Witnesses* with the first poem, in which Henry Stanley tells us that though David Livingstone has more solidity of character, more authenticity, than himself, he, the journalist Stanley, has the power to make Livingstone's public persona into whatever he wants. This sounds like another wishful parable of the poet as he confronts celebrity. Gods and heroes have charismatic power, yes. But they have no being outside of the writer's representations of them. Walker Percy takes advantage of the fact that William Holden has two bodies, the one with powerful sexual allure in 1961 preserved in his film performances, and the one that ages and dies. Percy's scene is "doubly real" for readers who survive Holden and have no chance of meeting him in the flesh. Likewise, every role of Garbo's, or Dietrich's, or Noel Coward's, on screen is likely to be affected by the spectator's sense that they are historical beings, extinguished lights preserved in shadow by the agency of celluloid. As revisionary historian, the poet (more than the novelist, who traffics in the contemporary) has the power to manipulate our response to bygone characters, enhancing the authenticity of readers who have been fissioned off from charismatic actors and actresses beyond their powers of touch. Indeed, this intensification of textuality to the point where it becomes coextensive with the real is one of the proud and enduring prerogatives of poets.

It may be that the 1980s and 1990s are especially susceptible to the remembrance of things past purveyed by movies, and at one remove by fiction and poetry about the movies. The nostalgia of the baby boomers whose lives were changed or nourished by movies, and even more extensively by television, has led to a kind of national repetition compulsion as remakes and sequels and pastiches continually recirculate the past through the present, often for feel-good effects that promote an aura of immortality as part of the package. Mark Crispin Miller has spoken of "an audience terrified of time itself" seeking to resist the ravages of age by demanding—and of course getting—the infantilized cartoons and kiddie serials of their childhood typified by the *Star Wars* and Indiana Jones movies, *Batman, The Flintstones, The Addams Family, Superman, Dick Tracy, Dennis the Menace,* and many more.[12]

At the same time, a cadre of American directors as proprietary about film history as the French auteurs of the 1960s has made allusionism a fetish, so that films since the early 1970s have offered cinephiles the pleasure of recognizing classic plots, scenes, characters, editing, lighting, and camera angles. Poets who make use of movie allusions thus have a potential audience that is well trained in responding to such fleeting and often esoteric references, though it would not be true to say that poets have learned the technique itself from the movies; quite the contrary, allusion is one device that cinema may be said to have borrowed from the Anglo-American poetic tradition. Modernism certainly intensified the practice, but anyone who has done source studies involving Spenser, Milton, Pope, and Blake knows how fundamental quotation and allusion have been to the medium of poetry. Postmodern moviemakers nurtured on the canonical masterpieces of Eisenstein, Chaplin, Hitchcock, Hawks, Lang, Ford, and others likewise pay homage to the old gods by constant imitation and appropriation, as if acknowledging that their works must of necessity possess a belated, secondhand quality appealing to a nostalgic audience that wants nothing more than more of what it fondly remembers.

As movie history takes this wistful turn, so poets of the last decade, themselves baby boomers responding to the same losses of middle age, look backward to connect their lives with the great icons of celebrity. Notice how Lucie Brock-Broido positions herself in relation to Marilyn Monroe for no other reason than to enforce an association with Monroe's glamour:

> How odd that she would die into an August
> night. I would have thought
> she would have gone out in a pale clear
> night of autumn, covered to the shoulder
> in an ivory sheet, hair
> fanned out across the pillow perfectly.
> *Fame will go by, and so long, I've had you, Fame.*
> From under the door, the lights leak
> into the hall & Sinatra going
> over & over in the bedroom on repeat
> & you were dying out.
> I was six, sitting in a sky blue metal chair
> in our kitchen.[13]

Tender is the night in this sumptuous evocation in the cinematic mode. Summer is too unpoetic for the death of a goddess, so the Keatsian poet summons a glossy "pale clear /night of autumn." Monroe is presented in pinup style, held for a moment in the camera eye, serenaded by Sinatra's crooning voice. Cut to the poet at six years in her comfy suburban milieu, who seems to participate mystically in Monroe's death. Because the sentimental diction is spread smooth across the two environments, Monroe's airbrushed death blends atmospherically into the cozy innocence of the speaker's family life. Brock-Broido quotes Monroe's statement about fame as a way of making an obvious connection to her own poetic enterprise;

"Fame is the spur" of poetry, as Milton wrote in his tribute to the prematurely deceased poet, Lycidas. (According to her friend, the poet Norman Rosten, Marilyn wrote poems from time to time, giving the Miltonic sentiment a surprising pertinence.)[14] Monroe "had" fame but continues to have it as well, thanks not only to her movies but to the obsession with her celebrity enacted in poems like this one and a multitude of others that use her life and death as locus for self-regard. There is no dramatic reason for Brock-Broido to introduce herself into this rhapsodic poem about Monroe's death—no effort at self-definition and self-renewal comparable to Graham's stationing of herself in a movie theater on the day of Kennedy's assassination. But the rules of sympathetic magic claim that one borrows the attributes of the divine by association with it.

At least this is the assumption in another, better-known poem on the same subject, Sharon Olds's "The Death of Marilyn Monroe." The opening stanza is the most carefully sculpted, in order to compose the same kind of stylish tableau as Brock-Broido's:

> The ambulance men touched her cold
> body, lifted it, heavy as iron,
> onto the stretcher, tried to close the
> mouth, closed the eyes, tied the
> arms to the sides, moved a caught
> strand of hair, as if it mattered,
> saw the shape of her breasts, flattened by
> gravity, under the sheet,
> carried her, as if it were she,
> down the steps.[15]

The sequence of predicate phrases brings the reader very close to the professional tasks of the ambulance medics, whom fate has chosen to manipulate this corpse after its fade-out. In one sense they are fulfilling a fantasy of the (male) moviegoing public: to see, to touch, to hold the sacred body. But Olds removes from their act any of the satisfaction of fantasy: it is a "cold" body and "heavy as iron," and the famous breasts have been "flattened by gravity." The conditional phrase "as if" further circumscribes the meaning of their act, though in a complex way. As moviegoers they have admired the Marilyn who was a screen persona; even if they had met the living Marilyn they would not have made contact with the fantasy object of their desire. The dead Marilyn ought to be emptied of all magical significance. But she continues to live because her effect on others never depended on reality, only on artistic illusion. Fame persists into the posthumous state, a fame that lends her greater presence than the medics or any living person of their acquaintance.

And so the next stanza begins, "These men were never the same." We hear how one had nightmares and depression, and another looked differently upon his wife and kids. "Even death / seemed different to him—a place where she / would be waiting." And in an enigmatic final stanza one of the medics stands in the doorway of a bedroom listening to an ordinary woman breathing. None of these men was loved or even noticed by Marilyn Monroe, yet they are touched by her because they touched her as she exited this life. For them, too, contact with a deity has fissioned an ordinary past from a mysterious, intensified, and poetic future. They are like the totality of the American public, traumatized by the premature deaths of their celebrities, living in a postmodern afterlife that has a peculiar resonance, an aura. Marilyn had two bodies, and the death of the actual one is made an occasion for a poem of public grief, even as the survival of her immortal self is measured in the undying memory of the medics.

The perpetual elegy of movie poetry, in which the spectator outlives the completed self of the cinema star and turns backward to regard and judge her, derives from a long tradition in which writers achieve fame by writing about the famous. Leo Braudy's survey of this tradition in *The Frenzy of Renown* takes note of how often writers triumphantly set their verbal artifacts in opposition to visual memorials, and in some cases, as with Pindar writing on the Olympic athletes, how the verbal memorial is the sole persisting presence of the real person in human memory. And yet, how different is the situation of the writer in the age of cinema. Braudy remarks that without the Gospels the life and death of Jesus "would have existed only, if at all, either as rumors or as a dimly understood story."[16] But adding one's drop of lyricism about Marilyn Monroe to the ocean of media imagery and commentary arising from her obsessively recirculated movies and photographs may seem a superfluous activity, unless poets achieve a unique lyric self-definition in the process. The darkest thing one can say about movie poetry is that it represents shameless attention-getting behavior in a culture of narcissism. The poet who insists on sharing the media scene with the enviable products of cinema technology might be compared to the rioters on Hollywood Boulevard in *The Day of the Locust* or comic figures like Rupert Pupkin in the film *The King of Comedy,* intervening jealously to say their piece in someone else's rightful spotlight. No doubt the popularity of pastiche poems designedly written to sound like movies, such as David Lehman's "Perfidia" or Nicholas Christopher's book-length B narrative *Desperate Characters* (1988), or the "poem-films" of British author Douglas Dunn, derives from this rivalry. It may also be that when poets focus on degraded film figures for consideration, like the Ritz Brothers in Frank Bidart's elegy, "To the Dead," or the "monster" with springs in his nose in Robert Pinsky's "Picture," they are making it easy on themselves as rivals in the sweepstakes for public veneration and artistic immortality.

Reading through volumes and journals of the 1980s and 1990s, one is astonished by how retrospective, how historicist, the practice of movie poetry has become. Henry Taylor has remarked how fascinated poets are by "films full of dead actors and antique cars," and how often these movies get ripped off into the poems that regard them.[17] Aren't poets excited by new movies anymore? Ever since Vachel Lindsay fell in love with Mary Pickford and Mae Marsh and set down tributes to them on the spot, at least down through Adrienne Rich's *hommages* to Godard, poets have generally responded to some film or personality of very recent acquaintance. John Berryman opens a poem already discussed, "This night I have seen a film." That sense of immediacy has yielded to something more plangent in tone, as poets turn inward to their memories of movies and theaters that brought them more visual pleasure than anything in their middle age. One finds in the most recent anthology of contemporary poetry at this writing, for example, Mark Doty in "Adonis Theatre" imagining a movie palace of the 1930s, Lynn Emmanuel in "Blonde Bombshell" recalling her childhood "in the dark of the Roxy," Elizabeth Spires in "Mutoscope" going all the way back to cinema's beginnings as she visits an "old Penny Palace" on the Brighton pier.[18] Edward Field's influence on this backward-looking company is enormous, both thematically and stylistically. A whole movement called "Stand Up Poetry," after the title of Field's first volume, has arisen to imitate the nostalgic mode. The Saturday matinee looms immensely in the foreground of their poems, full of retransmissions of the shoot-'em-ups and monster flicks, the voluptuous sexpots and the giddy slapstick of bygone days.

Two examples may indicate the direction of movie-haunted poetry at century's end. Diane Wakoski's *Medea* (1991) performs a retrospective journey in the manner of Jorie Graham, as she returns in memory to her early-teen years in California and recalls the betrayals, especially by men, that threatened to immobilize her as an artist and woman. But Wakoski regenerates herself by the agency of *new* movies, a passion of her later years. She declares herself the "Lady of Moonlight and Teenage Movies" and writes effusively, one might almost say girlishly, about Tom Cruise, Andrew McCarthy, Richard Gere, and other young leading men whom she casts as Jason to her Medea. Like Jason they *will* betray her, simply by being inaccessible to her desire. Throughout the book Wakoski identifies with the Mia Farrow character in *The Purple Rose of Cairo,* who dreams herself into a relationship with the duplicitous Jeff Daniels character, a screen figure who abandons her of ontological necessity. But Wakoski comments knowingly that "movies give me one of those parallel universes where I can live a different life than I was destined for."[19] After being abandoned by her leading man Mia Farrow still goes back to watch the glamorous *Top Hat*; and Wakoski returns to her fantasies of sexual engagement—and more than that, a motherly affection—with her leading men. The Yeatsian character of these poems affirms that new movies *are* redemptive, renewing as they do the romantic impulses that historical time conspires to annihilate in the aging poet.

The other direction is a progressive deconstruction of nostalgia and fresh enthusiasm alike. When Orpheus looks backward as a means of visually embracing his beloved, he causes her dissolution. There is a comic point to this classical mishap, and some poets have made such a good joke of the destructive backward glance that their irreverent poems now constitute a major genre of movie poetry. Bob Perelman, in his animated cartoon of a long poem, "Movie," thrusts Jacques Derrida into a Cary Grant-Katharine Hepburn classic, where the deconstructionist critic, intuiting the true intentions of his costars, chases them into the bedroom and sings their nuptials.[20] Amy Gerstler makes a movie gangster into a Kierkegaardian deity who tries on identities—"Jerusalem Slim on his final night in the garden. Mr. X, Dr. No, The Invisible Man"—to escape the fate of being unreal.[21]

The ultimate ironizing of movie history comes in a poem by John Ashbery, "The Lonedale Operator" (1984). The title refers to a one-reeler by D. W. Griffith (1911), and Ashbery's treatment of it makes a nice framing contrast to Vachel Lindsay's celebratory poem on Mae Marsh with which this study begins. Ashbery saw the movie as an undergraduate, and his unsuccessful efforts to recall it comprise the center of his prose poem:

> I can remember almost none of it, and the little I can remember may have been in another Griffith short, *The Lonely Villa*, which may have been on the same program. It seems that Blanche Sweet was a heroic telephone operator who managed to get through to the police and foil some gangsters who were trying to rob a railroad depot, though I also see this living room—small, though it was supposed to be in a large house—with Mary Pickford running around, and this may have been a scene in *The Lonely Villa*.

And so forth. Ashbery amusingly deconstructs the movie poem by choosing a film of no relevance to his inner life, except that like all memories imperfectly recaptured it signifies the bewildering losses of personal experience as they rush into the past. As he struggles to recall the film's narrative, in a syntax that mimics the jerky editing of the film, Ashbery sends up the solemnity and (to him) exaggerated emotion of the genre. Nevertheless, as with so many Ashbery poems, the reader is called upon to participate in the profound sadness of the ephemeral at the same time it is made an occasion for comedy. As he says in the final paragraph, "Anything can change as fast as it wants to, and in doing so may pass through a more or less terrible phase, but the true terror is in the swiftness of changing."[22] Twenty-four frames a second passing by the reader's eyes. That is the essential experience of cinema: every frame, and every film, a fissioning of the past from an ever-dwindling future. Even the meanest film—like *The Lonedale Operator*—can bring thoughts that lie too deep for tears.

Flat on their backs, the viewers of late-night TV achieve an exquisite intimacy with a talk-show host in this Cornell Capa photo. That TV keeps its audience figuratively supine is the dark suspicion of poets, including the author, who have witnessed the triumph of this visual medium. (Courtesy Cornell Capa-ICP-1957.)

Conclusion: "We're All You Know": Television and Personal History

HOMESICK IN LOS ANGELES

Overnight storms have unsmogged the mountains.
I can see their half-million dollar homes
rising like pantheons from the greener scrub.
Here in the basin iceplant gleams under eucalyptus
and bird of paradise so vibrant it seems to take wing.
For this twilight the city should become a single eye
observing its own lucent, lost perfection.

Cyclops waits indoors. My parents sleepwatch
as I tiptoe through the fluent chatter
of some latest Zsa Zsa, avoid the emerald eyes,
the dizzying abyss of her décolletage.
Everyone must see her new picture, she says,
a high-speed chase and numerous fornications.
Unnoticed, I begin to eavesdrop,
and how can the gaze not rest on her smile?

Use has more force than reason.
A Super Chief carried them from Iowa to these shores,
journey I reenacted with toy engines
while they called the stations from Boone to L.A.
Every mile swallowed into this cave of light,
gone with orange groves they tasted of in January
and the facade of Tara pointing toward the sea.

Moistened by rain, pink blossoms glisten
between fingers of the jade tree they planted.

It is brighter inside than the glow of any tree.
News briefs, reruns that kill an hour or two,
then game shows, a movie, and later news.
Every four minutes merchandise bullies them.
Mother and father, how shall I wield my love
against the raucous cannibal of this house?[1]

—1987

Rapid advances in the technology of the movies, as in the parallel cases of the automobile, the airplane, radio, and other new-century inventions, became a subject of anxiety in the literature of the 1930s. The changeover from silent to sound film had been a traumatic one for the film industry, and some critics with a strong art-historical bias noted with dismay the subordination of the visual image to the microphone in all too many movies in the aftermath of *The Jazz Singer*. But the dream factories very quickly integrated sound and light to produce flawlessly designed romantic glamour for a voracious public during the Depression, and by doing so moved ever closer to the center of American cultural life. Although most critics, and certainly the general public, welcomed each increment in the sophistication of film production as a fulfillment of the original promise of the medium, lurking in their congratulations was the fear that the teleology of film would lead the society toward some electrified future inimical to its welfare. That fear can be glimpsed in dystopias like *Brave New World, Nineteen Eighty-Four,* and *Fahrenheit 451* where the state uses film technology to control social behavior. But something else worried a few commentators in the 1930s: the miniaturization and (proposed) widespread distribution of the medium in the form of television.

Television is so vividly connected in our minds with network programming of the early 1950s that it surprises us still to be reminded that the phenomenon of "tele-vision" was introduced in 1922, in Paris, when Edward Bellin transmitted flashes of light a few feet, and more completely in 1925 when Charles Francis Jenkins developed the world's first working television system. By 1930 NBC had opened an experimental TV station in New York, and CBS followed suit in 1931. By the time of the 1939 World's Fair, where television was extensively displayed, the new medium had reached its takeoff point, though World War II delayed it from entering the market as a formidable rival, and usurper, of its parent technologies, radio and film.

Once the technology of television became feasible, or even thinkable, it began to worry the worldview of cultural critics. The persistent importance of Walter Benjamin's essay on "The Work of Art in the Age of Mechanical Reproduction" has much to do with the relevance of television as an implied example of his argument. Benjamin does not address the possibility directly, but his quotation from Paul Valéry could not be more apropos: "Just as water, gas, and electricity are brought into our houses from far off to satisfy our needs in response to a minimal effort, so we shall be supplied with visual or auditory images, which will appear and disappear at a simple movement of the hand, hardly more than a sign."[2] Benjamin's major concern was that any kind of popular and widely dispersed reproduction of images would lead to a redefinition of art, and, in his view, a degradation of the privileged relationship between artwork and public. The simulacrum, he complained, radically diminishes the aesthetic distance between spectator and artwork, and helps to strengthen the insidious effects of image multiplication in the culture. The sense of wonder derived from contact with the sacred cannot withstand ubiquity or familiarity, not to mention, in the case of television, the inferior quality of the visual image itself. If Benjamin had foreseen television he would have condemned it as the merest reproduction of a reproduction, as if the denizens of Plato's cave were to be supplied with a rude replica of the dumb show they had been witnessing so long on the cave wall.

Commenting on the movies in a state-of-the-culture collection of essays by different hands in 1938, Louis R. Reid remarked, "Television will mean a readjustment of human and economic values. Its sociological, educational, amusement entertainment, political implications, stagger the imagination. Its effect upon mankind is in the laps of the gods."[3] Similar prognostications filled the discourse about moving pictures throughout the 1930s and 1940s, until in the fall of 1946 the first mass production of television sets began, and the die was cast. For the middle-aged, like my parents, the availability of television was a watershed in their lives. I remember their hesitations and misgivings about whether to bring it into the home. Waiting a few years while technicians "got the kinks out" offered one reason for delay. And until there were compelling shows, with popular stars, they saw no need to purchase a set. Perhaps this new medium, which swiftly acquired nicknames like "the boob tube," "the idiot box," "the plug-in drug," "the glass tit," "the great time-killer," really wasn't such a good idea in a house with a college-bound only child. All this deliberating manifested anxiety about what the new invention might do to the rhythms and pleasures of everyday life in our small household. Clearly this was not going to be just a matter of radio with pictures, as it was first advertised, but a wholly new agency of power and pleasure that would fission the history of family life into significant before and after periods. But eventually there came the first set on the block and the first must-see program in the form of the Texaco Star Theatre, and then the fateful decision had to be made. Whatever my parents' qualms, my own enthusiasm for television knew no bounds. I had seen the future and I wanted it installed in our living room. And so in 1951 it came to be.

The first effect was one of family solidarity. Formerly, my parents had gone out to movies, leaving me with a babysitter, and on Saturday afternoons I had been sent to the matinee at the Bards or Baldwin theaters, usually with the same babysitter. Occasionally before my eighth birthday my parents found a movie that we might all enjoy; *King Solomon's Mines* and *Destination Moon* stick out in my memory as favorites, especially for my father and me. Television ended the dual-track experience and gathered us together nightly to watch visual fare we could all enjoy. This was the so-called golden age of television, when Milton Berle, Sid Caesar and Imogene Coca, Lucy and Desi, "Your Hit Parade," Jack Benny, Ernie Kovacs, and Jackie Gleason effectively welded whole families into happy units, and the society into an aggregation of families on the model of Ozzie and Harriet Nelson's. Coming from our various places in the house— my bedroom, the kitchen, the garage—we congregated at the imaginary hearth, and with that flick of the hand Valéry prophesied, we watched some entertaining version of ourselves dance across the tiny screen.

Television is the place where I educated myself in the movies. Los Angeles stations had a considerable stock of low-budget and British movies, though the major Hollywood studios for a brief time did not sell their libraries to television for fear of competition, and I watched virtually every movie I could, sometimes three per day. I became addicted to the visual narratives of the movies as I had become addicted to narratives in print. Indeed, each whetted my desire to indulge myself in the pleasures of the other, so that by the time I left high school, with hundreds if not thousands of movies under my belt, and an infinite appetite for books, my professional career followed the line of least resistance. I began my literary studies at UCLA with the assumption that I would read nothing but the prose I was accustomed to enjoying. Immersing myself in the required reading of the literary tradition, however, I developed a taste for poetry; or rather, the love of verse that came with my reading of Shakespeare in junior high grew in intensity as I discovered how many other fascinating poets like him—if not his equal—existed. Though I could not have easily explained why and how poetry enhanced my pleasure at the movies, and vice versa, I understood intuitively that something about the swift movement of intensely realized imagery in the lyric and narrative modes transferred to my appreciation of film form. When I came to read theorists like Eisenstein and Balazs I understood better why this was the case, and much of film criticism since the 1950s has taken as its subject the "poetics" of the film experience.

But television did not seem anything like poetry to me. The kind of sitcoms, cop shows, game shows, and "Playhouse" formula dramas that filled the airwaves struck me as the antithesis of what I admired in film, fiction, and poetry alike. The interjection of commercials increasingly repelled me from the medium, and I have never in my life been able to watch a show with canned laughter or other audience cues. No single program ever carried the concentrated weight of a good poem or story or movie; one had to sit before the flow of a whole evening's, or a whole week's variety, lulled into the duller rhythms of teleconsciousness, to acquire a few engaging "moments" of the kind books and movies provided so prodigally. As my parents became more and more fond of such programming, and later the talk shows that drove me to distraction, our solidarity dissolved back into the dual-track lives we had led before television came into the home. Now I was old enough to drive out to any movie I wanted, and they tended to stay at home and watch their favorite shows. They never read poetry, so that my increasing devotion to it came to be something else that divided us, as if it were a new

technology or a cataclysmic political event wedged between genera-
tions. Like some arcane body of knowledge, poetry put me on a
"higher" plane, alienated me from the interests and pursuits of their
lives; of course, they were delighted that I was elevating myself out
of the working class, and their loving encouragement produced in
me a species of remorse for the path I had chosen. I noticed that no
small amount of the poetry I read, including Shakespeare, was critical
of people like my parents. Since they never read it they were immune
to its condescension. With the arrogance of youth determined to
improve itself, and the inspiration of some classic texts, I imagined
them as prisoners of Plato's cave, and myself a wayfarer above-
ground, warmed by the rarefied sun of Truth.

My poem "Homecoming in Los Angeles" takes as its central
trope another cave, however. The common designation of TV as
Cyclops, the one-eyed monster, provided me with a hint of how I
could construct a lyric poem testifying to the sense of loss I felt, as
son and citizen, in a society increasingly dominated by the power of
television. Having spent my graduate years in Rhode Island, and my
teaching career in Michigan, I had numerous experiences of home-
coming. The literary topos of exile and homecoming, in any case,
was one I carried in my Jewish genes. I never touched down at LAX,
or revisited Culver City, without profound emotion, wondering
which memories would revive and which I would find to be affec-
tively extinguished. Because my parents still lived in the house I had
grown up in, my return to that street and that house always stirred
powerful anticipations as I monitored my feelings every step of the
way. How would I be received this time around? What hints would
I pick up of some irrevocable change in the family bond?

It never escaped my notice that after the first happy hours of
homecoming celebration and gossip, as dinner settled in the stomach
and conversation began to decelerate, the eyes of my parents began
to wander increasingly to the dark glass screen looming in the corner
of the living room. Eight o'clock was approaching, and some favorite
show. I obligingly encouraged them to watch, and they did, till bed-
time. This would be the routine throughout my visit. In one sense
their devotion to the vespers of television made me feel comfortable,
once again thoroughly at home. But in another sense the scene took
on the allegorical character of some *Kulturkampf* in which the ritual
of family reunion had been subverted by the monstrous rival who

devoured the attention and affection of my parents. One moment I was in Ithaka, and then with a flick of the hand I was in the cave of the Cyclops. Or I was in Babylonian exile, doomed to walk each evening the streets of my childhood while my parents watched *Wheel of Fortune* or *Maude,* gazing into the windows of every house on the street, every living room filled with that eerie blue glow. Was this the typical experience of my generation, I wondered. Was this the form of alienation that postmodern poets would undergo as their unique form of cultural rupture?

I came to feel, when I wrote the poem, that television had intervened between myself and the movies as well, just as it had in the society at large. I use the image of Tara in the poem for this reason. The facade of Tara was kept in a backlot of the Selznick studio not far from my house, and I occasionally climbed the fence to play hide and seek with friends among the abandoned ruins of movie history. When Desilu bought the Selznick property the sets were broken down or shipped elsewhere to make more room for television studios. I was aware of the poetic repetition of this radical change. In *Gone with the Wind* Tara is the sign of the antebellum splendor of the Old South, ruined in fact and memory by the depredations of the Civil War. Tara represents everything that Southerners will feel nostalgic about in the postwar era as they think back to the supposed chivalry and grace of a happy community. Indeed, nostalgia is encoded in the very name Tara, which points back to the glorious reign of the Irish kings before the British conquest. In my poem Tara signifies the splendor of Hollywood in the 1940s, when films like *Gone with the Wind* achieved an unrivaled glamour and (at the end of the decade) attracted kids like myself by their imperial and undisputed authority. Never again after television could the movies exert such absolute sway or command such undivided attention. Except for a few film scholars, perhaps, nobody in America has spent more time at the movies than they have in front of a television screen.

Television, then, becomes the sea of time and space in which contemporary people voyage, hour by hour, year by year. It effaces nature, it alters the texture of human relationship in the city. Types of the siren, "some latest Zsa Zsa," call to everyman less often from bar and brothel (as Joyce imagined in his novel of Ulysses, set just before the rise of the movies) than from the television set, and what viewer is immune from their nightly attractions? The whole of commerce is transacted in simulated form on the tube, and—if we extend the visual category to include computer monitors—the totality of information as well. "Television is our culture's principal mode of knowing about itself," Neil Postman claims,[4] an assertion reminiscent of the jeremiad delivered by newscaster Howard Beale in the movie *Network*. "This tube is the gospel . . . the most awesome propaganda force in the history of the world. . . . We're all you know!" Beale thunders at his herd of watchers. As cable programming and videotape rentals usurp the moviegoing habits of most Americans, with film libraries on demand via telephone cables looming ever closer, film history now depends upon the hardware of the television set for its very existence. The competition is over: movies, like all other parts of our information and entertainment network, have become essentially the software of our domestic media centers. In 1978 Jerry Mander was derided for titling his book *Four Arguments for the Elimination of Television*. There is no credible argument for its elimination, he was told. Quite the opposite, television will determine autonomously the grounds of discourse by which the non-television world will be interpreted and acted upon by a mass audience. We are not about to heave a log into the eye of this cannibal.

Mark Crispin Miller has remarked that "the impending closure of the world by TV entails . . . the homogenization of the spectacle, and the capitulation of the whole public, young and old, and the incorporation of all once-wayward elements, and the renovation of our country into one transcontinental shopping mall."[5] Perhaps this is too apocalyptic, or perhaps not. Like many similar pronouncements about the colonization of our imagination by television, however, it helps one to understand the dominant tendency in recent movie poems to speak elegiacally about the vexed romance between spectator and big-screen actors and stories. Since the time of Vachel Lindsay and Carl Sandburg the movie theater had been securely identified as a site of extraordinary revelation accessible to everyone. The negative facts of the matter—that the city of Hollywood was venal and corrupt, that movies were often trivial and stupid, that moviegoing endangered both the reality principle and the genuine operations of the imagination—paradoxically enhanced the paradisiacal character of movies by making them more needful of redemption, like the sacred places of Jerusalem, Rome, and London in the dominant myths of the West. Hollywood was, in Karl Shapiro's formulation, a *"possibly* proud Florence. "

Fighting for the soul of the movies was what so many poets, and novelists, happily did. This struggle to preserve and enhance the larger-than-life format and the oneiric nature of its narratives has been a national crusade since the first decade of this century. What seems so problematic in the 1990s is the prospect of technological advances that will permit the big screen to be swallowed into the little screen, so that the warfare will suddenly become moot, futile, quixotic. As living room screens become larger, capable of sharper definition, and even more ubiquitous, and multiplex movie theaters offer screens and viewing conditions comparable to a living room, the nature and destiny of the movies in the twenty-first century becomes increasingly uncertain. Of course they will continue to exist, and even thrive, but perhaps only on the condition that they are designed and directed for their principal hardware, the television set. This immense ontological shift in the identity of the movies may well cause poets to intensify their retrospective gaze, each generation borrowing its sense of wonder from the previous one, until the authentic experience of twentieth-century moviegoing finally disappears into the hoary idioms of poetic formula.

By this I mean that poets raised on television will depend on entirely different conventions of seeing when they look at and describe movies, not only current movies—themselves influenced powerfully by television practices—but the movies of the past. If earlier poems about the movies so often formed a school of the sublime, a tradition of joyful wonder, even when the sublime was being ironized for comic effects, posttelevision poems on the same movies must inevitably reflect the distortion of feeling caused by the intercession of the new medium. TV is the boundary break dividing an older piety from a more deconstructive, even mordant expression. The new poetry of Hollywood may glimpse its subject posthumously, as it were, as a cultural memory rather than as an authentic contemporary source of imaginative power.

There will be distinct advantages in this perspective, if we accept Marshall McLuhan's notion that TV watchers wear all of mankind as their skin. Much of postwar history has been made part of our consciousness through the mediation of television, beginning with the McCarthy hearings in the early 1950s, including the Kennedy assassination and funeral in 1963, and the Watergate events of 1973–74, down through the Gulf War and the Clarence Thomas–Anita Hill hearings in the Senate. The succession of network shows since the 1950s comprise a mythical history of America that literate viewers will ever afterward read as the dominant popular text of our time. Historicity is part of the worldview of the television generations, whatever their lapses of cultural literacy. Like recent critical theory, the new poetry of media lore will open itself to the diversity of realities enforced by television, rather than the more unitary (and coherent) story of the tribe fabricated by the classic movies and their admirers. TV is simply less discriminating, teaching its watchers to mingle imaginatively, and with a special kind of intimacy, among the totality of peoples, places, and things. John Fiske and John Hartley have referred to the "bardic" function of television in our culture for this reason.[6] As the centralized consciousness and primary socializing agent of our era, Fiske and Hartley assert, TV offers an audiovisual account of everything our public needs to know about itself, except perhaps the limitations of the medium itself. It is left for that other bardic medium, poetry, to call attention to the boundaries of its omnipresent rival.

As I write, there has so far been no great poem about television, though the subject has been treated on numerous occasions. "Good /poets steal, bad ones / watch TV," is Bob Perelman's opinion.[7] But good poets are watching TV also, though their reference to it is mainly negative. Galway Kinnell records the loathing of the human body he hears in commercials: "On the television screen: // Do you have a body that sweats? / Sweat that has odor? / False teeth clanging into your breakfast? . . . Piles so huge you don't need a chair to sit at a table?" Keith Waldrop notices how teenage girls stare at TV, "All they know bound into that bright box. . . . They watch, / uncomprehending, diaphonous movements in snow." Jorie Graham, too, sees only "flecks of / information . . . dots, dots / roiling up under the golden voice."[8] As channel surfing becomes a national mode of apprehension, thanks to the remote-control device and the abundance of cable-delivered channels, poetry about television is likely to have the mimetic form of early poems influenced by film montage: discontinuous, segmented, full of flickering leaps in time and space to simulate an epistemology constituted by the implosion (to use McLuhan's favorite term) of diverse visual and aural phenomena. As the primary discursive medium in our civilization, television offers a shared rhetoric of forms that is destined to infiltrate the traditional and experimental languages of poetry alike. The shape of such poems is likely to follow the lead of Allen Ginsberg's long oracular and disjointed work, "Television Was a Baby Crawling toward that Deathchamber." In that poem television is treated as a metaphor of the totality of American experience, indeed of cosmic experience, as our media have revealed it to us.

Eventually poets will treat television in sufficient variety and depth that a book like this one will be required to trace the subject through successive decades from the 1950s. There will be much to celebrate and deplore in the poems covered by that book. There will be a golden age to look back on fondly, a "crisis" as cable and VCR alternatives weaken the dominance of the networks, and perhaps technological threats to the vitality of commercial programming in the form of video games or some variant of what we now call Virtual Reality. The claims made for television as the *truly* democratic art will be matched by the savage indignation of many poets of the late twentieth and early twenty-first centuries as they excoriate the devastating effects of so much wasted time, so much social conditioning, so much trivial material bombarding an increasingly fractioned attention span. But who would write such a book, or such poems, unless he or she found the medium fascinating and important? It may be that in the cave of Cyclops one witnesses the strangling of love, the withering of a vital culture—this is the argument of my poem—but the whole truth is more complex than any one version of the encounter between spectator and medium. Vachel Lindsays have already been heard from, some Hart Crane has no doubt written a masterly "Chaplinesque" about the adept comedian of a popular sitcom; and all the rest of the sacred history will follow, as the new testament of our visual culture measures the distance between our mortal responsibilities and our unceasing dream of perfect entertainment.

Notes

Introduction

1. Dwight Macdonald, "A Theory of Mass Culture," in *Mass Culture: The Popular Arts in America,* ed. Bernard Rosenberg and David Manning White (Glencoe, Ill.: Free Press, 1957), 72. Macdonald would later develop this theory in his classic essay, "Masscult & Midcult," in *Against the American Grain* (New York: Random House, 1962), 3–75.
2. Walter Benjamin, *Illuminations,* ed. Hannah Arendt, trans. Harry Zohn (New York: Schocken, 1969), 221.
3. Gregory Battcock, "The Warhol Generation," in *The New Art: A Critical Anthology,* ed. Gregory Battcock (New York: Dutton, 1973), 21. Battcock argues that pop art was an elitist, not a democratic movement: "Pop Art became an art style that snickered at the poor taste and the common, uncomplicated communicative level of the masses" (23).
4. Carl Van Vechten, *Spider Boy: a scenario for a moving picture* (New York: Knopf, 1928). The portrait of the Invincible Film Company in Culver City, and the chief producer Sam Griesheimer, tells us much about how Hollywood was imagined in the 1920s. Carroll Graham and Garrett Graham, *Queer People* (Carbondale: Southern Illinois University Press, 1976), 156. As Budd Schulberg notes in an afterword, it is this novel, with its scenes of a Hollywood premiere and a brothel and a raffish underworld of starstruck hangers-on, that anticipates serious Hollywood fiction of the 1930s like Nathanael West's *The Day of the Locust,* Horace McCoy's *They Shoot Horses, Don't They?* and Schulberg's own *What Makes Sammy Run?* For a bibliography of studies of the Hollywood novel, see Harris Ross, *Film as Literature, Literature as Film* (New York: Greenwood Press, 1987).
5. Louis Simpson, "The Magic Carpet," in *In the Room We Share* (New York: Paragon, 1990), 53. According to Simpson, "Since movies were invented we have had no time for description of scenery and for long drawn-out transitions. Nor for the working out of an obvious plot." "Reflections on Narrative Poetry," in *Claims for Poetry,* ed. Donald Hall (Ann Arbor: University of Michigan Press, 1982), 413.
6. Stanley Cavell, *The World Viewed: Reflections on the Ontology of Film,* enlarged edition (Cambridge: Harvard University Press, 1979), 14. One could cite many expressions of the same viewpoint—for example, Arthur Miller's remark that film form is "the single great cultural invention of this civiliza-

tion. . . . The movie image is so overwhelming it's convincing in itself; the person is *there,* simply by being photographed." "A Conversation with Arthur Miller," *Michigan Quarterly Review* 29, no. 2 (Spring 1990): 159.

7. William Carlos Williams, "The Wanderer," in *The Collected Poems of William Carlos Williams,* vol. 1, ed. A. Walton Litz and Christopher MacGowan (New York: New Directions, 1986), 28. Williams does pay a brief tribute to Eisenstein's film *Que Viva Mexico!* in Book II of *Paterson.* See Christopher MacGowan's revised edition (New York: New Directions, 1992), 57–58.

8. Eugene Jolas, *Cinema* (New York: Adelphi, 1926), 80. Despite the title, Jolas's book has little to do with the movies. The same is true of Conrad Aiken's second volume of poems, *Turns and Movies* (Boston: Houghton Mifflin, 1916), a sequence entirely devoted to vaudeville performers. Such titles announce a forward-looking contemporaneity often belied by the poems themselves.

9. Henry Taylor, "A Panel of Experts on 'Blind Alley' Discuss the Influence of Cinema on Modern Poets," *Film Journal* 1 (Fall–Winter 1972): 39; David Lehman, "Picture This," *Pequod* 28–30 (1989): 118.

10. Edith Sitwell, *Taken Care Of* (New York: Atheneum, 1965), 223.

11. Delmore Schwartz, *Last & Lost Poems,* ed. Robert Phillips (New York: New Directions, 1989), 23.

12. Frank Norris, *McTeague,* vol. 8 of *Works* (Garden City: Doubleday, Doran, 1928), 84; Edith Wharton, *The House of Mirth* (New York: Scribner's, 1905), 139.

13. *The New Poetry: An Anthology,* ed. Harriet Monroe and Alice Corbin Henderson (New York: Macmillan, 1917), 109. The poem was reprinted in *The Soul of the City: An Urban Anthology,* ed. Garland Greever and Joseph M. Bachelor (Boston: Houghton Mifflin, 1923), 287.

14. Cavell, *World Viewed,* 189.

Chapter 1

1. *The Poetry of Vachel Lindsay, complete & with Lindsay's drawings,* 3 vols., ed. Dennis Camp (Peoria: Spoon River Poetry Press, 1984), 1:305–6. All citations of Lindsay's poems are to this edition and are given in the text.

2. *Letters of Vachel Lindsay,* ed. Marc Chenetier (New York: Burt Franklin & Co., 1979), 455.

3. Vachel Lindsay, *Art of the Moving Picture,* 2d ed (1922; rpt. New York: Liveright, 1970), 4.

4. *Letters,* 336.

5. See the discussion in *Letters,* 121–22. An editorial in the *Nation* pronounced in 1913 that movies warranted "little thought and no critical attention." See Michael Pressler, "Poet and Professor on the Movies," *Gettysburg Review* 4, no. 1 (Winter 1991): 164. Later in the silent era George Jean Nathan repeated the charge: "The movies are presently handicapped by the circumstance that they must all be fashioned with a single type of audience in mind, and that

type the lowest." *The World of George Jean Nathan,* ed. Charles Angoff (New York: Alfred A. Knopf, 1952), 460.

6. Cited in Harry M. Geduld, ed., *Focus on D. W. Griffith* (Englewood Cliffs, N.J.: Prentice-Hall, 1971), 34.

7. Frederick Palmer, *Palmer Plan Handbook: An Elementary Treatise on the Theory and Practice of Photoplay Scenario Writing According to Present Day Standards as Recognized and Employed by Successful Photo-Dramatists,* 2d ed. (Hollywood: Palmer Photoplay Corporation, 1922), 1:9.

8. Cited in Stanley Kauffmann with Bruce Henstell, eds., *American Film Criticism: From the Beginnings to Citizen Kane* (New York: Liveright, 1972), 68.

9. Henry Adams, *The Education of Henry Adams* (Boston: Houghton Mifflin, 1961), 383–84.

10. Richard deCordova, *Picture Personalities: The Emergence of the Star System in America* (Urbana: University of Illinois Press, 1990), 51.

11. Lindsay, *Art of the Moving Picture,* 56.

12. *Letters,* 298–300.

13. Lindsay, *Art of the Moving Picture,* 299.

14. Marjorie Rosen, *Popcorn Venus* (New York: Avon, 1974), 45. For an analysis of Mae Marsh's coquettish and flirtatious behavior (before marriage) in *The Mother and the Law,* in which madonna worship is coupled ambiguously with "unmistakably incestuous overtones," see Miriam Hansen, *Babel & Babylon: Spectatorship in American Silent Film* (Cambridge: Harvard University Press, 1991), 151.

15. Vachel Lindsay, "Queen of My People," *New Republic,* 7 July 1917, 280.

16. Molly Haskell, *From Reverence to Rape: The Treatment of Women in the Movies* (New York: Penguin Books, 1974), 54.

17. Anita Loos, "A Poet in Love," in *Fate Keeps on Happening: Adventures of Lorelei Lee and Other Writings,* ed. Ray Pierre Corsini (New York: Dodd, Mead, 1984), 162–65.

18. Vachel Lindsay, *Adventures: Rhymes and Designs* (New York: Eakins Press, 1968), 52.

19. Cited in Glenn Joseph Wolfe, *Vachel Lindsay: The Poet as Film Theorist* (New York: Arno Press, 1973), 135. He wrote in his unpublished manuscript, "To the movie fan, Egypt still exists. The Egyptian Theatre at Hollywood is a sort of beginning shrine, a sort of temple to them" (90–91). The unpublished manuscript, "The Greatest Movies Now Running," is in the Clifton Waller Barrett Collection, Alderman Library, University of Virginia, 22. Page numbers in parentheses in the remainder of this chapter refer to this manuscript.

20. "A Special Delivery Letter to My Particular Friends," box no. 16 of Lindsay archives, University of Virginia.

21. Geduld, *Focus on D. W. Griffith,* 34.

22. Lindsay, *Art of the Moving Picture,* 251–52.

23. John Berryman, "Homage to Film," *The Southern Review* 5, no. 4 (Spring 1940): 773.

Chapter 2

1. Hart Crane, "Chaplinesque," in *The Poems of Hart Crane,* ed. Marc Simon (New York: Liveright, 1986), 11.
2. See Edmund Wilson's essay, "It's Terrible! It's Ghastly! It Stinks!" in *The Shores of Light* (New York: Vintage Books, 1952), 662–68.
3. Alexander Pope, *Selected Poetry and Prose,* ed. William K. Wimsatt, Jr. (New York: Holt, Rinehart and Winston, 1961), 348. There are echoes in these passages, especially, of Othello's speech in act 5, scene 2: "I know not where is that Promethean heat / That can thy light relume."
4. Susan Jenkins Brown, *Robber Rocks: Letters and Memories of Hart Crane, 1923–1932* (Middletown, Conn.: Wesleyan University Press, 1969), 10.
5. Sergei Eisenstein, "Charlie the Kid," trans. Herbert Marshall, in *Sight and Sound: A Fiftieth Anniversary Selection,* ed. David Wilson (London: Faber and Faber, 1972), 49. Sherwood Anderson makes extended use of the Chaplin tramp figure in his poetic meditations on modern industrialism to refresh the reader's view of factory life as strange, grotesque, inhuman. Anderson's imagining of how Chaplin would usefully distort the encounter of man and machine anticipates *Modern Times* by five years. See *Perhaps Women* (New York: Liveright, 1931), 95–97.
6. *The Letters of Hart Crane,* ed. Brom Weber (Berkeley and Los Angeles: University of California Press, 1965), 68.
7. For a reading of Wordsworth's dream that emphasizes the political context see my *Ruins and Empire: The Evolution of a Theme in Augustan and Romantic Literature* (Pittsburgh: University of Pittsburgh Press, 1977), chap. 9.
8. *Letters,* 68.
9. *Letters,* 85.
10. Thomas E. Yingling, *Hart Crane and the Homosexual Text* (Chicago: University of Chicago Press, 1990), 117. On the subject of what Yingling calls Chaplin's "marvelous suspension of gender" see William Paul, "Charles Chaplin and the Annals of Anality," *Comedy/Cinema/Theory,* ed. Andrew S. Horton (Berkeley and Los Angeles: University of California Press, 1991), 109–30.
11. Delmore Schwartz, *Selected Essays of Delmore Schwartz,* ed. Donald A. Dike and David H. Zucker (Chicago: University of Chicago Press, 1970), 11.
12. Charles J. Maland, *Chaplin and American Culture: The Evolution of a Star Image* (Princeton: Princeton University Press, 1989), 63–64. Carl Sandburg in a newspaper feature of 1921 likewise refers to Chaplin's "large heart and contemplative mind," and recommends Hamlet as a vehicle for the comic he has just interviewed. Jean Cocteau suggests Prince Myshkin from *The Idiot* as a congenial role. See Harry M. Geduld, ed., *Authors on Film* (Bloomington: Indiana University Press, 1972), 263–66, 256. "I always knew I was a poet," Chaplin told Garson Kanin. See Kanin's memoir, *Hollywood* (New York: Viking, 1974), 128.
13. Parker Tyler, *Chaplin: Last of the Clowns* (New York: Horizon Press, 1972), 35. Later Tyler remarks, "The 'French' kick . . . the monumentally fragile

shrug; the deft, lightning-like adjustment of the derby; the cannily cosmic, single revolution of the cane; the gyration of the mustache that seemed to tickle his nose like some transcendent odor—all these things were child-aristocratic mannerisms, a heraldic defiance of the worst that reality could do, or not do" (74–75).

14. R. W. B. Lewis, *The Poetry of Hart Crane: A Critical Study* (Princeton: Princeton University Press, 1967), 70–73. A postwar influence is claimed by Gerald Mast, who sees Samuel Beckett's clowns in *Waiting for Godot* as derived from Chaplin and Keaton (Beckett wrote and directed a movie, *Film,* for the aged Keaton), and the name Godot as a play on Charlot, the French moniker for Chaplin. *A Short History of the Movies* (Indianapolis: Bobbs-Merrill, 1977), 153.

15. Alfred Kreymborg, *A History of American Poetry* (1929; New York: Tudor Publishing Co., 1934), 605.

16. Cited in John Unterecker, *Voyager: A Life of Hart Crane* (New York: Farrar, Straus and Giroux, 1969), 523.

17. Brown, *Robber Rocks,* 20.

18. Carl Sandburg, *Complete Poems* (New York: Harcourt, Brace and Company, 1950), 26. All citations of Sandburg's poems are to this edition and are given in the text.

19. "Since the Fleet with its twenty-five thousand gobs has left for Hawaii I have had a chance to face and recognize the full inconsequence of the Polly-anna greasepaint pinkpoodle paradise with its everlasting stereotyped sun-light and its millions of mechanical accessories and sylphlike robots of the age of celluloid." *Letters,* 324–25.

Chapter 3

1. Archibald MacLeish, *Collected Poems 1917–1982* (Boston: Houghton Mifflin, 1985), 145–46.

2. Wendy Steiner, *Exact Resemblance to Exact Resemblance: The Literary Portraiture of Gertrude Stein* (New Haven: Yale University Press, 1978), 17. For more on Stein and cinema, see P. Adams Sitney, *Modernist Montage: The Obscurity of Vision in Cinema and Literature* (New York: Columbia University Press, 1990).

3. Robert Penn Warren, "'Twelve Poets," *American Review* 3 (March 1934): 212–18.

4. Archibald MacLeish, *A Time to Speak* (Boston: Houghton Mifflin, 1940), 154.

5. *Letters of Archibald MacLeish, 1907 to 1982,* ed. R. H. Winnick (Boston: Houghton Mifflin, 1983), 140, 149. The poem is "Invocation to the Social Muse."

6. *Letters,* 142.

7. *Letters,* 157. See the discussion of *The Waste Land* as a cinematic poem in

Robert Richardson, *Literature and Film* (Bloomington: Indiana University Press, 1969), 104–18.

8. *Letters,* 153.
9. Gertrude Stein, *How Writing Is Written,* ed. Robert Bartlett Haas (Los Angeles: Black Sparrow Press, 1974), 159. Stein claimed that she developed her theory of the continuous presence before she had seen a single movie. She would go on to write film scripts, keeping in mind Jacques Viot's advice, "You have to remember in writing film stories that it is not like writing for the theater the film audience is not an audience that is awake it is an audience that is dreaming" (*Everybody's Autobiography* [New York: Random House, 1937], 210).
10. *A Time to Speak,* 85.
11. *The Dialogues of Archibald MacLeish and Mark Van Doren,* ed. Warren V. Bush (New York: E. P. Dutton, 1964), 89.
12. *Archibald MacLeish: Reflections,* ed. Bernard A. Drabeck and Helen E. Ellis (Amherst: University of Massachusetts Press, 1986), 99.
13. *A Time to Speak,* 40.
14. "MacLeish on Spain," *Cinema Arts* 1, no. 3 (September 1937): 59.
15. James Agee, *Agee on Film,* vol. 1 (New York: Grosset's Universal Library), 321. Agee sees in movies "the creation of a new dramatic poetry" and remarks that "for such new poetry, movies offer the richest opportunity since Shakespeare's time" (365).
16. Sol Funaroff, *The Spider and the Clock* (New York: International Publishers, 1938), 28.
17. *Archibald MacLeish: Reflections,* 64–65.
18. *Letters of Marshall McLuhan,* ed. Marie Molinaro, Corinne McLuhan, and William Toye (Oxford University Press, 1987), 193.
19. See Humphrey Carpenter, *A Serious Character: The Life of Ezra Pound* (Boston: Houghton Mifflin, 1988), 499, 595.
20. *Letters,* 282.

Chapter 4

1. Winfield Townley Scott, *New and Selected Poems,* ed. George P. Elliott (New York: Doubleday, 1967), 7–8.
2. Vachel Lindsay, *The Art of the Moving Picture* (2d ed., 1922; New York: Liveright, 1970), 159. The following quotations are on pp. 290 and 289, respectively. Lindsay notes characteristically, "The slums are an astonishing assembly of cave-men crawling out of their shelters to exhibit for the first time in history a common interest on a tremendous scale in an art form" (235). For a useful study of the resemblances, see Gerald Noxon, "Pictorial Origins of Cinema Narrative in Pre-Historic and Ancient Art," *Cinema Studies* 2 (Spring 1968): 1–56.
3. See Calvin Tomkins, "A Reporter at Large (Thinking in Time)," *New Yorker,* 22 April 1974, 124.

4. Alexander Marshack, *The Roots of Civilization* (New York: McGraw-Hill, 1972), 327.

5. *The Republic of Plato,* tr. Francis MacDonald Cornford (New York: Oxford University Press, 1971), 200.

6. Norman Mailer, *The Deer Park* (New York: G. P. Putnam's Sons, 1955), 33.

7. Cited in Scott Donaldson, *Poet in America: Winfield Townley Scott* (Austin: University of Texas Press, 1972), 343.

8. See *"a dirty hand": The Literary Notebooks of Winfield Townley Scott,* ed. Merle Armitage (Austin: University of Texas Press, 1969), 123.

9. Scott, *New and Selected Poems,* 150.

10. Winfield Townley Scott, *Alpha Omega,* ed. Eleanor M. Scott (Garden City, N.Y.: Doubleday, 1971), 125, 163.

11. Henry James Forman, *Our Movie-Made Children* (New York: Macmillan, 1934), 130–31. Subsequent references are given in the text.

12. Herbert Read, *A Coat of Many Colours* (London: George Routledge and Sons, 1945), 229. Read comments, "We have in France the *surrealiste* film—a film that is completely irrational in its content, a film that can only be compared with the dream, even with the nightmare, and which gains all its force and vividness by possessing the same characteristics as the dream."

13. William J. Perelman, ed., *The Movies on Trial* (New York: Macmillan, 1936), 147.

14. *Movies on Trial,* 151. Vachel Lindsay expressed a similar sentiment in the mid-1920s when he wrote that "we have started to rebuild the brain and fancy of mankind . . . Beginning again, we must begin as children. . . . the movies has [*sic*] made the thirteen year old imagination resplendent." See Vachel Lindsay, *"The Thief of Bagdad," Michigan Quarterly Review* 31, no. 2 (Spring 1992), 239–40.

15. Quoted in James Atlas, *Delmore Schwartz: The Life of an American Poet* (New York: Farrar Straus Giroux, 1977), 355, 107.

16. Delmore Schwartz, *Genesis, Book One* (New York: New Directions, 1943), 120. An interesting comparison would be Weldon Kees's poem of 1936, "Subtitle," in *The Collected Poems of Weldon Kees,* rev. ed., ed. Donald Justice (Lincoln: University of Nebraska Press, 1992), 3.

17. Sigmund Freud, *A General Introduction to Psycho-Analysis* (New York: Liveright, 1935), 115.

18. Schwartz, *Genesis: Book One,* 148.

19. Delmore Schwartz, "Paris and Helen," in *New Directions in Prose and Poetry, 1941,* ed. James Laughlin (Norfolk, Conn.: New Directions, 1941), 194.

20. *Selected Essays of Delmore Schwartz,* 439, 444.

21. Atlas, *Life,* 43. *Portrait of Delmore: Journals and Notes of Delmore Schwartz 1939–1959,* ed. Elizabeth Pollet (New York: Farrar Straus Giroux, 1986), 4.

22. Schwartz, *Last and Lost Poems,* 22.

23. The story is printed in *In Dreams Begin Responsibilities and Other Stories,* ed. James Atlas (New York: New Directions, 1978), 187–202.

24. For these Chaplin references see Delmore Schwartz, *Selected Poems: Summer Knowledge* (New York: New Directions, 1967), 47, 77. In Schwartz's writ-

ings on film Chaplin is constantly extolled as an ideal. "Everything characteristic of Charlie Chaplin connected him and related him to the entire human race" is a typical remark (*Selected Essays of Delmore Schwartz*, 473).

Intermission

1. Diana Trilling, "The Death of Marilyn Monroe," *Claremont Essays* (London: Secker and Warburg, 1965), 242. The context offers some exoneration. Speaking of writers who blamed Hollywood's "vulgarity and greed" for Monroe's suicide, Trilling writes, "I share their disgust with Hollywood, and I honor their need to isolate Marilyn Monroe from the nastiness that fed on her, but I find it impossible to believe that this girl would have been an iota better off were Hollywood to have been other than what we all know it to be, a madness in our culture."
2. W. B. Yeats, "The Hosting of the Sidhe," in *The Poems of W. B. Yeats,* ed. Richard J. Finneran (New York: Macmillan, 1983), 55.
3. Nathanael West, *The Day of the Locust* (1939; New York: Signet, 1983), 93. References in the text are to this edition.
4. Laurence Goldstein, *The Three Gardens* (Providence, R.I.: Copper Beech Press, 1987), 27. The poem first appeared in the *Southern Review* 18, no. 1 (January 1982): 166–68.
5. Quoted in Jay Martin, *Nathanael West: The Art of His Life* (New York: Farrar, Straus and Giroux, 1970), 273.
6. Grierson's comment is cited and discussed in William Stott, *Documentary Expression and Thirties America* (New York: Oxford University Press, 1973), 11–12.
7. See Geduld, *Authors on Film,* 240, 46. Compare Farrell's and Sartre's comments to that of a British working-class woman in John Fowles's story, "The Woman in the Reeds": "You know what it's like sometimes when you come out at the end of a film? You feel we're all nobodies; just a lot of nobodies they can do what they like in front of. We can never be like they are." See Laurence Goldstein, ed., *Seasonal Performances: A* Michigan Quarterly Review *Reader* (Ann Arbor: University of Michigan Press, 1991), 234. The same sentiment is captured in Alfred Hayes's poem, "Cinema," in *The Big Time* (New York: Howell, Soskin, 1944), 43–44. "No camera grinds us nights we groan and toss, / No lenses click us crouching in the upper tiers," Hayes writes. The leftist critique of the movies persistently emphasizes the way movie illusion mocks and diminishes the spectator's ordinary experience.

Chapter 5

1. Karl Shapiro, *Collected Poems 1940–1978* (New York: Random House, 1978), 31–32.
2. Karl Shapiro, *The Younger Son* (Chapel Hill, N.C.: Algonquin Books of Chapel Hill, 1988), 42, 22. For "thing poet" see 104.
3. Nathanael West, *The Day of the Locust* (1939; New York: Signet, 1983), 130. The quotations that follow are on p. 128.

4. Karl Shapiro, *The Bourgeois Poet* (New York: Random House, 1964), 54–55.

5. See Harold E. Stearns, ed., *America Now: An Inquiry into Civilization in the United States* (New York: Literary Guild, 1938), 66.

6. Kenneth Fearing, "Denouement," in *New & Selected Poems* (Bloomington: Indiana University Press, 1956), 31. The next poem cited is "Invitation," 12.

7. Schwartz, *Genesis, Book One,* 184.

8. Karl Shapiro, "Movie Actress," in *V-Letter and Other Poems* (New York: Reynal & Hitchcock, 1944), 15.

9. Karl Shapiro, *In Defense of Ignorance* (New York: Vintage, 1965), 205.

10. Neal Gabler, *An Empire of Their Own: How the Jews Invented Hollywood* (New York: Crown, 1988), 119.

11. Karl Shapiro, "The 151st Psalm," *Poems of a Jew* (New York: Random House, 1958), 6. See the poem "Israel" on p. 4 for Shapiro's celebration of "the battle for Zion" concluding in statehood for the Jewish people.

12. Shapiro, *In Defense of Ignorance,* 84.

13. Ibid., 35, 36. "His word was our poetic law," Shapiro remarked of Eliot in *Essay on Rime* (New York: Reynal & Hitchcock, 1945). He mixes praise of "Ash Wednesday" with scorn for the "jabberwocky" of *The Waste Land* and *The Cantos* (60, 45). Eliot was a favorite target of Jewish poets on the Left; see, for example, Sol Funaroff's radical revision of *The Waste Land* already discussed, and Kenneth Fearing's "American Rhapsody (I)": "That genius, that literatur, Theodore True, / St. Louis boy who made good as an Englishman in / theory, a deacon in vaudeville, a cipher in politics, / undesirable in large numbers to any community." *Poems* (New York: Dynamo, 1935), 25.

14. I. P. Fassett, review of *The Tents of Israel* by G. B. Stern, *The Criterion* 3, no. 10 (January 1925): 330. "We are all of us acquainted with at least one Jewish family, and so we know already everything that Miss Stern tells us," Fassett waspishly remarks.

15. Shapiro, *Essay on Rime,* 65.

16. Edmund Wilson, *Axel's Castle: A Study in the Imaginative Literature of 1870–1930* (New York: Scribner's, 1931), 120.

17. Thomas McGrath, "Ars Poetica; Or: Who Lives in the Ivory Tower," in *Longshot O'Leary's Garland of Practical Poesie* (New York: International Publishers, 1949), 8.

18. Karl Shapiro, *Reports of My Death* (Chapel Hill, N.C.: Algonquin Books of Chapel Hill, 1990), 35. It is noteworthy that Delmore Schwartz, even in an essay titled "The Literary Dictatorship of T. S. Eliot" (*Partisan Review,* February 1949), never made a connection between European fascism and the ascendancy of Eliot. In his 1960 review of Pound's Cantos 96–109, *Thrones de los Cantares,* Schwartz temporizes characteristically: "if Pound is, at times, anti-Semitic, he is also, at other times philo-Semitic." Like Pound's disciple Louis Zukofsky, Schwartz believed that the cause of modernist poetry was too important to damage by publicly protesting the anti-Semitism of its leading figures. See "Ezra Pound and History," in *Selected Essays of Delmore Schwartz,* 119.

19. F. Scott Fitzgerald, *The Last Tycoon* (1941; New York: Collier Books, 1986), 91, 15, 18. Subsequent page references are given in the text.

20. Shapiro, *Reports of My Death,* 137. One might have expected Shapiro to take more interest in Charles Reznikoff, an objectivist like Williams and a model for Ginsberg of the urban Jewish sensibility. Reznikoff used some film material in writing about his years in Southern California. See, for example, "Autobiography: Hollywood (I–XXVII)," *Poems 1937–1975,* vol. 2 of *Complete Poems,* ed. Seamus Cooney (Santa Barbara: Black Sparrow Press, 1977), 38–47.

21. Karl Shapiro, *Person, Place and Thing* (New York: Reynal & Hitchcock, 1942), 6

22. See Leslie Fiedler's two books, *Waiting for the End* (New York: Stein and Day, 1964), especially chaps. 5 and 6, and *To the Gentiles* (New York: Stein and Day, 1972), for lengthy discussions of the anti-Semitism of modernist writers, and the countervailing strategies of Jewish writers after World War II. In *After the Revolution: Studies in the Contemporary Jewish-American Imagination* (Bloomington: Indiana University Press, 1987), Mark Shechner examines how writers like Roth and Ginsberg use language as a social weapon against the assumed puritanism of their readers.

23. Isidor Schneider, *Comrade: Mister* (New York: Equinox Cooperative Press, 1934), unpaginated.

24. See the quotations and judicious discussion in Christopher Ricks, *T. S. Eliot and Prejudice* (Berkeley and Los Angeles: University of California Press, 1988), 41.

25. Shapiro, *The Bourgeois Poet,* 53–54.

Chapter 6

1. *The Selected Poems of Frank O'Hara,* ed. Donald Allen (New York: Knopf, 1974), 99–100.

2. Alan Feldman, *Frank O'Hara* (Boston: Twayne, 1979), 148.

3. Otto Friedrich, *City of Nets* (New York: Perennial Library, 1987), 344.

4. Friedrich, *City of Nets,* 436. Gore Vidal's novel *Myra Breckenridge* (1968), and its sequel, *Myron* (1974), are constructed playfully around the mythos of Hollywood decline. "It is now plain that the classic age of films has ended," Myra laments, "and will not return any more than verse drama . . . has a chance of revival." (See *Myra Breckenridge* and *Myron* [New York: Vintage, 1987], 95). Likewise Daniel Fuchs writes in his story of 1954, "The Golden West": "The handwriting was on the wall. The industry was dead. It was all over, the years of picturemaking, the work, the rush, the all-night session at the studio, the whole wonderful excitement and rapture." *The Apathetic Bookie Joint* (New York: Methuen, 1979), 188.

5. Douglas Gomery, "If You've Seen One, You've Seen the Mall," in *Seeing Through Movies,* ed. Mark Crispin Miller (New York: Pantheon Books, 1990), 65. One must note the HUAC hearings about Hollywood as a con-

tributory part of the crisis Hollywood suffered in the late 1940s and 1950s. Neither O'Hara nor his followers pays the slightest attention to this outrage against fellow artists. The Supreme Court decision in the *United States vs. Paramount* case of 1948 stripping the studios of their theaters damaged the financial well-being of the studios as well.

6. O'Hara, *Selected Poems,* 13–14.
7. Robert Pinsky, *Poetry and the World* (New York: Ecco Press, 1988), 96.
8. Jim Elledge, "'Never Argue About the Movies': Love and the Cinema in the Poetry of Frank O'Hara," *Frank O'Hara: To Be True to a City,* ed. Jim Elledge (Ann Arbor: University of Michigan Press, 1990), 350–57.
9. Parker Tyler, *The Will of Eros: Selected Poems 1930–1970* (Los Angeles: Black Sparrow Press, 1972), 27–29.
10. Feldman, *Frank O'Hara,* 149.
11. Marjorie Perloff, *Frank O'Hara: Poet among Painters* (New York: George Braziller, 1977), 153. One might pursue the connection between such litanies in verse and the not-so-trivial pursuit of film arcana in Wallace Markfield's *To an Early Grave* (New York: Simon and Schuster, 1964), the first novel to make of minor film history a ceremonial catechism. See the opening chapters, especially, where old friends traveling in a car to their mutual friend's burial site desperately quiz each other about old movies.
12. *The Collected Poems of Frank O'Hara,* ed. Donald Allen (New York: Knopf, 1971), 429.
13. Frank O'Hara, *Standing Still and Walking in New York* (Bolinas: Grey Fox Press, 1975), 17. "Movie-fed head" is on p. 95.
14. O'Hara, *Standing Still,* 160.
15. John Hollander, *Movie-Going and Other Poems* (New York: Atheneum, 1962), 4.
16. Robert von Hallberg, *American Poetry and Culture 1945–1980* (Cambridge: Harvard University Press, 1985), 181.
17. Rudy Kikel, "The Gay Frank O'Hara," *Frank O'Hara: To Be True to a City,* 338.
18. Allen Ginsberg, "These States, into L.A.," in *The Fall of America* (San Francisco: City Lights, 1972), 10. Laurel and Hardy reappear in Ginsberg's *White Shroud* (New York: Harper and Row, 1986), 21.
19. Vito Russo, *The Celluloid Closet: Homosexuality in the Movies,* Revised Edition (New York: Harper and Row, 1987), 72–74.
20. David R. Slavitt, *The Carnivore* (Chapel Hill: University of North Carolina Press, 1965), 10. A very different use of the Old West relevant to this list is Michael McClure's poem sequence, "The Sermons of Jean Harlow and The Curses of Billy the Kid," *Star* (New York: Grove Press, 1970), adapted to the stage as *The Beard* (New York: Grove Press, 1967). In both works the two overheated icons of popular culture rant and bitch at each other about sexuality and violence.
21. Edward Field, "Notes: Going to School at the Movies," *Telescope* 3, no. 3 (Fall 1984): 116.
22. Field, "Notes," 118.

Chapter 7

1. Adrienne Rich, *The Will to Change* (New York: Norton, 1971), 47–49. Though Rich included this poem in the selection from *The Will to Change* in the Norton Critical Edition of 1975, *Adrienne Rich's Poetry*, and in *Poems: Selected and New 1950–1974*, it was omitted from her later selected volume, *The Fact of a Doorframe* (1984).
2. Letter to the author, 19 January 1991.
3. Stanley Kauffmann, *A World on Film* (New York: Harper and Row, 1966), 415.
4. Quoted by Pauline Kael, *Kiss Kiss Bang Bang* (New York: Little, Brown, 1968), 113.
5. Cited by Toby Mussman, "Introductory Notes," *Jean-Luc Godard*, ed. Toby Mussman (New York: Dutton, 1968), 23.
6. Ludwig Wittgenstein, *Philosophical Investigations,* trans. G. E. M. Anscombe (New York: Macmillan, 1958), 8. The source is identified by Barbara Charlesworth Gelpi and Albert Gelpi in the Norton Critical Edition of Rich's poetry, no doubt after consultation with Rich.
7. Adrienne Rich, "When We Dead Awaken: Writing as Re-Vision," *On Lies, Secrets, and Silence: Selected Prose 1966–1978* (New York: Norton, 1979), 35.
8. Robert Hass, *Praise* (New York: Ecco Press, 1979), 3.
9. Adrienne Rich, "When We Dead Awaken," 39, 36.
10. John Kreidl, *Jean-Luc Godard* (Boston: Twayne, 1980), 178.
11. Robin Wood, "Alphaville," in *The Films of Jean-Luc Godard,* ed. Ian Cameron (New York: Praeger, 1969), 86.
12. This quotation and all others from the film are taken from *Alphaville: A Film by Jean-Luc Godard,* trans. Peter Whitehead (New York: Simon and Schuster, 1965). The quotation from *Capitale de la douleur* is on p. 67. More than twenty years later, Rich will say of America, "This is the capital of money and dolor." See *An Atlas of the Difficult World* (New York: Norton, 1991), 6.
13. Robert Duncan, *The Opening of the Field* (New York: Grove Press, 1960), 93.
14. Jean Cocteau, *Three Screenplays,* trans. Carol Martin-Sperry (New York: Grossman, 1972), 181–82.

Chapter 8

1. Wanda Coleman, *African Sleeping Sickness: Stories & Poems* (Santa Rosa, Calif.: Black Sparrow Press, 1990), 302.
2. Philip French, *Westerns: Aspects of a Movie Genre* (New York: Viking, 1973), 118, 122.
3. Louise Erdrich, *Jacklight* (New York: Holt, Rinehart and Winston, 1984), 12–13. Likewise, in Frank Chin's story "The Eat and Run Midnight People," the Chinese-American narrator imagines himself the John Wayne of *North to Alaska:* "John Wayne stepping outside and turning a piece of the outdoors into the goddamned Old West. His West." *The Chinaman Pacific & Frisco*

R. R. Co. (Minneapolis: Coffee House Press, 1988), 15. For the characteristic Latino-American view of Wayne, see the title story of Nash Candelaria, *The Day The Cisco Kid Shot John Wayne* (Tempe, Ariz.: Bilingual Press, 1988), 7–22. "Looking back," the narrator remarks, "I realized that Wayne, as America's gringo hero, was forever to me the bigoted Indian hater of 'The Searchers' fused with the deserving victim of the attacking Mexican forces at the Alamo." (21–22). For an iconography of Wayne roles, see Judith M. Riggin, *John Wayne: a Bio-Bibliography* (Westport, Conn.: Greenwood Press, 1992).

4. Wanda Coleman, *Heavy Daughter Blues* (Santa Rosa, Calif.: Black Sparrow Press, 1987), 84, 85.

5. George N. Fenin and William K. Everson, *The Western: From Silents to the Seventies* (New York: Grossman, 1973), 240.

6. Ralph Ellison, *Shadow and Act* (New York: Random House, 1964), 104. Ellison accounts for his fascination with archetypes, folk figures, and legendary heroes by saying of himself and his young friends, "We were under the intense spell of the early movies, the silents as well as the talkies" (xvi). The title essay of *Shadow and Act* is about the portrayal of blacks on film.

7. Don L. Lee, *Directionscore: Selected and New Poems* (Detroit: Broadside Press, 1971), 141. "Tony Curtis, Twiggy" is on p. 42.

8. Gwendolyn Brooks, *Blacks* (Chicago: David Company, 1987), 460.

9. Welton Smith, "Special Section for the Niggas on the Lower Eastside or: Invert the Divisor and Multiply," in *Black Fire: An Anthology of Afro-American Writing,* ed. LeRoi Jones and Larry Neal (New York: Morrow, 1968), 288.

10. Ishmael Reed, *Conjure* (Amherst: University of Massachusetts Press, 1972), 17. For more of Reed's response to the movies, see his novel *Reckless Eyeballing* (New York: Macmillan, 1988).

11. Wanda Coleman, *Heavy Daughter Blues,* 18.

12. Wanda Coleman, *Heavy Daughter Blues,* 19. "Casting Call" is on p. 67.

13. Gwendolyn Brooks, "The Leaders," in *Blacks,* 447.

14. Gwendolyn Brooks, ed., *A Broadside Treasury 1965–1970* (Detroit: Broadside Press, 1972), 48–49.

15. *Broadside Treasury,* 141.

16. "Black Art," in *Selected Poetry of Amiri Baraka/LeRoi Jones* (New York: Morrow, 1979), 106. Elizabeth Taylor returns as a bad example in "Poem for Halfwhite College Students," in which black youth are exhorted not to take Taylor and Richard Burton as their models, nor any other star: "check yourself, / when you find yourself gesturing like Steve McQueen, check it out, ask / in your black heart who it is you are, and is that image black or white" (109).

17. D. H. Melhem, *Heroism in the New Black Poetry* (Lexington: University Press of Kentucky, 1990), 257.

18. Larry Neal, "Malcolm X—An Autobiography," in *Hoodoo Hollerin' Bebop Ghosts* (Howard University Press, 1974), 8–9.

19. Robert Hayden, *Collected Poems,* ed. Frederick Glaysher (New York: Liveright, 1985), 86.
20. Donald Bogle, *Toms, Coons, Mulattoes, Mammies, and Bucks: An Interpretive History of Blacks in American Film,* 2d ed. (New York: Continuum, 1989), 269.
21. Hayden, *Collected Poems,* 172. For a similar portrait of the relation between the western hero and the vicarious sympathy of the moviegoer, see Gwendolyn Brooks's poem "Strong Men, Riding Horses," in *Blacks,* 329.
22. James Baldwin, *Go Tell It on the Mountain* (New York: Knopf, 1953), 44. "The gloom of Hell" is on p. 43. The following quote is on p. 45.
23. James Baldwin, *The Devil Finds Work* (New York: Dial, 1976), 75. "We were all niggers in the thirties" is on p. 25.
24. James Baldwin, "Staggerlee wonders," in *Jimmy's Blues* (New York: St. Martin's Press, 1985), 9.
25. See James Campbell, *Talking at the Gates: A Life of James Baldwin* (New York: Viking, 1991), 206.
26. "Birmingham Brown's Turn" is in *Rainbow Remnants in Rock Bottom Ghetto Sky* (New York: Persea, 1991), 33–37, and "Hattie and the Power of Biscuits" is in *At Redbones* (Cleveland State Poetry Center, 1990), 25. Birmingham Brown makes a comic appearance in Al Young's poem, "W. H. Auden & Mantan Moreland," in *Heaven: Collected Poems 1956–1990* (Berkeley: Creative Arts, 1992), 179. Moreland created the role of Charlie Chan's easily spooked chauffeur.

Chapter 9

1. Jorie Graham, *The Region of Unlikeness* (New York: Ecco Press, 1991), 5–6.
2. Jean Baudrillard, "Symbolic Exchange and Death," in *Selected Writings,* ed. Mark Poster (Stanford: Stanford University Press, 1988), 128.
3. Robert Frost, "For John F. Kennedy His Inauguration," in *In the Clearing* (New York: Holt, Rinehart and Winston, 1962), 30. Frost intended to read the poem at Kennedy's inauguration, but blustery and frigid weather persuaded him to recite the shorter lyric "The Gift Outright" instead.
4. Norman Mailer, *The Presidential Papers* (New York: G. P. Putnam's Sons, 1963), 28.
5. Mailer, *Presidential Papers,* 38. Stevenson is compared to Charlie Chaplin, Kennedy to Gregory Peck and Marlon Brando. "Like Brando, Kennedy's most characteristic quality is the remote and private air of a man who has traversed some lonely terrain of experience, of loss and gain, of nearness to death, which leaves him isolated from the mass of others" (48).
6. Don DeLillo, *Libra* (New York: Viking, 1988), 93.
7. Jorie Graham, *The End of Beauty* (New York: Ecco Press, 1987), 18.
8. David Rosenberg, ed., *The Movie That Changed My Life* (New York: Viking, 1991), 58, 4.
9. Walker Percy, *The Moviegoer* (New York: Knopf, 1961), 16. Binx speaks

about the spots of time that define a self in a movie culture: "Other people, so I have read, treasure memorable moments in their lives: the time one climbed the Parthenon at sunrise, the summer night one met a lonely girl in Central Park and achieved with her a sweet and natural relationship, as they say in books. . . . What I remember is the time John Wayne killed three men with a carbine as he was falling to the dusty street in *Stagecoach,* and the time the kitten found Orson Welles in the doorway in *The Third Man*" (7).

10. David Lehman, "Plato's Retreat," in *Operation Memory* (Princeton: Princeton University Press, 1990), 55. Surely Lehman has in mind a well-known passage by the film theorist Christian Metz, who defines the essence of cinema as "the failure to meet of the voyeur and the exhibitionist whose approaches no longer coincide." *The Imaginary Signifier: Psychoanalysis and the Cinema,* trans. Celia Britton et al. (Bloomington: Indiana University Press, 1982), 63.

11. Paul Monette, *No Witnesses* (New York: Avon, 1981), 106. Monette is having some fun with the image of Garbo we find in an essay like Roland Barthes's "The Face of Garbo": "The name given to her, *the Divine,* probably aimed to convey less a superlative state of beauty than the essence of her corporeal person, descended from a heaven where all things are formed and perfected in the clearest light." *Mythologies* (New York: Hill and Wang, 1972), 56–57. As early as 1927 Glenway Wescott noticed the enchanting face of Garbo becoming an American icon. "Now hired men . . . have the privilege of being in love with Miss Garbo, whose troubling face I find on a bright poster," he notes in a memoir, and later, "in the motion-picture theaters, thanks to the disastrous and vacillating ease in Miss Garbo's face—more fever." *Good-Bye Wisconsin* (New York: Harper & Brothers, 1928), 16, 24. In a novel composed mainly in the 1930s, H. D. describes the Garbo mystique: "She [Garbo] released from the screen the first . . . intimation of screen beauty. Screen? This was a veil, curiously embroidered, the veil before the temple." See *Bid Me to Live* (New York: Dial Press, 1960), 124.

12. Mark Crispin Miller, "End of Story," in *Seeing Through Movies,* 243.

13. Lucie Brock-Broido, *A Hunger* (New York: Knopf, 1988), 54. For an earlier poem that makes use of Marilyn's remark about fame, see James Schevill, "A Fame for Marilyn Monroe," in *The American Fantasies* (Athens, Ohio: Swallow Press, 1983), 164–65. Marilyn's fame has been amplified during the last two decades by the devotion of rock stars to her memory. Madonna is a virtual pastiche of her screen image, and Elton John recorded this generation's most famous song about her, "Norma Jean" (lyrics by Bernie Taupin).

14. Norman Rosten, "Dear Marilyn," *Marilyn Monroe: A Composite View,* ed. Edward Wagenknecht (Philadelphia: Chilton, 1969), 99.

15. Sharon Olds, *The Dead and the Living* (New York: Knopf, 1984), 10.

16. Leo Braudy, *The Frenzy of Renown: Fame and Its History* (New York: Oxford University Press, 1986), 173.

17. Henry Taylor, "A Panel of Experts on 'Blind Alley' Discuss the Influence of Cinema on Modern Poets," *Film Journal* 1 (Fall–Winter 1972): 38.

18. See Jack Myers and Roger Weingarten, eds., *New American Poets of the '90s* (Boston: David R. Godine, 1991), 58, 80, 360. Jason Shinder, editor of a forthcoming anthology of movie poems, *Screen Gems* (Harcourt Brace Jovanovich, 1994), has also composed a book-length sequence of poems on the history of American movies, beginning with *Fred Ott's Sneeze*.

19. Diane Wakoski, *Medea the Sorceress* (Santa Rosa, Calif.: Black Sparrow Press, 1991), 168. A recent poem that enacts the erotic surrender to a contemporary star is Ana Castillo's "Seduced by Natassja [*sic*] Kinski," *After Aztlan: Latino Poets of the Nineties* (Boston: David R. Godine, 1992), 19–21. After the speaker and Kinski spend the night together, "Natassja wants me forever," and the speaker reluctantly agrees, "As if I ever had a choice."

20. Bob Perelman, "Movie," in *The Best American Poetry 1989*, ed. Donald Hall and David Lehman (New York: Collier, 1989), 151–71. The closest analogy in fiction to such texts conditioned by the historicity of the movies is Robert Coover's *A Night at the Movies* (New York: Collier Books, 1987), especially the first story, "The Phantom of the Movie Palace," in which a projectionist edits old movies to suit his personal taste. The same trope for the author's unlimited power can be found in Theodore Roszak, *Flicker* (New York: Summit Books, 1991), David Thomson, *Suspects* (New York: Vintage, 1986), Gore Vidal, *Myron* (New York: Vintage, 1987), and the title story of Julio Cortázar's *We All Love Glenda So Much* (New York: Knopf, 1983). Digital video technology will make such personal reediting a possibility for everyone.

21. Amy Gerstler, "Slowly I Open My Eyes," in *Bitter Angel* (San Francisco: North Point Press, 1990), 40.

22. John Ashbery, "The Lonedale Operator," in *A Wave* (New York: Viking, 1984), 48–49. "Daffy Duck in Hollywood" is another poem in which Ashbery begins comically, in this case with operatic diction incongruously given to his fowl persona, and then concludes on a dour note as he notices how "All life is but a figment." See *Houseboat Days* (New York: Viking, 1977), 31–34.

Conclusion

1. Laurence Goldstein, "Homesick in Los Angeles," in *The Three Gardens*, 11. The poem appeared first in *Poetry*, May 1985, 73.

2. Benjamin, *Illuminations*, 219. Benjamin says later that the decay of the authority of the image "rests on two circumstances, both of which are related to the increasing significance of the masses in contemporary life. Namely, the desire of contemporary masses to bring things 'closer' spatially and humanly, which is just as ardent as their bent toward overcoming the uniqueness of every reality by accepting its reproduction" (223).

3. Louis R. Reid, "Amusement: Radio and Movies," in *America Now: An Inquiry into Civilization in the United States*, ed. Harold E. Stearns (New York: The Literary Guild, 1938), 18–19.

4. Neil Postman, *Amusing Ourselves to Death: Public Discourse in the Age of Show Business* (New York: Viking Penguin, 1985), 92.
5. Mark Crispin Miller, *Boxed In: The Culture of TV* (Northwestern University Press, 1988), 20. Miller remarks how "the generation [of the 1960s, the so-called Film Generation] that once laughed off TV . . . is trying still to laugh it off while disappearing into it" (15). Disappearing into it is precisely what the antihero of Jerzy Kosinski's prophetic novel *Being There* (New York: Harcourt, Brace, Jovanovich, 1970) seeks to do: "He wanted to see himself reduced to the size of the screen; he wanted to become an image, to dwell inside the set" (60–61). Though he is slow-witted and lacking in experience of the world, having been raised entirely within the walls of a protector's estate, Chance's TV-dominated consciousness makes him an ideal cultural icon, and the novel leaves him on the verge of becoming vice president of the United States.
6. See John Fiske and John Hartley, *Reading Television* (London: Methuen, 1978). Fiske has been the most eloquent defender of television against the charges of authors like Neil Postman, Todd Gitlin, Mark Crispin Miller, and the contributors to volumes like Donald Lazere, ed., *American Media and Mass Culture: Left Perspectives* (Berkeley and Los Angeles: University of California Press, 1987). The latter volume extends critiques by the Frankfurt School to deplore "commercial TV's stupefying norms" (13). The failure of such critiques, Fiske insists, is their "failure to recognize the intransigence of the people in the face of this system [of domination], their innumerable tactical evasions and resistances . . . their refusal of the position of compliant subject in bourgeois ideology that is so insistently thrust upon them." *Understanding Popular Culture* (Boston: Unwin Hyman, 1989), 162. In this more-leftist-than-thou critique, Fiske concludes that "television is a cultural resource that people use as they wish, not a cultural tyrant dictating its uses and dominating its users" (153).
7. Bob Perelman, "Movie," 166.
8. Galway Kinnell, *The Book of Nightmares* (Boston: Houghton, Mifflin, 1971), 42; Keith Waldrop, "Before Bed," *A Windmill Near Calvary* (Ann Arbor: University of Michigan Press, 1968), 7; Jorie Graham, "Who Watches from The Dark Porch," *Region of Unlikeness* (New York: Ecco Press, 1991), 106.

Index

Literary texts are listed solely under author.